Carry Forth the Stories

Carry Forth the Stories

A Journey into Indigenous Oral
Traditions with Implications for
Our Humanity

Expanded Edition

RODNEY FREY

Foreword by Leonard Bends

WSU
PRESS

Washington State University
Pullman, Washington

Washington State University Press
PO Box 645910
Pullman, Washington 99164-5910
Phone: 800-354-7360
Email: wsupress@wsu.edu
Website: wsupress.wsu.edu

For permission to reprint a segment of Tom Yellowtail's "The Little People," the author is grateful to the University of Oklahoma Press, and for inspiration from William Burke's "Salmon," to the American Folklore Society and the Confederated Tribes of the Colville Reservation.

This book is published with the assistance of a grant from the J.C. Smith Memorial Fund of the University of Idaho.

Library of Congress Cataloging-in-Publication Data is available.

On the cover: Huckleberries image courtesy of John Hartman;
Camas flower image by Rodney Frey

Dedicated to all the elders,
that their great stories will continue to be re-told,
and great stories will come.

Storyline

Chiwakíia
"to pray"

Foreword

As with all we do in the Native American world, we start this story, this *basbaaaliíchiwé*, with prayer to *Akbaatatdía*, the Creator. All things begin with words of life to the Creator, for without prayer, man's heart is lost and the soul wanders. So I begin in my Crow tongue. Listen intently now as I pray that you shall feel the words and understand.

Akbaatatdía, you have touched Rod Frey's heart to tell his story, *isbaaaliíchiweé*. Now touch those who read his words. Open their hearts as Rod has opened his and let them see the visions that Rod has seen and experienced. *Isbaaaliíchiweé ítchik*. His story is good.

Rod, who has a passion for understanding Native American traditions, culture, and practices, at a young age was tutored and mentored by individuals he crossed paths with and who helped him find himself in a world experienced by only a few non-natives. Rod, with a skittish yet inquisitive young mind, voluntarily placed himself in the hands and minds of these wise ones and experienced a life-changing approach to the sights and dreams of the world unknown and unseen by the contemporary people of this world.

As one of his mentors/teachers said "when you write down my words, they become dead words." But Rod, in his unique ability to tell stories, his unique "oral-nuanced transcription," has given life back into the written story.

With Rod's passion to teach his young students, and his compassion to share with those listening, he takes you into the world he experienced living and working alongside the wise ones. He helps those reading his words to have the ability to read with "heart knowledge," rather than just words on a sheet of paper. To the many who now sit in front of him, listen and you will have the opportunity to experience and understand the stories as were told to him by the wise ones.

Rod's passion to share what he experienced with each unique individual now seated before him, places each person in front of those old people, such as the late Allen Old Horn, Tom and Susie Yellowtail, Cliff SiJohn, and other Native American learned ones. Rod brings life back into the dead words that are written. Rod is set apart from anyone else's attempt to bring back and keep alive those old stories, like Burnt Face, Salmon, and other Native stories.

Rod's ability to engage his learners, assisting them to experience, illustrates his compassion for each person sitting before him.

Not only has he helped these individuals learn and experience the stories, in reading and experiencing this book you also will, for a moment, dwell in the world Rod experienced with the wise-ones, and will share with him his life in the Native world. You will share with him his time standing in front of and traveling within the Tin Shed and the Sweat House, and feel the urge to let go and experience Rod's journey.

Ahó
Baashoolichitche Bacheeítche "Medicine Rock Chief"
Leonard Bends, Retired Sundance Chief

Shóotaachi
"greeting"

Preface to the Expanded Edition

Shóotaachi. I extend a warm greeting to you who now hold this book in your hands—"*shóotaachi*," a common Apsáalooke greeting, literally meaning, "how are things?"

A special *ahó*, thank you, to my Apsáalooke brother, Leonard, for opening this journey with the words of a prayer to the Creator. May you be able to travel well, as you listen and hear the voices of the many "old people" and their stories, along with mine, that you'll encounter along the way.

After the 2017 publication of *Carry Forth the Stories: An Ethnographer's Journey into Native Oral Traditions*, the carrying forth of the stories continued. I was pleased for my mentors and teachers, who entrusted in me their most cherished stories, that this book won the 2018 Evans Handcart Award from the Mountain West Center for Regional Studies. Sponsored by the College of Humanities and Social Sciences at Utah State University, the award honors the top memoir for its "strong narrative and good storytelling," from "a personal perspective."

After retiring from the University of Idaho in 2017, I was asked to consider joining a team of lay chaplains at our local hospital, consisting of volunteers from a variety of backgrounds. With hesitation—knowing of the critical role chaplains play and I without such experience—I signed up in August 2018. I immediately found it extremely rewarding but also humbling and very challenging. Chaplaincy is to be approached with humility. After a career as a teacher, I became a student all over again. As a chaplain, I asked the question, "how can I best jumpstart a relationship with a perfect stranger, meaningful to that patient?" Digging deep, I turned to the *miyp* teachings and cherished stories offered to me by my Indigenous mentors, primary among them Tom Yellowtail of the Apsáalooke. I turned to certain "Awakening Stories" that had anchored my life's journey and followed those teaching stories into the *Ashkísshe* Sundance Lodge and on my healing journeys with cancer, where truly transformative stories awaited to be revealed. Those teachings and stories helped me *walk the halls* of Gritman Medical Center and into the rooms of perfect strangers to initiate meaningful relations with them. As I reflected on those teachings, distilled to their essence, to their "bones," they struck me that they are just as applicable for me as a chaplain, as they are applicable for us all, as we encounter the many strangers in our daily lives. Teachings that could easily speak to our shared humanity.

Upon further reflection on those critical *miyp* teachings, I realized that I had relied upon them earlier, toward the end of my academic journey, in the development of two primary components of a revised undergraduate General Education curriculum. From 2010–2015, I served on the University of Idaho's General Education Steering Committee, charged with proposing coursework reflective of "liberal education best practices" and then as Director of General Education, responsible for implementing the committee's recommendations. Indigenous teachings had direct application and were fundamental to essential components within General Education, a curriculum which represents about a third of the students' entire undergraduate coursework. And I realized that, as with a General Education curriculum, so too were these teachings applicable for the general public, for us all, as we encounter the many strangers in our daily lives.

This expanded edition of *Carry Forth the Stories* is now re-sub-titled, *A Journey into Indigenous Oral Traditions with Implications for Our Humanity*. Added in this edition are new chapters on my journeys in chaplaincy and General Education, along with a revision to the concluding chapter. They are all built on the foundational stories presented in the previous chapters of *Carry Forth the Stories*. While remaining valuable to ethnographers working ethically in collaboration with Native communities, in addressing my experiences as a chaplain and a General Education Director, *Carry Forth the Stories: A Journey into Indigenous Oral Traditions with Implications for Our Humanity* has application for us all, as we encounter the many strangers in our lives.

This expanded edition carries forth the Awakening Stories that began fifty years ago. A journey of unfolding stories that continues beyond the pages of this book.

Ahókaashiile "thank you very much."

Maakuuxshiichíilish "Seeking to Help Others"
Kw'lk'il Sqqi "Little Red Hawk"
Rodney Frey
24 January 2024

Basbaaaliíchiwé
"telling my story"

Preparing to Gather—Awakening Stories

Awakened early, before sunrise, I could no longer sleep. I had this deep urge to share something special, something gathered, something given to me that needed sharing—stories, many involving myself, many involving others. All vital to me. And I asked myself, why do I feel this desire so strongly? Would there be something of value in them, worthy of sharing, of value to others? Where would I even begin the telling? Trained in ethnography, it's always been easier for me to write about others, though with its own challenges, rather than to write about myself. And I thought, this could be awkward!

Story Responsibilities. Let me first respond to what, for me, is the most immediate and easiest of my cautionary, reflective questions. The Apsáalooke (Crow Indians of Montana) have an ancient term, *basbaaaliíchiwé,* literally meaning "telling my story." It has been the practice, still widely followed by the Apsáalooke and by other indigenous communities today, that upon some great deed or event occurring in a person's life, he or she would be invited by elders to re-tell that significant accomplishment, that event, in the company of family and friends, and perhaps the entire community. This practice was certainly exemplified in the storylines of such great stories as told by two of my teachers—in Lawrence Aripa's Four Smokes and in Tom Yellowtail's Burnt Face (Frey, Aripa, and Yellowtail 1995:15–20,

108–22). In both narratives, a young boy confronts and triumphs over seemingly overwhelming challenges, then returns to his family and community transformed. But it is a return that requires of the youth a re-counting of the deeds, of the lessons learned and "gifts" received, in front of family and community. The great deed would be brought to life again, distinctly re-told by one who had intimately experienced it, a "re-telling my story" in front of those assembled.

My urge to share with you comes from an acknowledgement of the responsibilities associated with *basbaaaliíchiwé*. The following essay is very much a re-telling of my own story, in fact, a series of stories, of gifts received, involving two seemingly separate journeys: one of my professional life, the other of my personal life. But these journeys are invariably interwoven and inseparable, each leading into and out of the other. They have oriented how I go about researching, writing, and teaching, have oriented me as an ethnographer. They have guided me in kinship and prayer, and most critically while on journeys of healing, when my young son, just a baby, faced his mortality, and later in my life while facing my mortality, they have guided me as a human being. These are stories that have created my world and re-defined me in relation to my indigenous teachers and hosts, as well as my academic colleagues, my students and my family, my Creator.

For years I attempted to keep my personal journey asleep from the gaze of the public, from my students, from my writings—that is, until the responsibilities associated with *basbaaaliíchiwé* were awoken in 2006. I had tried to unweave the private personal from the public professional, acknowledging that there was the former, but hushing disclosure of its storylines. I had some powerful experiences in the 1970s that at the time I felt were "personal." After considerable contemplation, I judged the value of their unique ethnographic insights warranted sharing them publicly, but without revealing that they happened to me specifically. A journey with cancer, the convergence of a stem cell transplant and a Sundance, facing my own mortality and stripping away all the irrelevant, and being given the most precious of gifts, is not a story meant to be kept to myself. At the depths of my humanity, I needed to reach out to humanity.

Among these many stories and events there were some that were so mysterious, so challenging, that they left me at times off-balance and uncertain, searching for meaning and understanding. My own healing journey with cancer is but one such story. While personally witnessing many such stories, knowing them as true, experiencing them as real, many still remain a mystery. Nothing in my middle-class, Euro-American upbringing, and nothing in my formal academic education, including that of anthropology, fully prepared me for these particular stories. Nevertheless, buried deep within the mysterious were insights into another world that in fact rendered my world a little more balanced and certain, offered a guiding hand while on a healing journey. I awoke with such a desire to share these stories

◆ ◆ ◆

Let's now gather some "huckleberries," led by Cliff SiJohn, a Schi̱t-su'umsh (Coeur d'Alene) elder and spiritual man, who shared a story from his childhood:

> One of my most powerful remembrances was when we arrived after the long ride from home to our family's traditional camp, high into the mountains, and the pickup and cars were parked, my dad just disappeared into the woods. No one would do any-thing, didn't unload the tipis or anything. Just stood around, said nothing. We'd first hear him singing, as he returned with a few branches loaded with *st'sha̱stq*, huckleberries. He'd come over to my brother and me and "dust us off," rubbing the branches over us. Then my father would take the bushes over to my grandmother. She'd carefully pull the berries off the branches, putting them into a cup, and then eat them. We never got to eat them, only her. Dad was talking Indian all along, talking about the power of the mothers, of reproducing, that the spirit of the mothers was like the Mother Earth, needing nourishment to reproduce. So she would take the first berries. We just stood there and watched!

Huckleberries. *John Hartman 2011*

It was hard work, hot, dusty, dirty work, but fun. Preparations, packing, the long trip to the mountains, to our family's camp, and then the gathering. It was a great honor, just like hunting, gathering—not for yourself, but for your family, for the people of the community that weren't able to make it up to the mountains. Then when we'd return, we'd knock on the doors, and see on their faces, on the faces of the old people, the joy. "We've been up to the mountains and we've brought you some berries," handing them a basket full. They knew it was hard work. We didn't expect anything back, nothing in return, though sometimes an elder would give you some dried meat, maybe even a Pendleton blanket. The "return" was seeing the appreciation on their faces. The *st'shastq* berries were meant to be shared.

(Re-told from a 1996 interview with Cliff SiJohn; also in Frey and the Schitsu'umsh 2001:187).

◆ ◆ ◆

Over the years I've had the opportunity of having Cliff SiJohn come to campus and visit with my students, speaking on a variety of topics dear to his heart. Cliff always loved to share some of the "Indian ways" of his family's traditions with these young people. Among the topics he'd inevitably want to address, the first would be the significance of gathering *st'shastq*—huckleberries. He'd talk of the importance of mending the cedar-bark baskets and preparing for the long trip to the mountain, of knowing when the berries were ready, and upon arriving on the mountain, offering prayer to the Creator, Mother Earth, and the berries, and then picking the berries with such care so as not to harm the bush. Cliff would then speak of the critical importance of sharing those hard-earned berries with those who are in need, with those who couldn't make it to the mountain, and of properly storing the huckleberries for future use. My students and I would come to learn of the nourishment only the huckleberries could provide.

As if changing the subject, Cliff would pause for a moment, then ask the students, "Why are you in school, taking this course, these courses? What are you going to do with this education?" After letting each student respond, Cliff would again pause, as he'd glance down at the floor. Breaking the silence, now looking out into the class, as if speaking directly to each student individually, Cliff would affirm, "You know, your education is a gathering of the huckleberries. With your huckleberry basket firmly strapped to your side, gather what your teachers, what your textbooks, what your fellow students and friends, gather what your life-experiences, in and out of the classroom, have to offer you. Be *attentive*; listen, *listen* with

Cliff SiJohn. *Frey 2002*

Cedar-bark basket. *Frey 2012*

all your mind, with all *your heart*. It's hard work. With great care place those berries in your cedar-bark basket. *Cherish* them. And then when you or someone you care for is in need, facing a challenge, needs a little nourishment, needs a little guidance, a little help, what are you to do? How will you *choose* to use the berries? What choices do you make? …Pull out some of those berries and use them, use them to help someone else in need. *Cherish your education*, cherish your huckleberries." And now with what you hold in hand, let's do some huckleberrying and see what awaits.

◆ ◆ ◆

As I re-tell my own stories in this essay I also seek to acknowledge and share the great stories of others—with hope that their stories will continue to live, to inform, and to inspire. These are stories such as Burnt Face, the Tin Shed and Sweat House, Salmon and Coyote, and the Rock Medicine Wheel. This essay is of two forms of re-telling, that of *basbaaaliíchiwé* and that of *baaéechichiwaau*. The Apsáalooke term *baaéechichiwaau* refers to the act of storytelling, of sharing the cherished narrative oral traditions of Coyote and Salmon and the other Animal First Peoples, those who brought forth and embedded the world with vitality and teachings. These are stories heard only on special occasions, at special times, as Coyote should only be told after the first frost. The phrase *baaéechichiwaau* literally means, "re-telling one's own." As applied to so many of the most treasured oral narratives, an individual should re-tell such a story only if he or she has the right to do so. It is a privilege granted by others. In re-telling a story there are considerations of etiquette and ethics.

I've been fortunate to have experienced many great events facilitated for me and many great stories shared with me by numerous, exceptional mentors and storytellers, all gracious hosts. I am so indebted. These are the stories, shared with care, shared deliberately, by Tom and Susie Yellowtail of the Apsáalooke (Crow) of Montana, by Lawrence Aripa, Lucy Finley, and Cliff SiJohn of the Schitsu'umsh (Coeur d'Alene) of Idaho, by Rob and Rose Moran of the Little Shell Chippewa and Warm Springs of Oregon (where Rob raised his family), by Mari Watters, and Josiah and D'Lisa Pinkham of the Niimíipuu (Nez Perce) of Idaho, by Janet and Rayburn Beck of the Shoshone of Fort Washakie, Wyoming, and by a host of others. These are stories granted to me, to be re-told. As the storytellers opened their homes to me, we shared food around a table and laughter and tears around daily lives. We shared from our hearts, and the stories transformed us. This essay is thus an ethnography of my own story landscape and of the story landscapes of indigenous others.

I don't fully understand why, but with so many of my teachers, we hit it right off from the start, we clicked, as if we'd known each other for years. It was 1974 and back behind his barn when I found Tom Yellowtail, an elder and Sundance Chief, feeding his pigs. We had met at the Crow Sundance a few days earlier and he had invited me to his home. He turned to me, and with that special smile in his eyes I'll never forget, welcomed me. Over the next few days, we shared a protracted introduction to each other, and Tom began feeding me as well. Jumping ahead, it was 1989. At a meal at the local café on the Coeur d'Alene Reservation, I was pitching the broad outlines of a possible research project to Cliff SiJohn. Not knowing me, Cliff was checking me out. Over the next few weeks he took cautious steps that would lead toward welcoming me into his home, and the enjoyment of many meals at the Coeur d'Alene Casino where he worked. It began quickly and extended for years, as Tom Yellowtail and Cliff SiJohn and others shared and entrusted their stories and their lives with and to me.

With this trusted sharing of stories came responsibilities, the responsibility of *baaéechichiwaau*. What was shared with me had to be shared with others, particularly with the young and the future generations. Stories are not meant to be kept, but made available.

In 1996 on the Coeur d'Alene Reservation I sat with Lucy Finley, a Schitsu'umsh elder, in her warm living room, her special dolls sitting here and there watching us. Lucy began the visit by asking if I needed something to eat, to drink. I was conducting an interview with her, on a Natural Resources Damage Assessment project dear to the tribe and her. Well into our conversation, with Lucy in the lead talking about the Jump Dance, Blue Jays, and her husband's *suumesh* spiritual powers, she paused and looked me in the eye, saying, "Rodney, these are stories, these are accounts of me and my husband, of what happened to him, that not even my family has heard. You need to pass on these stories."

Late into an evening during the summer of 1993, I was with Tom Yellowtail, at his cabin accessible only after miles of dirt road, far from the noise of the local Crow communities. He was ninety and we were recording a series of his cherished oral narratives that would be included in a book we were putting together, stories of Wise Man and the Little People, and Little Head (see Frey, Aripa, and Yellowtail 1995:91–96, 130–39, 122–30). Upon completing the last of his narratives, that of Burnt Face, Tom turned to me and said, "If all these great stories were told, great stories will come!" Through our endeavor, Tom hoped to pass along some of his most precious teachings, pass along the stories to all his "great-grandkids" yet to come. The stories are not meant to be kept.

Perhaps Lucy, Tom, and Cliff had each seen something in me, or had hoped that something would come out from me. Echoing the obligations of *basbaaaliíchiwé* and *baaéechichiwaau*, Lucy, Tom and Cliff, as with all my teachers, have granted to me the obligation, indeed the responsibility to re-tell the stories, mine and theirs, and with those stories, to seek to make a difference in the lives of others. Their stories certainly made all the difference in my life. This essay is an act of re-telling the cherished stories granted by others that became inescapably infused with my own stories.

Isn't this the case for us all? Have you, from your own life experiences, been granted great stories from your teachers, and shouldn't they be shared? It is the sharing of the great stories that ultimately defines us as humans, defines our humanity. We are the stories we tell. While our lives are short lived, the great stories should not be.

Be they in the stories of the Animal First Peoples, *baaéechichi-waau*, or the lessons one experienced in an event, a rite of passage, *basbaaaliíchiwé*, are all gifts that were integrated into and made an essential part of the fabric of the entire community. Each child, each elder, each person of that community is redefined in relation to that deed, to that lesson, to that person, and to one another. It is a sharing not only publicly acknowledging the transformational change in a youth, but offered as a potential transformative path for others in challenging times. As Four Smokes had triumphed over a great adversary, in the re-telling his courage may provide courage for others. A gift received was re-told and, in turn, gifted to others for their benefit, as a huckleberry to nourish, and as it became their own story, it then would be re-told. A swirling of story. And I awoke with such an urge to share these stories.

◆ ◆ ◆

Intermingled throughout this personal essay are etched a series of stories, vignettes, and narrative phrases, a montage of wondrous and often enigmatic stories and recounted transformative events. You will be hearing differing voices speak, my own, those of elders, such as Cliff, and perhaps even that of Coyote. Many of the stories are re-told and formatted in a style and manner reminiscent of oral-nuanced storytelling, with pacing and pauses facilitated by a poetic style. Many story snippets will be repeated, re-told through in a slightly different voice, from a different angle, in a different con-text. As with a great Coyote story, the repetition of key phrases, the repeating of critical messages is an essential didactic element of the narrative, rendering those messages that much riper with meaning. In the same way, this essay's storyline is left to unfold unanticipated, its plot and scenes (chapters) not fully revealed nor summarized for the reader beforehand. Our navigated lives, informed by choices, are infused with seemingly disparate reoccurring tales that require us to attempt to connect the dots. Gathering the huckleberries is hard work.

To assist you, the reader, these interspersed vignettes are identified and bookmarked by three centered diamonds ◆ ◆ ◆. As you engage these short stories, I ask that you attempt to listen attentively. As Cliff SiJohn always said, "be attentive, listen as the wind, brushing through the leaves of the trees, tells you something." *Stmi'sm* is the Schitsu'umsh term for this attempt to listen deeply and fully. How does this vignette relate to others, or to the themes of this chapter? Try to connect the dots. What might be revealed that is embedded deep within, and what might be discovered through your efforts? It takes a coming together of the two—discovering and revealing. Embedded within the stories and vignettes are what the Schitsu'umsh call the *miyp*, the "teachings from all things," the essential lessons, the huckleberries that would nourish. Discover what waits to be revealed to you in this essay. And then consider, "how might these *miyp* be applied in my life, and applied to help the lives of others?" How might your actions effect the actions of others? *'Itsk'u'lm* is the Schitsu'umsh term for "doing," and in this context, the "passing along through your actions that which is so cherished by others, that can nourish others." Prepare to gather some huckleberries.

I'm hopeful that these *miyp* offer lessons, insights, and implications for us all, for our humanity, and for you. A gift received is a gift to be shared. As these great stories, re-told here, were gifted to me by my teachers and intended to be shared with others, may they now be gifted to you, becoming part of your own story. May the gathered huckleberries pulled from my basket and shared with you, now be placed in your basket. May the huckleberries nourish those in need. We are the stories we share. As Tom reminds us, "If all these great stories were told, great stories will come!" And perhaps these are "stories that make the world" (Frey, Aripa, and Yellowtail 1995). And I woke early that morning with such a desire.

Putting words into print should always be a moment to take pause. In my efforts to re-tell the stories with integrity and respect, I do not intend to confuse or offend. I recall the words of one dear teacher, always ambivalent about participating in a research interview: "Rodney, when you put my words to print, someone can interpret them any which way. I wouldn't be there to clarify." Is what I have presented in this essay been nuanced enough to offer clarity of meaning? Can it stand on its own? I know some readers may have family or cultural traditions that discourage naming those who have passed, or publicly discussing or exhibiting images of certain ceremonies, for example. Will a particular vignette cause offense? As I dig deep and reflect on these concerns, I rely upon the guidance of and seek to be true to my own family traditions. I recognize and respect the sincere concerns of others, but I must turn to the example and tutelage of a grandfather and elder brothers, of my elders. I seek to acknowledge, honor, and share only that which they have granted and entrusted to me, and through me intended to be passed on to you, the reader. And thus I continue to write, remembering the words of Cliff, "Tell it from your heart and you'll have clean hands."

◆ ◆ ◆

When the Lapwai Niimíipuu students gathered at the University of Idaho to give a presentation to a large assemblage of students and faculty, each felt a bit intimidated. But their teacher, D'Lisa Penney Pinkham, had each begin by voicing his or her name and identifying their Niimíipuu family, doing so with confidence. It's the place to begin a story.

◆ ◆ ◆

A Birth Name. Where to start a re-telling, to start the story? As good as any, and perhaps the best, I'll start with a birth name, a family, and my early years.

I was born in 1950 and given the name Rodney Paul Frey by my parents, Wallace and Jeanne Frey, who were of German and English ancestry. Dad worked all his life on the railroad, and Mom was a "stay-at-home-mom," providing me with a stable upbringing. I am the husband of Kristine Roby and father of Matthew Frey, from a previous marriage.

I was raised and baptized a Christian, having taken confirmation in the Methodist Church. In our church youth reading group, we read a book that continues to resonate with me: Viktor Frankl's *Man's Search for Meaning*. In choosing a narrative of hope and love over despair, hate, or anger, one can triumph over even the direst of circumstances, as Frankl attested as a survivor of Auschwitz.

While supportive, my parents never fully understood my journey into the stories of the indigenous, so alien to their own upbringing. I owe them thanks for preparing me with such core values as honesty, being attentive, being willing to explore, and taking responsibility for my actions. They indulged my youthful curiosity about the Anasazi, "the ancient ones," allowing me dig a huge trench alongside our house to sculpt and model cliff dwellings, and taking summer trips to Mesa Verde and Chaco Canyon. I doubt there would have been an invitation to enter the Tin Shed and Sweat Lodge, the homes of my indigenous hosts, without the foundation provided by my mom and dad.

My public schooling experiences also helped set the stage for my awareness of and interest in other cultures. I attended an inner-city high school in Denver, with a graduating class of 799, over a quarter of whom were African-American, in addition to Asian-American and Hispanic students. Such a wondrous diversity that I embraced in the classroom and on the track. I was a runner, and for a "white boy," pretty good at it: a member of a state-champion track team, nicknamed "the Fox." My senior year I anchored our mile relay team. Our team traveled together to meets throughout the state. We practiced hard and depended upon each other. We shared disappointments, and together we celebrated our accomplishments. On this predominately African-American team, I participated in difference; yet in those fluid moments as the baton was handed off, there was no difference, and it made all the difference. In retrospect, this was preparation for entering onto the landscapes and into the lives that were yet to come.

Upon entering college, the first in my family to do so, my track team experiences helped prepare me for what I found expressed in that first anthropology course—an appreciation of diversity. My academic pursuits led to ethnography, the anthropology of the "living ones," and bachelor's and master's degrees from Colorado State University, and a PhD in 1979 from the University of Colorado. My dissertation research was under the caring guidance of Deward Walker, professor of anthropology, and Davíd Carassco, professor of religious studies. I emerged "educated" from a comfortable, white, middle-class, Protestant landscape, with a profound appreciation for difference.

But my experiences over a three-year period during the 1970s, as a graduate student on the Crow Indian Reservation of Montana, were what fundamentally defined the intersecting paths of my life-long journey. Among the stories from that period, the following four made all the difference.

◆ ◆ ◆

The Tin Shed. It's June, 1974. I remember it as a warm and very pleasant afternoon, that day at Crow Agency, Montana. I was about to begin my first ethnographic research, having just finished my master's degree. I had the opportunity to work with the Apsáalooke, literally, "children of the large beaked bird," or in the colloquial, Euro-American-derived term, "the Crow." I was invited by the Crow Tribe and the Indian Health Service (IHS) to be part of a three-member team of graduate students to assist with helping improve health care delivered by the IHS physicians to their patients. My particular research focused on improving communications by helping inform and educate the professionally trained but inexperienced non-Indian doctors who served in the IHS. The physicians were having a difficult time communicating with their tribal patients, especially the elders and the more traditional members. Working with the elders, I helped put together an extended essay on how tribal members categorized and approached illness and healing, all from their perspectives, an essay the doctors would use to better understand and hopefully communicate with their patients.

On that June day, under the shade of an old cottonwood and sitting on a well-worn wooden bench, I found myself introducing the project to an Apsáalooke elder. Experienced in the ways of his people, Allen Old Horn is an "announcer," one who has a Medicine Bundle of sacred objects through which he prays, that in this instance provide protection in the proper use of spoken words and confer his right to speak aloud in public for others. He would stand with those who needed someone to speak publicly for them. Perhaps the person was young, inexperienced in the use of words, fearful of misusing them; perhaps he or she needed the words of a respected elder. There might be one who had served his country in active duty, having faced the enemy, and now returned home, distinguished; or another who had faced cancer, the treatment having taken its toll, but now healthy. The great deed or challenge each had experienced would now be brought to life again, distinctly re-told through Allen's articulate and booming voice in front of those assembled. At a giveaway, during a Sundance, at the half-time of a high school basketball game, or some other public event or celebration, with his deliberate and projected voice, Allen would relay to all those assembled what another wished conveyed. It was another expression of *basbaaaliíchiwé*. Allen Old Horn facilitated for others their re-telling of what had been transformative.

The Tin Shed, Crow Agency, Montana. *Frey 1974*

I had surmised that if Allen was willing he'd be a wonderfully well-informed interviewee for the project. Now, as we sat there under the cottonwood, Allen was very patient with my many questions. With the cassette tape recorder on, I asked about kinship, ceremonies, language, and my questions kept coming, bombarding him with youthful enthusiasm to learn.

After a while, enough was enough, and Allen held out his hand, stopping my next question in mid-sentence. He pointed to a corrugated-metal building, some fifty yards to the north. It likely housed highway equipment, trucks and tractors, or so I imagined. Allen turned to me and said, "*You see* that tin shed?…it's kinda like our way of life…you can sit back here and talk about it…but *not really understand*…it's not 'til you go *inside: listen…feel it…*feel the damp…see it from the *inside* looking out…that you really know what it's all about…you've *gotta go inside*." As the conversation continued that summer, Allen and others would ask, "When you leave that tin shed, what are *you going to do* with what you've been given? With it, how might you *help others*?" (Re-told from 1974 interviews; also in Frey, Aripa, and Yellowtail 1995:5–8.)

◆ ◆ ◆

The Wheel. That same summer of 1974 I was introduced to one of the most amazing ways of looking at and experiencing the world, the uncanny ability of so many Apsáalooke individuals to simultaneously walk distinct ways of life—for example, embracing both the Sundance and Christianity, and doing so with such ease.

This ambidextrous ability was exemplified in the lives of Tom and Susie Yellowtail. Tom was an *akbaalíak*, a traditional healer, and the Sundance Chief for his people. He was also a devout Baptist, knowing his Gospels. Susie danced alongside her husband in the Big Lodge, practiced Western biomedicine, and was among the first American Indian registered nurses in this country. Susie was appointed to Presidential Councils, and traveled widely throughout the United States representing Indian peoples. In the Sundance Lodge, Tom danced with Eagle plumes and the Eagle-bone whistle, and prayed to *Akbaatatdía*, "the one who made everything;" in the Little Brown Baptist Church he read from the Good Book and prayed to Jesus Christ. In the Sundance Lodge, Susie applied *baaxpée*, "Indian medicine"; in the Indian Health Service Hospital she prescribed Western biomedicine. But the Bible and the stethoscope were never brought into the Sundance, and the Eagle-bone whistle never blew in the church. And while the Eagle feathers of an *akbaalíak*, "one who doctors," might be fanned over a patient in the hospital, the prayers and songs of the *akbaalíak* are offered only in the privacy of the patient's room, distinct from the care provided by physician and nurse. Tom and Susie were able, with competence, to effectively communicate and participate with others, indeed nurture and support others, from diverse communities, so distinct and seemingly mutually exclusive.

Years later, it was October of 1993, in Chicago, Tom stood under his Eagle-feather headdress and in full regalia, and shared the podium with some of the world's foremost religious and spiritual leaders—priests, rabbis, imams, including the Dalai Lama. It was the one hundredth anniversary of the Council for a Parliament of the World's Religions. Tom's Apsáalooke prayers for world peace were easily heard, mingling and merging with more than 5,000 other adherents and spokespeople from the world's different religions—Christian, Muslim and Jew, Hindu, Buddhist and Taoist, and American Indian.

Tom Yellowtail, who became one of my most prominent and enduring teachers, offered the following understanding of how to travel the distinct ways of life. Using imagery he felt I could relate to, he began by saying, "The world is as a great Wagon Wheel, a Medicine Wheel." Tom was intimately familiar with the Wheel, as depicted by the Rock Medicine Wheel to the south of his Wyola home, and as incorporated into the Sundance Lodge and the pattern of its dancers (Frey 1987:150–76). The term for the Medicine Wheel is *Annashisée*, meaning "place of the big lodge." Another term for the Sundance lodge is *Ashé isée*, the "Big Lodge."

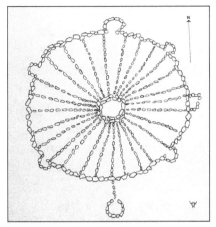

An approximation of the Big Horn Medicine Wheel. *Frey 1987*

From its perch high atop the Big Horn Mountains of Wyoming, the rocks of the Medicine Wheel have endured since time immemorial, the focus of countless pilgrimages and prayers. Its twenty-eight spokes made of rows of rocks were linked by an outer rim of rocks some eighty feet in diameter, with a central rock cairn some two feet in height. As Tom had told in his favorite story, it was Burnt Face, a young boy, horribly disfigured, deeply scarred, who first traveled so long ago to these mountains to fast and offer prayer, who assembled these rocks as a gift to the *Awakkuléeshe*, "Little People," who inhabited the area (Frey 1987: 89–92, 68–69).

Imagine the Apsáalooke Sundance Lodge from the eye of a soaring eagle. The Big Lodge is anchored by a forked cottonwood tree, the Center Pole, from which twelve overhead poles radiate out to shorter posts to form the rim of the Lodge some seventy to eighty feet in diameter, all enclosed by cut trees and brush, its door opens to the rising morning Sun. The cottonwood tree had been cut from its roots days before and planted four feet into the ground at the location that would become the center of the Lodge. For three and sometimes four days, more than one hundred participants would fast from food and water, and offer prayer and dance for loved ones. To the beat of the drum and song, and with Eagle-bone whistles in their mouths and Eagle plumes in hand, men and women charge the Center Pole, with its mounted Buffalo head to the west and Eagle to the east, each suspended from its fork, and then dance back to their stalls, and then charge again, and again. Each dancer has made his or her own individual vow to the Creator to give of him or herself for a loved one in need, each dancer distinct in intentions and expression from the other. Nevertheless, all the dancers are united as one as they blow their Eagle-bone whistles to the beat of the drum, and as they stand before the Center Pole and offer burnt tobacco in prayer, or as they receive a blessing or healing, or even a visit from Buffalo, or Eagle, and be given a special gift, a "Medicine."

A common Apsáalooke name for the Sundance Lodge is *Ash-kísshe*—referring to "representation lodge." With one meaning referring to its structure—a replication of the world, a microcosm of the greater macrocosm, a reflection, a mirror. Each of the unique spokes are dancing, among the many collective diverse spokes, all in unison, united by the ubiquitous spirit of Whistle and Drum, under the gaze of the Center Pole, of *Akbaatatdía*, the Creator, the *axis mundi*, anchoring and permeating the many spokes equally. The image of the Wheel is seen and danced and experienced, and brought forth.

And Tom went on to say, "The spokes of the Wagon Wheel, the Medicine Wheel...are the *various paths* to the *hub*...the *different* religions...the different peoples of the world...each with their *own* ways...their own languages...their *own* traditions...but each spoke is *equally* important...that Wheel just *wouldn't turn* if some spokes

The Crow Sundance Lodge, the "Big Lodge," Wolf Mountains, Montana. *Frey 1993*

Tom and Susie Yellowtail at home in Wyola. *Frey 1976*

were longer than others…if some were taken out altogether…*all* the spokes are needed if the Wheel is gonna to turn…but all the spokes are linked to the *same hub*…the same Creator…each religion…each spoke might call the Creator by a different name…but the prayers of all religions are heard by the Creator…if the Wheel is to turn." Spokes unique, spokes collectively diverse; a hub and rim unifying, ubiquitous, universal.

◆ ◆ ◆

A Prayer for My Son. The summers with the Apsáalooke in 1974 and 1975 were indeed extraordinary, as I delved into such diverse realms as traditional healing and powwows, gender roles and Sundances, and was introduced to some incredible teachers, who would host me in their homes for years to come. During those two summers I was able to camp and enjoy meals with families at both Sundances, and in fact, assist in the construction of the 1975 Lodge. As the Sundance Chief, Tom was in charge of running them. At the 1975 Sundance my wife and six-month-old son Matt were able to join me. I remember the grandmothers, so intrigued with this blond-haired, blue-eyed, white baby, that they asked if they could "borrow" him for the afternoon. Matt was wrapped tight in a beaded cradleboard and rocked on the laps of virtually every grandmother in the twenty-some camps of the Sundance encampment that day. With a smile on his face, without a cry, he seemed to enjoy it!

By this second summer I had begun learning some of the personal stories behind a few of the dancers, of their hopes and challenges. While standing at the Lodge door, I felt a little of the tremendous sacrifice they sought to give for loved ones over these three days of going without food and water, under the hot July sun. I felt something flow out from the Lodge. At the door of that Sundance Lodge, my knees buckled as tears unrestrained fell from my eyes. I swirled in a wave of heart outpouring.

The winter of 1976 found me back in Colorado, pursuing my graduate studies in Fort Collins. One late afternoon, my wife and I, along with Matt, were on a short road trip, on our way home. Suddenly, Matt went limp on us, unconscious. Holding his seemingly lifeless body in our arms, we rushed our son to the nearest hospital, where all sorts of tests were run, including an MRI. During those desperate moments, lasting an eternity, this twenty-five-year-old father reached out in any way I felt I could be heard, prayed with all my heart that my son would recover and be safe. And at that spontaneous moment, what came into my heart were the stirrings emanating out of Sundance prayers, led by Tom Yellowtail. At that moment I vowed to fast from food and water, alone on a hill for three days for my son's recovery. Matt recovered, we never learned what had actually caused this episode. That summer of 1976 I asked Tom if he would help me fulfill my promise to fast, so I could honor my son. Generously, Tom agreed and prepared me—with a cleansing Sweat bath, in the use of the Pipe and Tobacco, with a fan of Eagle feathers, with how the hot coals and cedar were to be used during my morning and evening prayers, and helping me select a location up in the hills, far from the curiosity of others.

Even with my background in anthropology, this urban-raised, white, middle-class young man had no idea what to anticipate, though I had sincere desire to offer myself, to suffer a little, for the joy of my son's recovery. During the day, Tom had me walk up from

my camp site to a higher butte to pray under a tree. Each day as I
walked to the hill, I passed close by a den of rattlesnakes. Tom had
mentioned possible visitors and how to use the feathers. Alone, so
distant from others, as I came up to the snakes each day, for some
reason, I sat down right before them, with the Eagle-feather fan in
front of me, and had an odd sort of dialogue with those I would
have normally jumped back from under any other circumstances.
Words were not exchanged, but we communicated. There was no
fear, no apprehension, just this silent conversation, and then I'd
get up and move to the hill top. Thinking back upon it now, I must
have been crazy!

During this fast in the hills there was another who would visit.
I had gone two full days and nights without food and water, under
the Sun's watch, offering my morning and evening prayers around
a small fire, and actually felt fine. I was going into the last evening,
after the sun had set, and thinking about coming down, back to the
warmth of Tom's home the next morning. "I really accomplished it;
I really did it myself," I thought. And then it hit, I was overwhelmed
with intense anxiety and fear. My heart was racing, the palms of
my hands sweating, I wanted to run, but run where? I remembered
what Tom had said about the power of tobacco and prayer. So I lit
a cigarette, faced into the moon-lit shadowy east, and began the
prayer, from all my heart. Holding the cigarette in front of me, a
first, then second, and a third cigarette was lit from the previous, in
a continuous long prayer. The rapid palpitations continued.

And then he appeared, out of the dark, clear and vivid, not
more than twenty feet to the south of me—one of the Little People.
Standing there, some three feet tall, he said nothing, just looked at
me, and *I knew*. As fast as it had first rushed over me, the fear and
anxiety were gone, as was my visitor. And I realized that I had not,
in fact, accomplished anything on my own, with my efforts alone,
but this fast was the culmination of the many prayers of others, of
Tom, of a Little Person, of my family, of the efforts of many, part of
an interconnected world. I voiced my deep thanks and had a good
night's sleep, that last night on the hill. At the time I knew little of

the vast traditions associated with what the Apsáalooke term the *Awakkuléeshe*, the Little People.

Coming down off the hill the next day, Tom and I took a Sweat bath together. Tom asked about what happened, and I told him of my visitors. I re-told my story. Moments later, Tom turned to me and asked if I would care to join him in a few weeks to continue my prayers for my son, this time in the Sundance Lodge. I did. As with the fast on the hill, I had not anticipated my first Sundance, and had no awareness of what lay before me. But I did have a sincere desire to pray for my son's health, to continue my pledge and give thanks. So began my crossings over. I continued dancing, as to "blow the Whistle" in the Big Lodge once entails doing so four times, and I completed two such cycles—my eighth Sundance in 1996. (Re-told from experiences; also in Frey 1987:86.)

◆ ◆ ◆

Let me tell you the story of Burnt Face. This was Tom Yellowtail's most cherished story.

In the days they moved about the country,
   from place to place,
      along the rivers,
         the Bighorn River,
            the Yellowstone River;
      along the mountains,
         the Rocky Mountains,
            the Bighorn Mountain;
      in the valleys,
         the Bighorn Valley.
This one group of Crows is camped there.
It's evening,
   meals had been cooked,
      fires are dying down.
Over there, they're running through camp,
   chasing each other,
      having fun.
   A boy *falls*.

His face lands in the hot coals of the fire pit.

It's a *deep* burn!

Some time passes.

He comes out of his tipi.

They gather around.

His sisters, his brothers, his friends.

They see it,

a scar, *all over* the right side of his face.

Someone calls out,

"hey, Burnt Face!"

Some laugh.

Months follow,

he feels *bad*,

ashamed.

At ten years old, the young boy keeps to himself,

traveling *alone*,

setting up his camp *far* from his family and his people.

Then it comes to him.

He'll go to the mountains,

to fast,

to pray,

seeking help.

It may take him awhile,

He may not even *make it off* the mountain.

He travels alone to those high mountains of the Bighorns.

He wears out each of four sets of moccasins his mother had made.

He eats the last of his food.

There, *high* on the mountain, the sunrise and sunset are clearly seen,

he goes without food and water,

offers daily prayer with the Indian tobacco,

with the carved stone pipe his father had given him.

Under the watch of the Sun,

he moves huge rocks,

there, that one,

there, another

forms a great Wheel,

an offering,
twenty-eight spokes with a rock hub,
like the Sundance Lodge.
It takes him awhile.
It's an *offering*,
showing his sincerity.
a gift to whoever might come,
perhaps to the *Awakkuléeshe*,
the Little People,
who inhabit this area.
And they do come, there,
the Little People;
they'd been watching him.
They take him in,
adopt him;
He calls them his "Medicine Fathers,"
his *scar* is removed.
It's a *new born* child's face.
He travels back home.
It takes awhile,
returns to his people,
They don't recognize him at first.
"who are you?"
They ask him to tell them his *name*,
to *tell his story*,
to his family, to his friends, to everyone.
Burnt Face *re-tells* his story,
of his fast,
of the rock wheel,
of the Little People,
of his name.
He becomes a healer amongst his people,
he applies "medicine," *baaxpée* to the lives of those in need,
all the while keeping his name,
to always remember.

There, the trail ends.

(Re-told based upon Tom Yellowtail's original telling of Burnt Face circa late-1970s and repeated until his passing in November of 1993; also in Frey 1987:90–92; Frey, Aripa, and Yellowtail 1995:108–22; Frey, Yellowtail, and SiJohn 2008:185–205.)

◆ ◆ ◆

As a young ethnographer, what was I to make of these extraordinary experiences and distinct, diverse teachings? A Tin Shed? A Rock Medicine Wheel? Burnt Face? And the *Little People*? Truly mysterious! Truly so "other" than anything my young life had prepared me for, even the anthropology curriculum I had taken. As I began to travel into the Tin Shed and the other stories, was I listening attentively to Allen and Tom and Susie? Had I been attentive to Lucy? To Cliff? Was I attentive to one of the *Awakkuléeshe*? Had I participated fully in their stories, in my experiences with them? Should I ignore them? Perhaps I should rationalize them in some academic, theoretical manner? I know the lessons and meanings within the stories didn't always reveal themselves immediately. Was I patient enough?

Yet how could I but acknowledge these stories, what had been so special and profoundly transformative? They were now embedded deep in my emerging professional and personal journey. How could I but accept them in the manner in which they were given? Though yet embryonic in my journey, these four teachings and experiences, accompanied by their generous storytellers, would in turn prove to provide the best possible preparation for the many mysteries yet to come. The Tin Shed story provided the best course for my entry and continued passage as an ethnographer, while the Medicine Wheel provided an awareness of the possibility of multiple paths, none of which need be mutually exclusive. In Burnt Face I glimpsed a pathway of potential transformation, and with the experience of the Little People I was jump-started well within that Tin Shed, awakening further a path not previously acknowledged, nor even imagined possible. So began an ethnographer's journey into Native oral tradition.

Despite this auspicious initiation, haunting me from the very start and still today are two prevailing questions, one personal, the other professional. As I continued on into the Tin Shed, would I be able to "connect the dots?" It would be hard work. Would I as a human being someday reach a better appreciation and understanding of the experience of the Little People and of the personal transformations that resulted and continue to be brought forth? Could I re-tell my story? And would someday I arrive at a position, with some degree of confidence, that I as an ethnographer, as a teacher, as a writer, could effectively disseminate, with permission from my host teachers, that which is held so cherished by them, and share the heart knowledge and practices found within the Tin Shed? Could I re-tell the stories of others? In any case, as I share the huckleberries I received, may you, in turn, be able to *stmi'sm* "listen," be attentive to the stories, and place what berries might be revealed to you into your own cedar basket, to share with others. To carry forth the stories. This essay is a weaving of the threads of cherished stories and oral narrative traditions granted by others, with the threads of my own personally-experienced story events, to re-tell, re-create the evolving tapestry that is my story, *basbaaaliíchiwé.*

◆ ◆ ◆

Basbaaaliíchiwé—re-telling my stories; *baaéechichiwaau—re-telling* their stories. Entering the Tin Shed? Traveling the spokes and perhaps reaching a hub? Encountering Burnt Face, and the Awakkuléeshe? And huckleberrying the entire time? I awoke with such a desire.

And it all starts with story.

'Me'y'mi'y'm
"telling stories"

Swirling with Coyote—
Re-telling the Stories

Everyone is having a tough time of it,
    There, the Rock Monster is rolling around,
        Over there, the camps *aren't safe.*
There, First Peoples go to Coyote,
    they ask for his help.
        "What's in it for *me?*" he responds.
"Mice, *all* the mice you want," they say.
Agreeing to the terms,
    Coyote seeks out the Monster.
There, the Rock Monster is rolling around.
Coyote taunts and challenges the Monster,
    "You are *so ugly!*"
Coyote gets the Rock Monster to chase him,
    There, *away* from the camps of the people.
They go this way, then that,
    creating the flat of Rathdrum Prairie,
        the hill that is Plummer Butte,
            much of the lands we see today.
Coyote begins to tire out,
    The Rock Monster *keeps on coming.*
Coyote gets an idea.

There, through the bushes toward the cliff,
  there is a ledge overlooking the lake.
    Coyote runs toward it.
The Rock Monster rolls right behind him,
  rolling through those huckleberry bushes.
Coyote jumps *onto* the ledge.
The fast rolling Rock,
  covered in huckleberry juice,
    falls into the lake,
      drowning
Lake Coeur d'Alene is *made blue.*
Soon the Human People will be here,
  the landscape embedded throughout with the stories.
Each time this story is re-told,
  the Coyote *comes alive,*
    swirls around you,
      talks to you,
  and the *blue* in the lake is continued.
There, the trail ends.

(Re-told as originally conveyed by Lawrence Aripa in 1991; also
in Frey, Aripa, and Yellowtail 1995:71–75, and Frey and the
Schi̲tsu'umsh 2001:127–131.)

◆ ◆ ◆

I was an adjunct faculty member at the University of Montana from
the fall of 1979 through spring of 1980, attempting to fill in for
the renowned scholar Joseph Epes Brown (a student of the Lakota
elder, Black Elk, and author of *The Sacred Pipe*), and teaching his
courses on American Indian religions while he was on a year-long
sabbatical. It was that summer of 1979 at the Sundance that I first
met Joseph, when he asked if I'd like to come to Missoula. What an
honor and great opportunity, but very daunting to fill in for such a
distinguished professor in my first teaching position. During this
formative year I learned of Agnes Vanderburg, who was well-known
for her storytelling and wisdom. She was an elder and teacher of the

"Coyote's 'Blue' Lake Coeur d'Alene," looking east from Indian Cliffs, onto Lake Coeur d'Alene, with St. Joe Baldy in the distant background. *John Hartman 2002*

Bitterroot Salish of Montana. Each summer beginning in 1981 she held a Culture Camp at a remote site on the Flathead Reservation, which continued annually until her passing. The summer of 1983 I set up my small, twelve-foot tipi among the many that made up the camp and became one of Agnes' students. The days and evenings were filled with beading and basket making, with shared food and stories, and the youthful excitement of the students. She was such a great teacher and storyteller.

In 1981, while teaching at Carroll College, a small, Catholic, liberal-arts college in Helena, Montana, I sponsored a conference on Montana storytelling, with raconteurs representing varied genres. A cowboy storyteller had just completed his session, and, with his strong booming voice, had easily delivered his stories squarely into the laps of each person in the audience, concluding each story by stating a single moral message. Next up was Agnes Vanderburg. With neither the physical frame nor self-amplified voice of the previous teller, in fact, preferring not to project her voices through an artificially electrified microphone, she began her stories. Soon all were moving their chairs in a little closer and closer yet, to catch every one of Agnes' deliberately spoken words. In no time, everyone seemed completely engaged, eyes moving this way, then that as Agnes pointed here, then looked there, leading the way through an unfolding story landscape. Upon finishing, and unlike the previous storyteller, she simply returned to her seat, offering neither commentary nor explanation, nor a clear moral lesson like those delivered in Aesop's fables.

You had to work for Agnes's stories. They would not be delivered to you, unwrapped and ready for use. Layered with multiple meanings, her stories spoke as easily to that six-year-old child who sat in the front row, as they did to the thirty-six-year-old Indian man standing to the side, as they did to the religious studies scholar of sixty seated in the back row. For there was something that might be revealed and awaited discovery for each and every one who was willing to travel the territory of Agnes' stories. As a master storyteller, this was indeed part of her magic. (Re-told from a 1981 experience; also in Frey and the Schitsu'umsh 2001:282.)

In 1983 I had Agnes again return to Carroll College for a conference presentation and the opportunity to hear her stories. As the audience anticipated being part of her magic, Agnes came to the podium and said, "It's not storytelling season, it's over." She turned and sat down. In reflection, I realized we must have had our spring thunder, signaling the end of the appropriate time for telling Coyote stories until the first frost returned in the coming fall. It was a great reminder of just how the stories are intimately embedded in the landscape and its seasonal cycles. They emanate out of particular seasons of warmth and growth, cold and preparation, and the specific landscapes of river bends, rock outcroppings, hills and mountains. Through her deliberately spoken words, you could travel these story landscapes, around this river bend, over that hill, and there was no other landscape, no other season. But on this day, in this season, it was not the time to travel Coyote's landscape.

❖ ❖ ❖

Doesn't it all *really* begin with story? Over the many years, I'd often hear a story merged within a conversation, or re-told as a stand-alone. Stories meant everything to my teachers. Stories such as Burnt Face, or a creation story involving Salmon or Coyote, not only defined the world, guiding people at each juncture through its landscapes, but when told with such care, these stories also brought the world into existence. Now that's a beginning!

From the first time I ventured into the indigenous Tin Shed, stories seemed to fill the air. Regardless of the community, be it at Crow Agency in 1974, or at Lapwai on the Nez Perce Reservation, or Plummer on the Coeur d'Alene Reservation in 1989, I have been surrounded by stories. During visits on the Blackfeet and Flathead Reservations in Montana during the 1980s, and the Confederated Tribes of Warm Springs Reservation of Oregon in the early 2000s, or the Spokane Reservation of Washington in 2014, I heard stories re-told. And they continue today.

Stories seemed to be interwoven throughout people's lives. They might be heard just before taking a Sweat bath, after an evening meal, as we were setting up a tipi, as we visited late into the night at a Sundance encampment, or perhaps during the early morning hours at a wake for a distinguished elder. While we traveled in his pickup to Sheridan, Wyoming, to get a week's worth of groceries, Tom Yellowtail would often tell one story, then another, then still another, as a particular hill came into view, a riverbed, or an open plain. Stories embedded in the terrain of the landscape; stories embedded in the activities of people's lives.

And there was that moment at his remote cabin in 1993, late into the night, and Tom, after retelling his most cherished narrative—that of Burnt Face—spoke those prophetic words: "If all these great stories were told, great stories *will* come!"

❖ ❖ ❖

Even before experiencing the power of storytelling from various Indian elders, I experienced it as a nervous graduate teaching assistant. At the time, 1973, I was working on my master's degree in anthropology at Colorado State University. I was to give my very first lecture to some two hundred freshmen on any topic of interest to me. At the time I had a fascination with eighteen and nineteenth century European peasant society. But how would I attempt to lecture these students on a topic so esoteric and removed from their lives, a potentially "deadly" topic for these freshmen? So I told a story. I had researched a day-in-the-life of the Sibiriaks, the European emigrants to Siberia during the days of Tsarist Russia. With these ethnographic details I created an account, a storyline of what one might experience upon walking into a Sibiriak village—the smells of the dung heap just outside the village, the two-storied houses lining the main road, with livestock pens on their first floors, the sounds of a wedding, describing what people were wearing and how they were interacting with one another. While I am not so sure what the students might have learned and remembered, I did seem to hold their attention as they engaged in the story. And while I know I cannot remember much about my own studies on nineteeth-century European peasantry, I can still vividly remember the details of that story and the feeling I got in telling it.

Soon after the Sibiriak story, I was introduced to a very innovative but little-known work edited by Elsie Clews Parsons entitled,

WRITING RESOURCE

"Tools to Shape Texts: What Creative Nonfiction Can Offer Ethnography," an article by Kirin Narayan, offers a thorough introduction on the placement of creative nonfiction within the discipline of anthropology, advocating nonfiction's importance, along with practical tips on how to use creative nonfiction writing in ethnography. *Anthropology and Humanism* 32, 2:130–144. huminst.uic.edu/docs/default-document-library/narayantools-essay.pdf

American Indian Life (1967). Originally published in 1922, Parsons had gathered the prominent ethnographers of the American Indian of her day, such as Franz Boas, Alfred Kroeber, Robert Lowie, Edward Sapir, Paul Radin, and Clark Wissler, and had each write fictional stories with plots and characters, always adhering "strictly to the social facts," that could depict the "thoughts and feelings of the Indian...[which is] impossible in a formal, scientific report" (1967:13). Hence what I subsequently refined into a key course learning activity: "creative nonfiction ethnography." I asked my students to first research, via the library, the pertinent material culture, social, and religious structures, as well as the worldview underpinnings of their particular topic—a day-in-the life, a social or ritual event, even a seasonal round. Then they were to imagine and create a believable and culturally appropriate storyline and set of characters, with themselves as the protagonist.

By attempting through creative nonfiction to engage in the life of someone so removed from our own, we can experience at least a little of what Allen Old Horn had urged—"go *inside,*" "*feel* it," "see it from the *inside* looking out." In a 1973 classroom and in a 1974 field experience, the seeds were sown for a pedagogy I would later develop as an instructor.

◆ ◆ ◆

In 1992, while a faculty member and director of an outreach campus for Lewis-Clark State College in Coeur d'Alene, Idaho, I was asked to serve on the local school district's Language Arts Committee. The district had begun the process of selecting new fourth-grade language arts textbooks. I was particularly interested in how American Indian literature and stories were being represented and pedagogically conveyed. In a review of current adopted texts, I discovered that the students of this non-Indian school district, just to the north of the Coeur d'Alene Reservation, had very little language arts or social studies curriculum exposure, at any grade level, to the rich heritage of the people for whom their city and school district were named. I also learned that this review involved a very competitive national market within which publishers were championing their particular richly-illustrated and designed series. What I found was deeply disturbing.

At the fourth-grade level there was no contemporary Native literature represented, only simplified and shortened narrative oral traditions. In my review I found the stories were re-written in a manner that minimized indigenous perspectives, and focused more on rendering the stories accessible to the sensibilities of a non-Indian teacher-student clientele. Far too often story characters and plot lines were romanticized to fit Euro-American stereotypes. These were stories framed with little or no indigenous historical or cultural context offered. And most disturbing was how these stories were introduced to the student. In language implied or even overt, these were stories viewed as mere fantasy, part of a "primitive" people's "quaint beliefs and practices," as simplistic, imaginary "myths and superstitions." Implicit was the premise that these stories are reflective of early human attempts at explaining experiences in the world, that otherwise could not be understood. The stories were seen as false and misplaced explanations formed without the benefit of informed science. This focus on an explanatory function promoted stereotypes and misrepresentations by a community that needed to be much better informed about their

 STORIES THAT MAKE THE WORLD

The Coeur d'Alene school district, specifically its teacher's guide, served as the basis for the book *Stories That Make the World: Oral Traditions of the Indian Peoples of the Inland Northwest as Told by Lawrence Aripa, Tom Yellowtail and Others* (Frey, Aripa, and Yellowtail 1995). I have always been gratified to hear from Lawrence's relatives, and separately from Tom's relatives, that upon "reading his stories, they could hear his voice speaking to them."

neighbors and their city's namesake (Frey, Aripa, and Yellowtail 1995:xiii–xvi; 175–176).

Working in collaboration with the elders of the Schịtsu'umsh, I developed our own curriculum materials, including a teacher's guide, text materials, and video tapes of storytelling by elders, and held teacher workshops to introduce the materials. The workshops were led by Lawrence Aripa and Cliff SiJohn, with support funding provided by the Idaho Humanities Committee. Using an approach to stories developed by folklorist Alan Dundes (1966), the curriculum provided a review of the "texts," i.e., on the nature of key themes and motifs infused in the stories, the "texture," i.e., a discussion of storytelling techniques, the dynamic of orality and the "power of words," and the "context," i.e., the purposes of the stories, including their didactic roles and the critical function of vitalizing and perpetuating, of "making the world." They had little to do with explaining the world. In order to better present the oral nuance and dynamics of these oral traditions, and influenced by the pioneering work of Dell Hymes (1981) and Dennis Tedlock (1972), the stories presented in the curriculum were formatted using a poetic style, with pacing, pauses, and emphasized words noted. I was beginning to appreciate the importance of aligning the content of the stories with their pedagogical means of dissemination, linking the "what" with the "how."

While the curriculum and workshops were fully endorsed by the Coeur d'Alene Tribe's Culture Committee, some members of the district's school board opposed the curriculum, stating that it "espoused non-Christian, satanic materials." Nevertheless, the fourth grade Schịtsu'umsh language arts curriculum was adopted for use in the district's twenty-two elementary schools.

This project demonstrated that the rich oral traditions of indigenous peoples and an appropriate associated pedagogy can be integrated into a non-Indian school district, helping bring alive the depth of beauty and meaning of these stories for all to appreciate.

◆ ◆ ◆

To tell of the narrative traditions is to *'me'y'mi'y'm.* What I've learned from my Apsáalooke teachers, such as Tom Yellowtail, and my Niimíipuu mentors, such as Josiah Pinkham or Mari Watters, is remarkably akin to what I have learned about the meaning of story as lived by the Schítsu'umsh. For the Schítsu'umsh—the Coeur d'Alene Indians—the act of re-telling their stories is termed *'me'y'mi'y'm,* "telling stories."

The place to begin the stories is with their source. As the Schítsu'umsh elders would say, "Our stories came to us from *K'u'lntsutn,* 'he who creates himself,' the Creator." Before the Jesuits arrived in 1842 and still for some Schítsu'umsh today, the Creator is addressed as the *Amotqn,* "the one who sits at the head mountain." In either case, it is the same Creator (Frey and the Schítsu'umsh 2001:109–11). The stories have been with the Schítsu'umsh "since time immemorial," since the time of the Animal First Peoples and Chief Child of the Yellowroot, *Sp'ukhwenichelt,* his name literally meaning "son of light." *Sp'ukhwenichelt* is one of their culture heroes. He helped transform the landscape around Lake Coeur d'Alene, ridding it of the "man-eaters" and monsters, and inundating it with tools, tastes, and teachings, planting it with the "gifts" the humans would need (Frey and the Schítsu'umsh 2001:144–151). Sent by the Creator, as an extension of its volition, meaning, animating force and life, the Animal First Peoples prepared the world for the coming of Human Peoples, deeds etched in the landscape and its stories.

Buried deep within these stories are what is termed the *miyp,* the "teachings from all things" (Frey and the Schítsu'umsh 2001:182–86, 270–71). The *miyp* are the foundations for what the Schítsu'umsh call their *hnkhwelkhwlnet,* "our ways of life in the world," for their indigenous knowledge and practices. The *miyp* are understood as enduring, solid as "bones." Within any given story there can be many and varied bones from which to learn. The many-layered *miyp* engrained within a Coyote story could elicit a laugh from and provide a lesson for old and young alike. The *'me'y'mi'y'm* provided an affective tone to life, as well as a didactic form for life, framed within self-paced instruction linked to a listener's particular experiences

(Frey, Aripa, and Yellowtail 1995:171–77). These are the stories handed down orally from their grandparents and their grandparents before them; these are stories "since time immemorial," with the *miyp* within the stories steadfast, unchanging.

The Schitsu'umsh classify their narrative oral traditions into Animal People/First People stories, such as those of Coyote and Salmon, called *'me'y'mi'y'm q'esp schint*, "he/she/they are telling stories and learning about the time before the human beings"; and stories involving the Human Peoples, such as those of Burnt Face and Four Smokes, referred to as *'me'y'mi'y'm łu schint*, "he/she/they are telling stories and learning about the human beings" (Frey, Aripa, and Yellowtail 1995:12–13; Frey and the Schitsu'umsh 2001:183).

Revealing the *miyp*. In the act of re-telling their most cherished stories, the Schitsu'umsh attempt to teach children the *miyp*—what they will need to know to live their lives, to live life well. In the stories, the *miyp* communicate to future generations what is most treasured, what is most important.

These stories can speak to each person, be they a Schitsu'umsh youth of ten years, an elder with a wealth of sixty years of experience, or a non-Indian scientist. These are stories that can offer "aha moments." Like Agnes Vanderburg, Native storytellers seldom attach specific Aesop-like moral commentaries, e.g., "and that is what the story means," to their stories. The storyteller would not want to emphasize a particular lesson, and forgo the possibility of the many other lessons that could have been revealed. As the listener grows in experiences from year to year, upon hearing the same stories re-told, they may discover new *miyp*. The *miyp* was always there, the difference being in the life-experiences each participant brings into the story, and his or her willingness to listen and participate. But be it a ten-year-old or a sixty-year-old, both must engage the story by being attentive and actively listen, they both must do some work to engage, if the treasures buried deep are to be uncovered.

I've learned by working with the elders, such as Cliff SiJohn, and language specialists of the Coeur d'Alene Tribe that this discovery process is best approached and appreciated from their Native perspective. The English term "discovery," for example, is loaded with many meanings, some of which may mislead and distort that which we seek. What have been the implications of Columbus "discovering" the American Indian? There are two *snchitsu'umshtsn* (Coeur d'Alene language) terms that better convey the meaning and significance of the "aha moment." The first term is *chetche'in'nts*, "to reveal, disclose, or uncover," implying that something that had been hidden, something that had always been there, is now revealed. And the other term is *hischits*, "it is my discovery," referring to the great effort one must assert in being attentive and listening, all the while not knowing what might result, what might be revealed. It takes both. And then comes the recognition, the "aha moment" and you have, through your great efforts, discovered one of the *miyp*, uniquely appropriate given your particular background and life experiences: "It is my discovery." As with Agnes' stories, you had to work for it. But it is not *"my* discovery" in the sense of ownership (aka Columbus), but "my" in the sense of linking you in particular to the *miyp*, while acknowledging access to what countless others before you had gained access to. The process of "revealing" and "discovery" is consistent with the interactions between participants, one electing to reveal something to someone else, the other actively paying attention, discovering what might be revealed. When we re-tell our stories, there are thus responsibilities of both the story-teller, and of the story listener, and perhaps of another participant.

◆ ◆ ◆

During the spring of 1991 I witnessed a remarkable re-telling. Basil White, a Kootenai elder, was sharing the rather lengthy narrative, "The Animals and Sea Monster," to a largely non-Indian audience. As he spoke, I recall his words as deliberate and precise, using all the techniques of an accomplished raconteur to bring the story alive. The unfolding storyline wove this way and that, with a multitude of beings appearing at every juncture, Muskrat and Frog, Magpie and Woodpecker, Sea Monster and Coyote. I felt the uneasiness of many in the audience, with plot development and characters that did not fit their linear, Euro-American notions. But if you listened, Basil provided a rare and authentic opportunity. And he provided a wonderful example of a retold story.

A few days later I consulted a not-readily-accessible publication of Kootenai narratives, recorded sometime around the turn of the last century (Boas and Chamberlain, 1918). In that collection was the story Basil had retold. As I scanned the pages, I could hear Basil's words. Remarkably, Basil and his family had kept the story of the Animals and Sea Monster fundamentally intact, kept all the bones and *miyp* together, from generation to generation, for some ninety years, without deleting some of the bones, without adding others, all within the oral tradition of re-membering. He and his family did so without reliance on the written word. As it happened, that evening's performance was audio-recorded, transcribed, and with Basil's assistance and approval, included in *Stories That Make the World* (Frey, Aripa, and Yellowtail 1995:196–213). Basil demonstrated the responsibility of the storyteller in keeping the bones together, as well as the long-term and immediate dynamics of re-telling, re-membering, re-turning to the original.

◆ ◆ ◆

The Bones and Flesh of the Stories. The *miyp*, the teachings, are revealed as the narrative oral traditions are engaged, heard, and experienced. The stories are understood by the elders as a living being, a person with flesh and bones. As one Schitsu'umsh elder has related, a "story is like a person, with a skeleton, muscle and flesh…you have to keep all the bones together; you can't add new ones or take away some…they all have to be there" (Frey and the Schitsu'umsh 2001:191). The story itself, as a living person, has the responsibility to reveal to the other story participants what is embedded deep within. The oral narrative traditions, such as stories of Coyote and Chief Child of the Yellowroot, are richly layered with these essential *miyp*, with the "bones" (Frey and the Schitsu'umsh 2001:191). The bones include the narrative's storyline, its essential and perennial teachings—the *miyp*—as well as its ontology principles that define what is real and true. These are bones that were first established and embedded into the oral traditions and, thus, the landscape by the Creator and by the actions of Coyote and the other Animal First Peoples. These bones and *miyp* remain remarkably consistent from telling to telling, storyteller to storyteller, year after year, from time immemorial to the present. While enduring, the bones can be forgotten, only to be re-discovered, re-membered, as in the process expressed by the Greek term *anamnesis*—"a recollection or remembering from a past incarnation." The *miyp* are revealed only in participatory interaction with those who are attentively engaging, and what is revealed is only what is relevant and important to the story listener.

◆ ◆ ◆

In the summer of 1991, during a teacher's in-service training retreat at a camp resort along the shores of Lake Coeur d'Alene, I witnessed another most remarkable re-telling. Some thirty public school teachers from around the state were attending the multi-day workshop to learn how to more effectively and appropriately infuse narrative oral traditions into their language arts and social studies curriculums. A few of us were sitting around the evening's camp fire, when one of the teachers shared a Lakota story, animated and detailed with a complex storyline, lasting some twenty minutes. None of us had ever heard it before. Immediately following the re-telling, Mari Watters, a Niimíipuu elder and accomplished storyteller, and one of the workshop instructors, said, "Let's see if I got it." She re-membered the narrative, complete with identical storyline and characters, with all the *miyp* bones, just as Basil White had, but doing so her way, using her particular storytelling techniques to re-animate the bones of the story. (Re-told from the 1991 Mari Watters re-telling; also in Frey, Aripa, and Yellowtail 1995:152–53.) We all traveled within that Lakota story, that evening along the shores of Lake Coeur d'Alene, twice.

◆ ◆ ◆

Bringing the Bones Alive: Techniques of Telling. In the act of story-telling, the flesh and muscle of the story are added, re-animating and bringing life back to the bones, to a "living person." The breathing of life back into a story is accomplished through the techniques and styles of telling used by Schitsu'umsh raconteurs and elders. The bones are the enduring and perpetual underlying structures, what is stable, that give substance and form to the agile flesh, what is supple, and thus to a living story.

The elders are skilled in incorporating various techniques of storytelling as part of their bringing the story alive (Frey, Aripa, and Yellowtail 1995:147–54; Frey and the Schitsu'umsh 2001:188–204). These include an array of techniques, such as the inclusion of explicit references to particular locations, to rivers and mountains, to a rock outcropping, and the use of deictic words in the narrative texts, words like "here" and "there," to anchor the unfolding story lessons to a specific place and landscape. Those raconteurs are skilled in using deliberate pauses and voice intonation, and in complementing their auditory communications with body language and hand gesturing. As a well-respected Schitsu'umsh storyteller, Lawrence Aripa would project differing voices for each of the characters of his stories, and especially delighted in creating the deep burly voice of the Creator chastising Coyote for some misdeed.

This multi-dimensional storytelling session is thus more akin to a theatrical performance, a play acted out by a raconteur. The stories were typically inlaid with patterned phrase and scene repetitions, helping build tension within the storyline, emphasizing key points, and assisting in the remembering of the varied and lengthy narratives, a mnemonic device to keep the "bones" together. It would take Coyote five successive attempts at tricking the Swallow Sisters before breaking the damn at Celilo Falls, with each attempt fully described, until succeeding in releasing the Salmon upriver—three and five being the typical pattern for such scene repetitions in Plateau stories. For the Pend d'Oreille of Montana, the extensive use of repetition would contribute to the full cycle of Coyote narratives, with all his adventures and misadventures in going upriver, starting at Celilo

Falls on the Columbia, taking three full winter nights to complete the re-telling (Frey, Aripa, and Yellowtail 1995:150). Above all, the stories were re-membered, never memorized word for word, as that was too "rigid and dead." The appreciation of the re-telling as "re-membered" is so appropriate. There is a re-uniting, a renewed membership, a re-turning to and re-kindling of the kinship with all those within the unfolding story, alive with Coyote and Burnt Face, and with fellow listeners.

Along with other techniques, each elder might prefer and rely on a certain set of these skills, so one storyteller's style differs from that of the next. While varied in technique and style, the intent of each storyteller is always the same—to draw the listener into the story as a participant. As a re-membered story, the raconteur could freely adjust a pause here, add a repetition there, and give an inflection to that phrase, even add a phrase or two of local color and relevance to better engage the listeners. As a living being with each re-telling, the story is brought to life (Frey and the Schitsu'umsh 2001:191).

◆ ◆ ◆

The spring of Joseph Epes Brown's year-long sabbatical found me in Missoula, Montana, teaching a set of his Native American courses. One course in particular allowed me an opportunity to share examples of narrative oral traditions. On the scheduled day for the lesson, I was not sure if we had our first frost yet. So we drew the window blinds, turned off the overhead lights, and had a dog one of the students always brought to class stand guard at the door. It's been told that if a Coyote story is told out of season, in the summer, snakes and bears like to join in! The last of the stories re-told that day was "Coyote and the Lizard." It was a trickster story par excellence, abbreviated here:

Coyote, as always, was hungry for a little snack, and seeing Lizard high on a tree trunk, asked him to come down for a little visit. Knowing what Coyote really wanted, Lizard refused the offer. Insistent, Coyote repeated his request. Finally, Lizard tells Coyote that he, the Lizard, has an important task, that of "holding up the sky." If he should let go from the tree and came down, the sky would fall. Then Lizard said, "I'm really getting tired, could you relieve me while I rest? I'll come back." Fearing that the sky might fall, Coyote agrees and the two exchange places. And Lizard takes off for his "rest." But as time passes, and passes, Lizard doesn't return, and Coyote is himself getting exhausted, gripping tight to the tree's trunk. He just cannot hang on any longer, and sees a little ditch near the tree. That's it, he'd jumped into it before the sky falls, and he'll be safe. Coyote jumps and waits. But the sky didn't fall and the Lizard never did return.

That Sunday morning, the eighteenth of May 1980, the sky *did* fall on Missoula, as some five hundred miles away Mount Saint Helens erupted and a thick layer of fine ash settled over the city. Now I am not suggesting anything, but perhaps the coincidence is another reminder of how the stories are anchored to the cycles of the landscape, and of the power of story itself.

◆ ◆ ◆

Consider the responsibilities of the storyteller. A storyteller's primary responsibility is to keep all the bones of the story intact, anchoring the story to the *miyp*, and of not adding, nor deleting, nor inventing new bones. Recall that a "story is like a person, with a skeleton, muscle and flesh… you have to keep all the bones together; you can't add new ones or take away some…they all have to be there" (Frey and the Schitsu'umsh 2001:191). The storyteller's goal is also to bring the listeners—the audience—into the story as participants, not as observers of the story. The goal is to render the story accessible. "When you tell the story, you've gotta go inside and become the Coyote, or the Mole. Feel it as they feel it." And as one elder encouraged, "tell the story with heart" (Frey and the Schitsu'umsh 2001:191). It is the responsibility of the storyteller to welcome all the listeners, inviting them to participate in the story, regardless of their background and level of experience. The techniques of re-telling these ancient stories include the use of voice, intonation, and inflection, body language, unique idiosyncrasies and gestures, the spoken word itself, and the very selection of words that make the story accessible to everyone. These are techniques that seek to accommodate the differing experiences of the listeners, so that each are welcomed into the story's landscape. Again, there are no "morals" attached to the stories, no "this is what the story means." As elders have insisted, doing so could prevent the possibility of the many meanings that are hidden within from coming out.

With their techniques of storytelling, our elders attempt to bring life to the story, adding muscle and flesh to the bones, animating the skeleton with a beating heart, bringing the story-person back to life. A story should move about, be alive, with you participating in it, regardless of your particular background. The "glue" that connects the *miyp* with the changing and varied participants is the ability of the storyteller, and of the listener-participants, to connect through a deep understanding and appreciation of the other participants, as if part of one "family." This dynamic is the capacity to have empathy for someone else, both the human and the animal beings associated with the story. It is encapsulated in the Schitsu'umsh term, *snukwnkhwtskhwts'mi'ls*, "empathy"—a deep understanding of someone else's condition or situation. As applied throughout this essay, empathy is defined as that capacity to understand or feel what another being (be it human, animal or spirit) is experiencing from the perspective of the other—the capacity to place oneself in another's cognitive and/or affective position.

The essential competency of the storyteller is *snuk-wnkhwtskhwts'mi'ls*, the ability to effectively project one's self into the characters of the story, be it Coyote or Chief Child of the Yellowroot, and to help listeners discover the *miyp* they convey. And the storyteller must have the capacity and competency to deeply appreciate and know the varied listeners who are seeking to engage the story, each with their own differing names and backgrounds. He must be able to welcome a diverse audience into the story.

Through the eyes so much can be revealed. From 1992 to 2003 I had the opportunity to serve on the Idaho Humanities Council's Speakers Bureau, with a program topic on American Indian stories of Idaho. It brought me to communities throughout the state—small and large, rural and urban—sponsored by various civic groups and schools, with audiences as likely to be adults as children. While diverse, the groups typically shared in having little background in these indigenous narratives and their delivery of style, but a common desire to learn. I found that if I was to engage such diverse audiences, it required more than simply the intrigue of the novel storylines and their characters, and my rather animated storytelling techniques, though they greatly helped. In each presentation of the same story, I certainly sought to retain the essential storyline actions reflective of the story's perennial "bones." But if the story was to come alive and engage the audience I needed to gauge their level of engagement. I've always found it amazing how the eyes, in association with body language, can be windows into the reactions and attentiveness of a person. Students may think they can go incognito by sitting in the back row of a class, but they cannot. If a story was to succeed, I needed to feel and appreciate something of the ongoing responses among the members of my diverse audiences to the unfolding story. In presenting a story I'd always seek to remember, not memorize it. I needed a degree of flexibility to adjust or add a word here or there, to repeat a certain phrase, and to bring emphasis to a word by heightening its intonation. The "skin and muscle" could not be rigid. Given these surface adjustments to the storytelling, I could more effectively bring almost any audience—even those in the back row—into the story. When the eyes are all in sync so too is the participation.

Over eight years of observing Lawrence Aripa re-tell Four Smokes, Coyote and the Green Spot, and so many other of his favorite Schi̲t-su'umsh narratives to audiences of adults or elementary students, I saw how each time he'd maintain the deep integrity, the "bones" of the story. On each occasion he'd vary some of the words, intonation pattern, and the facial expressions, eyes this way and that, and hand gesturing, bringing a dynamic to the telling that welcomed the participation of his audience members.

◆ ◆ ◆

I've always found that in attempting to articulate and then convey my indigenous research to my students, especially in the context of an interactive seminar with its shared questions, that the ideas and subtleties of the research itself become better crystallized and new angles revealed and enunciated. One such example occurred during a fall semester while I was teaching an upper-level anthropology class on the Plateau Indians at the University of Idaho, and discussing the skills necessary for a successful storyteller and story-listener. In that classroom context, it was clear that if a story were to come alive and be meaningful, the prerequisite for both the raconteur and listener was the capacity for empathy. Then I encountered the Schitsu'umsh term, *snukwnkhwtskhwts'mi'ls*, which perfectly expressed this necessary ability to bring the story to life. For me, field research always continues and becomes more fully realized with discussion and dissemination, as in the classroom. Isn't the case that to convey an idea to someone else requires clear understanding of what you seek to convey? Something *chetche'in'nts*, revealed; something *hischits,* discovered.

◆ ◆ ◆

Consider the responsibilities of the listener. Of primary importance to the listener is to become a participant in the story, not an observer viewing the story from outside. As one elder stated, the stories are like canoes, you untie them when you start out, are told to stay on course when you wander off, and then tie the story up when you finish for the night (Frey, Aripa, and Yellowtail 1995:172). Everyone has to paddle the canoe if the canoe is to travel the rivers and you are to be able to explore the landscape of the Animal First Peoples and discover the gifts embedded within. Some Schitsu'umsh add to the end of their story the phrase, *tsi'łhnkhukhwatpalqs*, "the trail ends." It is the understanding that the story participants have been traveling and exploring a landscape, which is now coming to an end. As Cliff reminds us, the listeners seek to go "inside and become the Coyote, or the Bear, or the Mole," and the Animal First Peoples "come alive" and "swirl around you as Turtle is saying his thing or as Chipmunk is saying something...All these things suddenly come alive" (Frey and the Schitsu'umsh 2001:202).

But the stories only come alive, are real and true, full of meaning and vitality, when all participate and contribute; a story is an event of interaction with its participants. And while traveling in the story, the participant must be attentive to what gifts that may await, to what might be *chetche'in'nts*, revealed. As Vic Charlo, a Bitterroot Salish writer and elder, once told me, the "stories are what we explore with" (Frey, Aripa, and Yellowtail 1995:172). And should the participants no longer paddle, should they no longer "feel it as [the Animal First Peoples] feel it," no longer "swirl with Coyote," should they no longer demonstrate their participation in the story, the storytelling would cease, the elder stopping in mid-sentence.

And as with the storyteller, if the listeners are to participate in the paddling, the essential competency is their ability to *snuk-wnkhwtskhwts'mi'ls*, to deeply listen and understand, and be able to project into and have a deep appreciation of the characters of the story, be they Coyote, Chief Child of the Yellowroot, or Chipmunk. Listeners must bring into play empathy for others. Only in doing so can the *miyp* these characters embody be revealed to them.

◆ ◆ ◆

During the 1970s I was welcomed into the home of Tom and Susie Yellowtail, living with them for a number of summers, extending to year-round on a couple of occasions. These two individuals lived extraordinary lives, with wonderful stories to share. On numerous occasions people from throughout the United States would pay them weekend visits, hoping to learn more from Tom and Susie. They were gracious hosts and remarkable storytellers. Susie, one of the first American Indian registered nurses in the country, received her education "back east," and changed her name from "Susie Walking Bear" to avoid frightening her patients. She toured as chaperone to "Miss American Indian" winners, served on a couple of Presidential Commissions, and was always in demand as a speaker on college campuses. But over the years, after hearing Susie repeat her stories, they became so familiar to me that I grew less attentive as they were re-told, sometimes tuning them out. And then there was

Tom, always seated right beside Susie, listening, listening to stories he knew so intimately, having heard them for literally decades, even experiencing some for himself. Tom would laugh, and he'd shed a tear, and he'd so deeply listen that it was as if he'd never heard Susie's stories before! Susie was indeed a great storyteller, bringing to bear all the necessary competencies. And Tom was indeed a great story listener, participating in the unfolding landscape of that story as it was brought to life. Participating anew, swirling with Susie. (Re-told from experiences; also in Frey, Aripa, and Yellowtail 1995:153–54.)

◆ ◆ ◆

Orality. Deward Walker, my dissertation chair at the University of Colorado, insisted that if I were to work with the Apsáalooke I needed to learn their language. To better engage and understand my indigenous collaborators and garner trust with them, it was critical that I learn the language of my hosts. During the 1970s and 80s, the Crow population was fully bilingual, with an estimated 80 percent fluent Apsáalooke speakers. It was the primary language heard at all public events and in most daily conversations, and used by all the elders. Besides Tom and Susie Yellowtail, my teachers included Hu Matthews, Rose Chesarech, and Mary Helen Medicine Horse. In 1979 I was perhaps the first to use a Native language to satisfy the University of Colorado's language requirement. While I was never fluent, my minimal competency in the language opened doors and revealed insights. I was able to grasp many topics of discussion and certainly knew when I was the brunt of a joke! Offering a simple greeting in Apsáalooke demonstrated to potential collaborators that I was dedicated enough to go the extra steps to enter the Tin Shed on their terms. The lack of the use of personal pronouns—he, she or it—in the language led to the realization of how meaning was contextualized. In a conversation or during a storytelling the context and circumstances would reveal the gender of the subject or character. There was an informative use of the suffix, *shéeluk,* meaning "it is said" or "he/she said it" in oral narratives, which was also noted by Robert Lowie (1960) using his orthography as *tsə ruk.* You might hear if told in English:

Everyone is having a tough time of it, it is said,
  There, the Rock Monster is rolling around, it is said,
    Over there, the camps *aren't safe*, it is said.

Patterned clusters of "verses and scene" in a narrative were marked by use of these suffixes and gave a distinctive oral-nuanced cadence to the storytelling (Frey, Aripa, and Yellowtail 1995:151–52, 217–18). And with the "future and non-future verb tense" structure, lacking past, present, and future verb forms, I was introduced to a non-linear, cyclical understanding of time itself. The nature of orality was taking on meaning of altogether new dimensions for me.

◆ ◆ ◆

The varied storytellers, indeed the very words they speak, share certain qualities. They share qualities in communicating through the *oral* tradition, through what is called "orality." Orality is not a form of communication simply devoid of writing; it is not to be equated with illiteracy. Orality has unique forms of communication, from the nature of disseminating information to the storing of that information. As expressed by poet Henry Wadsworth Longfellow, "The human voice is the organ of the soul." As distinct from literacy, the orality of storytelling has implications for the meaning conveyed (Frey, Aripa, and Yellowtail 1995:141–47; Frey and the Schitsu'umsh 2001:188-204).

Consider the physiological nature of this auditory experience, of this clustering of phonemes, of distinguishing sounds within the act of storytelling. As a heard experience, orality is a transitory, effervescent incident, here one moment and gone the next, a continual stream. No permanence, no objects. And further, the sound emitted envelops and surrounds the listener, involuntarily unifying him or her in that momentary event. Once spoken, the word is heard, is registered and envelops a recipient. Ears unlike eyes are not as easily closed to the influx of a physical stimulation. At this physiological level, "Orality is thus a transitory *event* that *unifies* the listener *involuntarily* with the sound and its sources" (Frey, Aripa, and Yellowtail 1995:143).

Consider the syntactic and semantic nature of the story experience, of this clustering of morphemes, of meaningful units of sound within the story text. Indigenous texts are often characterized by their general lack of function words, words that provide relationship and connect thoughts, such as prepositions, "about," "for," "of," "with," and conjunctions, "and," "but," "or." In fact, indigenous texts are generally noted for their rather terse, stark use of words and descriptive phrases altogether. Niimíipuu scholar Archie Phinney pointed out that in the combined indigenous oral literature of Coyote, "No clear image is offered or needed" of this trickster (Frey, Aripa, and Yellowtail 1995:149). This was indeed the case for all the Animal First Peoples, lacking not only imagery but detailed descriptions of their actions, their motivations, and of the landscape on which their exploits unfolded. Hence to complete the thoughts between words and phrases, to know the gender of a character, to complete the image of Coyote, or of a landscape, each listener is called upon to engage the story text and add the connections, to make the links, to complete the picture. It's hard work. A story is only whole when its participants are an integral part of it, integrated within a larger context of interpersonal relations and a particular landscape. No passive listening allowed, no viewing from afar. But everyone can also connect the dots a little differently, discovering this meaning or that meaning, embedded within the richly layered story, relative to his or her own experiences and maturation level—lessons specific and relevant to him or her alone. Meaning is contextualized.

◆ ◆ ◆

In 1974, while involved in the Indian Health Service project attempting to improve healthcare delivery for Apsáalooke, I would randomly visit homes in Crow Agency, introducing myself and the project. Virtually everyone welcomed this stranger into their homes, asking me to join in in whatever they were doing at the time, be it watching TV in the living room, having a meal with the entire family seated around the dining room table, or on one occasion, stacking bales of hay in the back corral. As I introduced the project, everyone seemed to like the idea, seeing it as important and wanting to help, many even voicing the notion that they could "turn the tables on the docs" and "teach them something." But as the conversation turned into a semi-structured interview, with more specific questions about how they understood illnesses and the terms they used for sickness, they responded elusively, or not at all. Few wished to talk about an illness he, she, or another person had. I was beginning to understand the power of the spoken word, of speaking something into existence. (Re-told from experiences; also in Frey, Aripa, and Yellowtail 1995:154–55).

◆ ◆ ◆

Finally, consider the indigenous spoken word itself. Through my understanding of the Apsáalooke oral-based language I glimpsed for the first time a most remarkable attribute of the oral tradition—words spoken aloud have the potential to create reality (Frey, Aripa, and Yellowtail 1995:xviii, 154–58; Frey and the Schitsu'umsh 2001:197–99; Frey 2004:163–64). People were reluctant to talk about an illness, for fear of bringing it about. That summer of 1974 I also noticed that "goodbye" was seldom spoken, but instead I'd hear, *diiawákaawik*, "I'll see you later." "Goodbye" was considered "too final," possibly leading to not seeing that person again. Bestowed by one's *biilápxe* during a Bundle ceremony, an "Indian Name" was not only descriptive of a quality sought for someone, but which actually helped to bring that quality about in the person's life. There was Allen Old Horn's Medicine Bundle, as a public "announcer," a "camp crier," helping protect his use of words when spoken aloud for another, typically younger person. And then I was introduced to an Apsáalooke expression, *dasshússua,* literally meaning "breaking with the mouth" (Frey 1987:164; Frey, Aripa, and Yellowtail 1995:155). For the Apsáalooke, that which comes from the heart through the mouth has the transformative power to bring about that which was spoken. With this understanding I began to realize that indeed, the words of a story don't so much describe the world, as "stories make the world." When "the fibers of the words are woven into the exquisite tapestry of a story, the words bring forth the deeds portrayed…The world is made and rendered meaningful in the act of revealing Coyote's story of it" (Frey, Aripa, and Yellowtail 1995:156, 214). When Tom, Cliff, Lawrence, or Mari wove their words into a fine tapestry of their stories, in their acts of speaking the story aloud, the "world is made" and rendered meaningful. Always the biggest challenge for my students was to make the jump that in this act of re-telling the story of Rock Monster covered in huckleberry juice drowning in Lake Coeur d'Alene, just maybe the *blue* of the lake is perpetuated?

When all these orality elements and dynamics—the storytelling techniques, the physiological experience, the syntactical qualities, and the power of the spoken word—come together and coalesce, they can transform a passive audience into participant travelers within an unfolding landscape. Coyote swirls around you and talks to you. As the elders have said, a story is only brought to life when all those in the canoe of the storytelling session—the storyteller and participating audience—equally help with paddling up the river, exploring the territory together, with the raconteur guiding the way (Frey, Aripa, and Yellowtail 1995:172). Traditionally, when participants began waning, disengaging from a storytelling session, they would cease to provide verbal or visual cues acknowledging their continued engagement—for example, ceasing to periodically voice, *éeh*, "yes." Without feedback, the raconteur would stop the re-telling, immediately, regardless of whether the story was completed or not (Frey, Aripa, and Yellowtail 1995:148). The paddling had ceased. As an interaction between storyteller and listeners, the raconteur monitors participation, fluctuating an emphasis here, employing a technique there, and guiding participants within and through a territory. The storyteller's responsibility is to encourage the listeners to remain paddlers, engaging them as participants, while keeping the canoe on course, navigating each bend and fork in the river of the story's landscape, the story's bones. In turn, the listener-participants' responsibilities are to fully engage the story, keeping the canoe moving, and to listen deeply, discovering what might wait within, "a gift," unique for each participant, unique each time the story is engaged.

The elements and dynamics of orality bring about the transitory intersection of those participating, an event always in the making, anchored to the *miyp* "bones," allowing you and the Coyote to swirl and talk with each other. This multi-dimensional expression, when conducted in the native language, is understood akin to "ceremony," as the ritual act of participating in the renewal of the world, in a shining through of the sacred, a hierophany. By re-telling stories of Coyote, stories of creation and rejuvenation, during the dormant winter, the flowering of the coming spring is brought forth. The orality of storytelling renders reality as an ephemeral event, participatory and unifying, performative and transformative, at each unfolding moment. In giving voice to story the world is brought forth and perpetuated.

Literacy. The contrasts between orality and literacy (the written word, another sort of symbolic clustering), could not be more stark and revealing, with critical implications. This contrast is not to suggest each is in exclusion of the other, as any particular language system may have what I will identify as elements of both orality and literacy. For example, the pictorial arts among the Apsáalooke, such as pictographs on a stone wall, winter counts painted on a buffalo hide, beaded designs on a dance regalia, the sacred objects of a Medicine Bundle, or architectural style of a tipi, can entail qualities suggestive of literacy.

As we know, writing is itself a technological invention, involving some sort of physical medium or surface (wood, clay, or stone surface, hide, parchment, paper, computer screen) and some sort of marking device (etching or imprinting device, ink and pen, press, electronic keyboard), to record and share a standardized symbolic code (an alphabet with consonants and vowels). An early example is represented in Sumerian cuneiform of some 3,500 BCE. Fundamentally a series of pictographs stamped on clay tokens, cuneiform was used for recording ideas and numbers associated with economic transactions. With the Semitic languages, such as Arabic, Aramaic, Hebrew, and Phoenician, a consonant system was developed as early as 1,050 BCE, and with the Greeks, vowels were added as early as 400 BCE. Among the Olmec and Maya of Mesoamerica, we have forms of writing dating back at least to 900 BCE. This is the technology that has moved the once oral traditions of Gilgamesh and Homer to what we now can hold in our hands. The organic nature of orality is anything but technologically based.

The dynamics of literacy are further revealing, in contrast with orality (Frey, Aripa, and Yellowtail 1995:141–47). First consider the physiological nature of the literacy experience. Literacy is composed of visual images and symbols, of written words fixed to the pages of a book, to a material object, an object with some degree of permanence, having a quality of "thingness." A story is accessed and conveyed through the physicality of visible and tangible pages of a book. The eye of the reader can scan the lines of the pages at his or her own pace, voluntarily, stopping here to reflect on this word, on that idea, backward scan, moving on, speed reading through this section, skipping that altogether, and putting the whole thing aside, at his or her pleasure. It is not an involuntary engagement as with orality. To the extent that the medium mediates and influences what is viewed, the world envisioned via literacy tends to be understood as made up of objects with some degree of a permanence, a world objectified, with you, the reader, as a detached, independent viewer.

Consider the syntactic and semantic nature of literacy. Anchored from a much more formalized and standardized set of grammatical rules, literacy seeks to render meaning independent and autonomous of an interpersonal context, independent of the reader. A sentence, a story itself, has a completeness unto itself, with minimal need of an infusion of links and connections made by a reader. The author endeavors to convey a constant and indelible denotation, remarkably detached from an immediacy with any particular audience. A preposition added here, a conjunction there, personal pronouns throughout. Coyote is delivered to the reader richly adorned with imagery and motivation, a landscape endowed with color and texture rather than left to the reader's imagination to connect the dots. If the communication is to be successful, both author and reader would need to subscribe to a shared grammatical convention, for example, formalized in APA style for the social and behavioral sciences, MLA format for the humanities, or Chicago Manual of Style for anthropologists, to inform, structure, and encase the dissemination and the accessing of meaning. In contrast to orality, meaning is decontextualized.

Taken together, the qualities and attributes of literacy contribute to an understanding of reality as made up of discrete objects, with some degree of concreteness and permanency, to be observed from afar, as if behind the neutrality of a thick glass pane. Born out of this duality is an impetus to invest in and bring forth an ideational story separate from and descriptive of the physical experience, in beliefs and theories about reality, in hypotheses, propositions and equations that are predictive of "sense datum," material objects known through direct experience, in analytical treatises. It certainly can be argued that the dynamics and nature of literacy not only supported, but was a precursor and, if not, a precondition for the emergence of the scientific method as derived from such philosophers as René Descartes and John Locke, as will be discussed subsequently. Born out of this dualism is also investment in story that is separate from and descriptive of experience, in sonnets and poems and prose, in essays, short stories and novels, in the great tradition of Shakespeare and Dickens, in literary stories—stories that seek to "suspend disbelief" about reality, taking the reader to new imaginary worlds created by their authors. The literacy of science and literature can *objectify*, render reality as made up of objects; and can dichotomize, render reality *objectively*, separating an observer's hypothesis or sonnet from the observed sense data or nature's configuration, extricating self from other.

◆ ◆ ◆

Cliff SiJohn repeatedly reminded me over the years that there was something very special about the act of telling of these stories. In re-telling of the "First Peoples, they come *alive…*they *swirl around* you as the Turtle is saying his thing or as the Chipmunk is saying something…they *swirl around* you and you see the *Indian medicine*… this is Chipmunk talking to you…this is Coyote talking to you… this is the Elk and the Deer and the Eagle, and this is Hawk…all these things *suddenly come alive*…they are just as alive as they were a thousand years ago." (Re-told from 1989 and 1997 interviews; also in Frey and the Schitsu'umsh 2001:197.) "They come *alive*…they *swirl* around you."

◆ ◆ ◆

The contrast between orality and literacy could not be more revealing. The shift is from viewing stories as explanations about and descriptions of the world and of Coyote and a blue lake, as predictors of reality or suspenders of disbelief about reality, to experiencing the stories as the world, as intensifiers of what is most real. The shift is from understanding an author of a novel or a scientist of a theory as its originator and you the observer, to experiencing the unfolding of a story with its storyteller in concert with you, with the other engaged listener-participants, and with Turtle, Chipmunk, and Coyote, all as co-facilitators, as co-creators of that transitory intersection, all swirling together, "alive as they were a thousand years ago," and a lake made blue. The shift is from compartmentalized concrete cubicles, to dynamic participatory amalgamations, from abstracted beliefs about, to direct experience with. Or put more bluntly, as one of the elders repeatedly told me, "Rodney, when you write it down, my words are dead," an estranging of my being from the world, calcifying its vibrancy.

◆ ◆ ◆

In 1977 and 1978 I was hired by Montana State University as an adjunct professor to offer college courses for students home for the summer break. That first summer we used a room at the local Catholic Church at Crow Agency for our classroom, and had ten or so students enrolled, all of whom were successfully pursuing their graduate studies. Of the courses I was to teach, one was on American Indian Religion. Imagine this "white boy," a rookie instructor at that, teaching a course on Indian spirituality to Indians! Well, I moved forward as best I could, prepared extra hard, and attempted to focus on traditions far from the Crow country, on the ceremonies and oral traditions of the Diné (Navajo) of the Southwest, the Kwakwaka'wakw (Kwakiutl) of the Northwest Coast, and of the Inuit (Eskimo) of the Arctic, for example. And it seemed to be working out, as we had some great discussions about some practices relatively unfamiliar to my students. I worked hard on those lectures, researched them thoroughly, but interestingly, my students were not taking detailed notes on these fine lectures, in fact, no notes at all. Well, I thought this could serve as a teaching moment. So for the first exam, an essay exam, I'd base it almost entirely on my lectures and not on the readings, and when their graded exams were returned, they'd realize the value of taking notes. The exam questions were handed out and the exam began. The students wrote, and wrote, and wrote some more. And when I graded their essays, without an exception, their responses were outstanding, conveying back what I had conveyed and then much more, all in their own words, all earning grades of A. It was a teaching moment, a teaching moment for me! While all these graduate students had demonstrated a high capacity to successfully navigate the academic world of the university, doing so with tremendous competencies in literacy, they were also all primary Crow speakers, with competencies in orality and in listening deeply, all without a reliance on note-taking to remember.

 HEAR THE STORIES

While lacking the interaction and intimacy of sitting before as elder and engaging in an unfolding story brought to life, recordings can offer the opportunity to experience a little of the orality of stories. To hear stories from Cliff SiJohn, Lawrence Aripa and other elders, visit the website *Schitsu'umsh Lifelong Learning Online* (Frey and the Schitsu'umsh 2002), at www.lib. uidaho.edu/digital/L3/Sites/ShowOneSiteSiteID50.html.

Despite the stark contrast, a competency in literacy is not so great that it precludes a continued competency in orality. They need not be mutually exclusive. As Mari Watters and Basil White would later demonstrate, within the oral tradition, the bones of the stories, or of a white guy's self-assured lectures, are not easily forgotten, but can be remembered and re-told with vitality. (Re-told from experiences; also in Frey, Aripa, and Yellowtail 1995:144).

◆ ◆ ◆

Traveling in Agnes Vanderburg's stories? In the act of *re-telling*, a lake is *made* blue? The *Awakkuléeshe*? A burnt face *made* as a newborn child's face? When you tell the story, you've got to go inside and *become* the Coyote? Story as *living* being? The sky *falling*? Not speaking of illness and *dasshússua*? *Orality* and *swirling* with Coyote? Stories *remembered* and great stories *will* come? *Literacy* with firm bones intact yet flesh solidified *firm*? I accepted these assertions on face value, patient, trusting my teachers, but still all a great mystery!

Yet I asked, could the "dead" words still bear fruit, a huckleberry or two? Could the words etched on paper and their stories even be brought back to life, if only a little?

I woke with such a desire.

Smłich
"salmon"

Resuscitating Salmon from the Bones—
Re-telling as Pedagogy and Perpetuation

Salmon is a *great* warrior.
He's going up the Big River,
   the Columbia River,
      along the trail there;
         Salmon goes up river.
            Salmon *always* goes up river.
Salmon comes to a wooden platform along the river's bank;
   it's built to catch the salmon;
      it's not so well made;
         Old Man Spider is working on it.
Old Man Spider is working on a dip-net;
   with the twine;
      it's not so well made.
"What are you doing?" Salmon says.
"Oh,
   I'm just making a platform,
      preparing a dip-net.
         I thought I might try my luck at catching a salmon or two;
            they might take pity on me," Old Man Spider says.
Well,
   Salmon goes over to the platform there

piles up rocks,
　　moves the logs,
　　　here and here.
　Salmon picks up the dip-net,
　　threads the twine,
　　　here and here.
Salmon puts the dip-net into the river,
　just like that,
　　lands a salmon.
He goes back up the bank of the river,
　to Old Man Spider.
"Well,
　there are a lot of salmon in that river.
　　Everything is ready.
　　　I dipped out one salmon;
　　　　left it there for you," Salmon says.
"Soon the human people will come to this place.
　When the people come,
　　this is the way they'll fish the salmon,
　　　Old Man Spider *teach them this*," Salmon says.
"There's a big camp of people up river;
　the Dove people," Old Man Spider says.
"The chief has a beautiful daughter.
　The one who can split the five pieces of elk antler,
　　each as long as a spear point,
　　　he can marry his daughter," Old Man Spider says.
Salmon goes up the river,
　to the camp of the Dove people.
　　Salmon *always* goes up river.

◆ ◆ ◆

As we began this essay with story, a series of stories, let's continue with another, a little longer story, the creation narrative involving *Smlich*, the Schitsu'umsh word for "salmon." As I've entered the Tin Sheds of indigenous peoples, I've always been greeted with stories. Story is the place to begin. As I've entered my first class meetings each semester, I've always welcomed my students with stories, the place to begin. This particular story is one of my favorites, having re-told it and brought it to life with students and at public gatherings for over two decades. And perhaps Salmon can provide for you an opportunity to gather a huckleberry or two.

I encourage you, the reader, to become a speaker or listener. Have someone read and speak the text to you, so that you can experience its orality. Listen, and with attentiveness and empathy, attempt to relate to Salmon, Dove, and Spider, see from their perspectives. To gain a sense of the oral nuance and storytelling dynamic I have formatted the story in a poetic style. By representing each verse on the written page as a separate line, the rhythm and pacing can be more clearly conveyed. It is a literature meant to be told aloud, heard in the company of others, a literature based in orality. In this re-telling, see if you can begin to travel Salmon's landscape.

Next, try to re-member and re-tell the story to others. As you do, seek to maintain the storyline, characters, and "bones" within the story, while applying empathetic storytelling skills to the members of your audience—adjusting words, pacing, intonations to draw them into the story. Without changing the bones, consider adding an unanticipated twist in the unfolding story that might garner a smile or even a laugh. Later in our story, watch for an unexpected reference to the gray wolf, for example. As a storyteller, you can easily judge if listeners are engaged or drifting off.

In the text you'll also notice the periodic repetition of the phrase— "Salmon goes up the river, Salmon *always* goes up river." Traditionally, audience members would acknowledge their participation by periodically voicing *éeh*, "yes." Without such acknowledgment, the story would cease. To help transform a passive audience into story participants I'd have listeners voice aloud the second phrase—"Salmon *always* goes up river." When some would be slow to respond, I'd wait, looking them in the eye. In doing so, the participants become part of the story's pacing and its re-telling.

Vary the length of your pauses between each verse; short pauses are indicated by commas and semicolons, and longer pauses by periods. Certain words are italicized for emphasis. Your voice should oscillate; not be a monotone. You will notice that certain verses as well as sequences of actions are repeated throughout the text. Note how many elk antlers must be broken? How many wolf brothers? How many times does Salmon repeat the phrase—"And soon the human people will come to this place"? It will take Salmon a particular number of attempts to successfully complete an endeavor. Throughout the Inland Northwest the numbers which govern these patterns are typically three and five. The patterns of repetition not only highlight the key actions of the story, but help draw the listener into the rhythm of that story. "Salmon always goes up river. Salmon *always* goes up river."

You will also notice that the use of the language is rather terse. Descriptions of the landscape and the characters that roam that land—Salmon, Dove, and Spider—are only minimally conveyed. In fact, the motivations of those characters are seldom explained. It is left to the active imagination of the story listener to complete the images of the landscape and the actions of the characters. It is for this reason that the visual images we have provided only hint at the descriptions of Salmon or Dove. As Archie Phinney, a Niimíipuu who worked with his mother Wayi'latpu to provide a comprehensive study of his people's oral literature (1934), once stated, there is "no clear picture" of the physical images of the Animal First Peoples "offered or needed."

With your particular techniques of telling, bring flesh to the bones, allow your audience to travel the story's landscape and swirl with Salmon, allow the story to again come alive. In the experience of re-telling and hearing the story, in the patterns of repetition, and in the minimal use of the language and visual imagery the listener is transformed into a participant within the story. And the voice of Salmon and of the elders who have told his story becomes a little more immediate and personal and the swirling can begin.

◆ ◆ ◆

Salmon goes up the river,
    to the camp of the Dove people.
        Salmon *always* goes up river.
Along the way he sees something on the path,
    a piece of flint,
        hmmm—a sharp piece of flint?
            Salmon picks it up,
                puts it under his *fingernail.*
Along the way he sees something on the path,
    hmmm—a small pouch of salmon oil?
        Salmon picks it up,
            puts it in his mouth,
                just behind his *cheek.*
Salmon goes up the river;
    Salmon *always* goes up river.

◆ ◆ ◆

The story of Salmon is one of the many great stories told by the indigenous people of the Plateau. This is the area of the Inland Northwest and Columbia River Basin, a river drainage of over 13,000 miles, stretching from its mouth at the Pacific Ocean near Portland, Oregon, to its headwaters in British Columbia, Canada. As with the other Animal First Peoples, such as Coyote and Fox, Rattlesnake and Grizzly Bear, and Rabbit and Jack Rabbit, Salmon travels a primordial landscape and helps prepare the world for the "coming of the Human Peoples."

There are many stories of Salmon's people. In the story of Coyote and the Swallow Sisters, the two Sisters had captured all the salmon people in a large pond near Celilo Falls on the Columbia River. With his skills at deception and trickery, Coyote is able to free the salmon to go up stream and turns the Sisters into swallows, who now signal the return of the salmon each year. There is also the story of Coyote and the Woman. Coyote sought a particularly beautiful woman as his wife, but the people refused to allow the marriage. Coming down river, stopping at each village with his request, he is denied. In anger, Coyote makes the great river falls near Spokane, Washington, and Post Falls, Idaho. As a result, the salmon are now prevented from going up river, and the people cannot fish for them.

Before 1855, when the first of a series of federal treaties was signed with the indigenous people of the Columbia River Basin region, there were over fourteen million Chinook, coho, and sockeye salmon, as well as steelhead, that swam up the Columbia annually. It has been estimated that for many of the tribes of the region the salmon contributed up to 40 percent of the entire aboriginal diet. The indigenous people have always given the greatest respect to Salmon, honoring him and the fish he brought. Each year with the coming of the salmon up the river, and at sites such as Celilo Falls, Priest Rapids, and Kettle Falls, the people would hold the First Salmon ceremony. During the five-day ceremony, homage would be paid to Salmon, and salmon would be gathered in great quantities from specially constructed weir-traps and dip nets.

Today it is estimated that fewer than 2.5 million salmon return annually to spawn in the Columbia River and its various tributaries. The number of native sockeye salmon is even fewer, with often less than a dozen making their way back through the 950 miles of rapids and eight hydroelectric dams along the Columbia and Snake Rivers to Redfish Lake in central Idaho. In former times thousands of sockeye salmon would return to Redfish Lake to spawn each year, hence its name. For those salmon who once headed for Canada, none have passed beyond the Grand Coulee Dam in central Washington since its completion in 1942.

◆ ◆ ◆

Salmon goes up the river;
   Salmon *always* goes up river.
      It's a *big* camp.
There are many young men,
   sitting on a log there;
      each had tried to split the pieces of antler;
        their heads are held down.

"I'll split the antlers,
   Rrrr," Grizzly Bear said.
      But he *couldn't*.
All who tried,
   each had *failed*,
      hold their heads down.
"It's up to you;
   None of us could break them,
      try your hand at it," the young men say.
"*Well*,
   if the chief asks me,
      I'll try my hand at it," Salmon says.
Salmon goes into the chief's tule mat lodge.
   The chief is there.
      His daughter is there.
"Come on in," the chief says.
Salmon's and Dove's eyes meet.
   They care for each other very much.
      She particularly loves his *handsome red head*.
"Try to split the pieces of antler," the chief says.
"Thank you for the invitation," Salmon says.
The pieces of antler are laying there,
   on a small tule mat.
"Do you want me to split this antler here,
   here?" Salmon says.
Salmon points his finger to the antler;
   moves his fingernail here and here.
Salmon holds the antler to his mouth;
   kisses the antler.
Salmon twists the antler;
   splits it into pieces.
"*Ah*," the chief says.
Salmon takes another antler.
"Do you want me to split it here,
   here?"

Salmon moves his fingernail along the antler;
    puts it to his mouth.
Salmon twists the antler;
    splits it in two.
"*Ah*," the chief says.
Salmon takes the third elk antler.
"Do you want me to split it here,
        here?"
He moves his finger;
    puts the antler to his mouth.
The antler splits into several pieces.
"*Ah*," the chief says.
Salmon takes the fourth antler.
"Do you want me to split it here,
        here?"
He moves his fingernail along the antler;
    takes it to his mouth.
The antler splits into pieces.
"*Ah*," the chief says.
Salmon takes the fifth antler,
    the *biggest* of all.
"Do you want me to split it here,
    here?" Salmon says.
Salmon moves his fingernail along the antler here,
    here and here again;
        takes it to his mouth,
            takes it to his mouth again.
Salmon twists the antler
    and twists the antler.
        It splits into *several* pieces.
"*Ah*,
    ah," the chief says.
The chief of the Dove people is true to his word.
    Salmon and Dove are allowed to marry.
        They care for each other very much.

She loves his *handsome red head.*
"The people will be very angry that we got married.
    Hold *tight* to my belt,
       close your eyes;
         you'll be safe.
           The arrows won't hurt you.
             They're after me," Salmon says.

◆ ◆ ◆

That morning they were particularly spirited—an animated class of fourth graders. Lawrence Aripa walked in, suitcase in hand, and made his way to the front desk beside the teacher. An introduction was made, amid a partial simmering of the high energy. But once Lawrence began speaking in an unfamiliar rhythm, and bringing out from the well-traveled suitcase, one by one, each item of his powwow dance regalia, a quiet filled the room, eyes and ears became attentive in anticipation. Each item that emerged—a porcupine hair head roach, then a pair of beaded moccasins—was accompanied by a story—stories of their meanings, stories of particular importance to Lawrence from his years of powwow dancing. Stories blended into stories of Coyote and Four Smokes, and the students were transported to landscapes none had previously witnessed, none had experienced, and none would soon forget.

◆ ◆ ◆

With such a smile on his face, Lawrence Aripa would tell of Four Smokes or Coyote and the Rock before an audience of fourth graders in their classrooms or teachers at workshops (Frey, Aripa, and Yellowtail 1995:15–20, 71–75, 177–79; Frey and the Schitsu'umsh 2001:127–31). At his family's annual winter Jump Dance, storyteller Cliff SiJohn would take care to include the children in the ceremony. At one such dance, he paused the dancing to have the children come to the center floor and with deliberate patience, Cliff told stories, sang songs, and recalled the power of what the children were witnessing, capping it off with a giveaway of toys and candy, so they would remember the Jump Dance when at play. Even when his sight had been taken and he was confined to a wheelchair, Cliff loved nothing more than to come to my classes each year and take my students "huckleberrying."

As Lawrence so aptly demonstrated as he opened his worn suitcase and stories flowed out, a most effective way to have my students enter the Tin Shed is through story. In my teaching, I use story for pedagogy. I attempt to fill the classroom with story, including having elders come to my classroom to share their stories, as Cliff SiJohn and Josiah Pinkham have done so often.

I have myself attempted to demonstrate and model for my students the power of storytelling (though first I confirm that we've had our fall frost). My all-time favorite re-tellings are those of Burnt Face and Salmon, a "resuscitation" from the "bones." So ubiquitous to the Plateau, Salmon, in all his adventures, was the perfect entry point onto this landscape. Over the years I've had former students comment on how they can still vividly remember my re-telling of Salmon, though evidently not much else from the course. So much for those great lectures! And so it is with story.

Certainly my own style and technique of re-telling and animating the stories has been influenced by years with Tom Yellowtail and Lawrence Aripa. I also credit my passion for narrative oral traditions to David Carrasco, who was a professor of religious studies at the University of Colorado. I was his graduate teaching assistant, and he served on my dissertation committee. David's charismatic enthusiasm brought his classes alive, as his students entered into the ancient Aztec story of Quetzalcoatl, the Feathered Serpent, and the other Tin Sheds David constructed for them. It is David, now at Harvard with a joint appointment at the Harvard Divinity School, who I thank for introducing me to the great scholar of religion, Mircea Eliade, and the notion of the "hierophany" (Eliade 1954; 1958; 1959).

As an essential learning activity in my classes, I have students themselves re-member and re-tell authentic stories, but only those narratives that can be appropriately and publicly shared (Frey, Aripa, and Yellowtail 1995:232–40). As we learned from Agnes, in some traditions Coyote stories are only re-told during the winter. Following the ethics of *baaéechichiwaau*, some stories are meant only for the ears of family members, and are not to be shared publically. Students research whether a story is appropriate to share, its seasonality, and any other associated etiquette. I also have students attempt to re-tell a narrative that has been recorded in its native language, with an English interlinear transcription, along with a free translation. For the Apsáalooke, students consider the written texts of Robert Lowie (1960); for the Niimíipuu, such texts can be found in Haruo Aoki (1979), Hauro Aoki and Deward Walker (1989), and Archie Phinney (1934); and for the Schitsu'umsh, Gladys Reichard (1946, 1947). In so doing, elements of the storytelling nuance, such as deictics, phrase repetitions, quotative suffixes, verb tense forms, and personal pronoun usage (which are often removed or rendered into standardized English when a story is edited for publication for a wider audience), can be identified and reintegrated into the re-telling. With these rich texts, students can also more readily access the "bones" of the story and the *miyp* "teachings" embedded within. In the re-telling, it is critical that the student retains all the bones, not adding new ones, not forgetting the perennial ones, and not changing the storyline, characters, and scenes. But in seeking out a narrative for re-telling, I also have students select a story that somehow speaks to them, for which they have found some sort of affinity and attraction, be it a lesson or character engrained in the narrative.

It then becomes the responsibility of the storyteller, using his or her particular repertoire of storytelling techniques, to reanimate the bones with flesh, to bring it alive for the audience now transformed into participants within the unfolding story. In essence, it becomes an act of *resuscitating* the bones imprinted on the printed page. The same story might be animated by one student raconteur with extensive use of dynamic intonation and differing voice inflection for each character, while another storyteller might apply visual body language and hand gesturing to help bring the narrative alive. In each case, experiencing the stories from the inside looking out can bring a whole new awareness of their meanings.

As the students engage in their stories, I ask them to be attentive, to listen closely, to *stmi'sm*. I ask them to participate, to "paddle," to do and engage, to *'itsk'u'lm*. The students are asked to attempt to *snukwnkhwtskhwts'mi'ls*, to feel with empathy, Salmon and Dove. I ask them to apply a little of their empathy to those they encounter along the story's landscape. Only by doing so can the stories reveal their *miyp*. Embedded deep within are the bones, the *miyp* await revealing, *chetche'in'nts*, await discovery, *hischits*. Only in doing so can Salmon come alive and again swim upriver. Because Salmon always goes up river!

In the endeavor, I'd remind my students with the words Cliff SiJohn shared with me, "Watch and you'll see the storyteller become the Coyote!…When you tell the stories, you've gotta go inside and become the Coyote, or the Bear, or the Mole. Feel it as they feel it, and tell the stories with your heart [gently patting himself on his chest], not up here [pointing to his head]. If you tell it with your heart, you'll have clean hands" (Frey, Aripa, and Yellowtail 1995:216).

Following the re-telling, I have students reflect on any revealed and discovered meanings, submitting a short "reflective write." While the experience of re-telling a story in front of others can make some students anxious, I have found that they appreciate the resulting benefits. It has been rewarding to have my students, after first fully engaging the stories and bringing them to life as part of the course assignment, later re-tell them, fully animated, with all the bones, before a group of local elementary or high school students, extending the life of the stories and rendering them accessible to others.

◆ ◆ ◆

The people are standing around watching.
The young men with their heads down,
   are there.
     They get *angry* when they see Salmon with Dove.
Salmon rushes across the camp toward the river.
   He's halfway to the river before anyone moves.
The women tease the young men with their heads down.

"There goes Salmon *getting away* with Dove;
   none of you are doing *anything*," the women say.
All the men grab their bows and arrows;
   run after Salmon.
They shoot at him,
   but the arrows *glance off* Salmon's back,
      off his back,
         off his back.
There's all this noise,
   shouting and commotion.
Porcupine is sleeping in his lodge,
   away from the camp.
He hears all this noise,
   pushes open the flap of the lodge door.
He sees what's going on,
   puts on his moccasins,
      his quills and so on.
Porcupine starts down the hill;
   but he's *pretty slow.*
      He goes back into his lodge,
         back to sleep.
There's all this noise,
   shouting and commotion.
Rattlesnake looks out his lodge.
   He's an old man.
He sees Salmon with Dove.
   He's *angry.*
Rattlesnake takes out one of his poison fangs,
   puts it on an arrow shaft.
He shoots the arrow;
   it hits Salmon *in the back* of the head.
      The arrow-point stays in Salmon's head.
Salmon tumbles,
   falls over,
      falls into the river.

The river carries Salmon down the river.
Dove is there,
   crying.
The five Wolf brothers are up there;
   they are great hunters.
They see what's happening;
   see Salmon go down the river.
They come down,
   take Dove to their own camp,
     take her *way up* in the mountains,
      and make her do all the work.
       They're very cruel to her.
All day and night,
   the wives of the five brothers watch over Dove.
She's very unhappy;
   she feels bad.
     She spends her time *crying,*
      crying.
The river carries Salmon a *long* way,
   down river,
     a long way.
Branches along the way tear his flesh,
   from his bones.
Salmon is washed up onto a sandbar there.
His flesh is gone;
   only the skull and the backbone are there.
     The sun bleaches those bones *white.*

◆ ◆ ◆

This particular re-telling is a resuscitation from the bones. As you will shortly see, a resuscitation from the bones is also a critical theme within the story itself. This particular re-telling was originally inspired by a written rendition of a 1930 re-telling of Salmon by the Sanpoil elder William Burke (Ray 1933:142–45), along with the 1927 re-telling of Salmon by the Schitsu'umsh elder Dorothy Nicodemus (Reichard 1946 and 1947:119–21). I had not heard it told aloud previously. From these enduring bones of the written story come the key characters, and scenes and their sequences, as well as the underlying teachings and possible huckleberries. The Salmon story is part of a shared tradition throughout the Plateau. In addition to Burke and Nicodemus, you can for example read versions of the Salmon narrative as told by the Okanogan elder Humishuma, "Mourning Dove," first published in 1933 (Mourning Dove 1990:93–96) and the Niimíipuu elder Wayi'latpu, collected in 1929–30 (Phinney 1934:222–27). While the spoken languages of Burke, Nicodemus, and Humishuma are Inland Salishan, Wayi'latpu's is in the Sahaptian language family. This ubiquitous story is embedded in a shared landscape rather than of a particular linguistic or tribal tradition.

While each of our original storytellers told the narrative slightly differently, each with his or her own emphasis and storytelling techniques, each adding flesh to the perennial bones in his or her own way, I have sought to maintain the integrity of the Salmon narrative to reflect the spirit of the tradition and the land from which it is anchored. I've sought to retain the shared underlying bones found in all these renditions—the enduring teachings or what the Schitsu'umsh call *miyp* "teachings from all things." In my attempt to transform the bones of the printed word into a living story much of the wording and formatting of this re-constructed text has been influenced by over two decades of participant interactions with elders, audiences, and the story itself. It is a pedagogical attempt to resuscitate the bones by adding vibrant flesh, as any raconteur would seek to do. It is an aligning of the essential parts of this interrelated Salmon tradition to provide an interpretative text that bridges this re-telling for you, encouraging your participation within a living story. Here and elsewhere, my goal is to convey as authentically as possible in a written format the style and voice of an indigenous storytelling. Yet to recapture the elegance, beauty, and power with which the Indian elders, over countless generations, have spoken the Salmon story into being, is virtually impossible.

◆ ◆ ◆

Mouse,
   the Sly One,
      comes along.
         He's looking for something to eat.
She finds the bones of Salmon.
Salmon had been chief to Mouse.
   Mouse *feels bad.*
She goes back to her camp;
   gets a pouch of salmon oil.
Mouse sings a song, rubs the skull and the backbone with the oil,
   a *first* day passes.
Mouse sings, rubs the bones with the salmon oil,
   a *second* day.
Song is sung, the bones are rubbed,
   a *third,*
      a *fourth* day.
Mouse sings and rubs the skull,
   the backbone with the salmon oil,
      on the *fifth* day.
The flesh *comes back* to those bones.
   Salmon has *life.*
"Oh,
   I've been *sleeping* a long time," Salmon says.
"You *haven't been* sleeping,
   you've been *dead*!" Mouse says.
"*Oh!*" Salmon says.
Salmon is strong,
   returns back to the river,
      along the path *there.*
His wife is nowhere to be seen.
"The Wolf brothers have taken her,
   they are *cruel.*
      She spends her time crying.
         You must go for her," Old Man Spider says.

Salmon goes upriver;

Salmon *always* goes upriver.

◆ ◆ ◆

I first glimpsed the excitement and approval of elders in having non-Indian students re-tell their most cherished traditions when Chris Bain, a fourth-grade teacher in the Coeur d'Alene School District, had his students publicly perform Schitsu'umsh narrative oral traditions. With youthful energy, using stories recently approved by the Schitsu'umsh and developed for use in the 1992 language arts curriculum, the students brought the stories alive. Lawrence Aripa and Cliff SiJohn were delighted to see their stories recounted in this fashion.

◆ ◆ ◆

In my Plateau Indians course at the University of Idaho, circa 2012, I had a student who could have taught the course himself. Frank Finley was well versed in his own family's Salish traditions, including basket-making, and was in fact a faculty member of the Salish Kootenai College in Montana. Frank offered to present a mini-workshop on making twine, and from it, what are called by Plateau peoples "cornhusk and sally bags." My students discovered that the act of re-telling the stories and of making twine from dogbane are similar, having remarkable parallels. As part of his presentation, Frank demonstrated how to fashion twine from sticks of dogbane, and, in turn, he had the students attempt to do the same for themselves. Each student was given a three-foot-long dogbane branch, something that had once been alive, flexible, and growing. Held in hand, the dried dogbane branch was stiff, inflexible, and seemingly without life. The students were instructed first to use their feet to carefully step on the branch, and then use their fingers to work the rigid dogbane. Then with hands, effort, some skill, and a little water, the students rolled and twisted the freed fibers into twine. Each student transformed what had been rigid and dead into something flexible, exceedingly strong, and useful—into twine, something now alive. To do so, each student had to first access the essence of the dogbane by removing its hard woody material and revealing its strong, fibrous threads. With continued effort and skill, the twine could then be transformed into a "living" bag or basket.

The stories the students were then engaging and remembering as part of their learning activity were much like the rigid sticks of dried dogbane, stories fixed on the pages of a book, without "life." But with their own efforts and skills in listening, they would first attempt to get down to the story's very fibers, strong and flexible, discover the "bones" in the story. Then with continued effort, applying storytelling skills and their energy to the story, each student would attempt to breathe life back into those bones, those fibers, put flesh on the bones and render his or her story alive, flexible enough to invite an audience into the story; indeed, transforming them into participants of the unfolding narrative. The student storytelling and twining experiences were an illustration of the power of indigenous participatory learning.

◆ ◆ ◆

Salmon goes up the river;
   Salmon *always* goes up river.
He comes to the camp of Whitefish here.
   Whitefish is making a three-pronged fish spear.
"What are you doing?" Salmon says.
Whitefish keeps whistling.
"What are you doing?" Salmon says.
Whitefish keeps whistling.
"What are you doing?" Salmon says.
Whitefish turns,
   grabs Salmon,
      pushes the spear into his arm.
"This is what I'm going to do with it;
   I'm going to use it *on you*," Whitefish says.
"*Ouch*,
   that's hurting me," Salmon says.
Salmon pulls the spear from his arm;
   looks it over.

"That's a *pretty good* spear." Salmon says.
Salmon grabs Whitefish;
   pushes him down.
      Salmon jabs the spear into the back of the neck of Whitefish.
"Soon the human people will come to this place.
   When the people come,
      they'll use the three-pronged spear;
         this is the way they'll fish for the whitefish,
            Whitefish *teach them this*," Salmon says.
Salmon goes up the river;
   Salmon *always* goes up river.
He comes to the camp of Rattlesnake.
   Rattlesnake is in his old tule mat-covered lodge,
Salmon hears a song.
   "I shot Salmon.
      I shot Salmon.
         Salmon was chief.
            He's chief no more."
Salmon goes into the lodge;
   Rattlesnake sees him from the corner of his eye.
The song changes.
   "I'm so sad that Salmon is dead.
      I'm so sad that Salmon is dead.
         Salmon was chief.
            He was a good chief."
Salmon says nothing.
He picks up a piece of burning wood from the fire;
   touches it to the dry mat-lodge;
      jumps back.
         The flames *leap up*.
Rattlesnake is trapped;
   can't get out.
      Rattlesnake is *all ashes*.
From one of Rattlesnake's eyes crawls a *small* snake;
   it's a *rattlesnake*.

"Soon the human people will come to this place.
   When the people come,
      you'll be *the rattlesnake,*
         crawl on its belly.
           Take this gourd
              put it on your tail.
                  Always *warn* people before you strike.
                     Rattlesnake *teach them this,*" Salmon says.
Salmon goes up the river;
   Salmon *always* goes up river.

◆ ◆ ◆

As Cliff so often repeated, when re-telling of the Animal First Peoples, "they come *alive*…they *swirl around* you as the Turtle is saying his thing or as the Chipmunk is saying something…they *swirl around* you and you see the *Indian medicine*…this is Chipmunk talking to you…this is Coyote talking to you…this is the Elk and the Deer and the Eagle, and this is Hawk…all these things *suddenly come alive*…they are just as alive as they were a thousand years ago." As Salmon comes *alive*…and *swirls* around you…reality is perpetuated. The re-telling is anything but quaint beliefs and false explanations about reality.

◆ ◆ ◆

I recall with clarity my first, albeit brief, encounter with "swirling," with the feeling of Coyote coming alive and talking to me. In 1978 I was a graduate student at the University of Colorado, teaching a course to some seventy undergraduates. On this particular day I planned to share the Diné (Navajo) creation account, setting aside the entire class session to do so. Using what I felt was a reliable publication from the Navajo Community College, for days prior to the presentation I had been going over the storyline, its characters and scenes, the varied worlds from which the *Yei*, the "Holy Ones," had emerged into this the Fifth World. This was the story of Changing Woman, and her hero twins, Monster Slayer and Child of the Water, who traveled the land, overcoming most of its "monsters," preparing the world for the coming of Human Peoples. With my students attentive, I started in. Using my own words and style of telling, I seemed to give life to the story, certainly engaging the students. I saw it in their eyes; I felt it with their presence. And then it happened, some twenty minutes into the re-telling. So distinct, so vivid, I was no longer telling a story, but was within it. I was traveling with the *Yei*, witnessing new, fresh events unfold right before my very eyes. While preparing for this story I couldn't recall having ever read these events. I seemed to be in a place and time transcendent of the mechanics of voicing words, in a place and time made of words. Frankly, it was unnerving and I stopped short my re-telling. I apologized to the students and dismissed class early, my heart still rapidly palpitating. When I got back to my office, and re-read my notes, the "fresh events" I experienced as "new" were indeed in the text all along. I don't honestly know what my students experienced that day, but I surely swirled, if only momentarily. Lifted from the dusty pages of an obscure publication, words once dead were, if unwittingly, in part resuscitated, a story brought back to life, if only momentarily. Bones firm and stable, flesh vibrant and supple. And a story continues to be perpetuated…as does the world.

◆ ◆ ◆

Salmon goes upriver;
   Salmon *always* goes upriver.
He finds Dove in the camp of the Wolf brothers.
They're out hunting.
   Their eyes meet,
      they care for each other very much.
         She particularly loves his *handsome red head.*
"What do the Wolf brothers do when they return from the hunt?"
   Salmon says.
"They first go down to the river to wash," Dove says.
Salmon goes down to the river,
   into the waters.
      His knife is ready.

Dove calls out.
  "Come,
    I'm hungry,
      I'm hungry," she says.
The first Wolf brother,
  the oldest,
    comes back.
"I *smell* Salmon," he says.
"How could that be?
  He's dead," Dove says.
"*I'm not so sure?*" he says.
The first brother goes down to the river to wash.
When he's in the waters,
  Salmon is there;
    takes out his knife.
      The Wolf brother *floats down* the river.
The second Wolf brother,
  the next oldest,
    comes back.
"I *smell* Salmon," he says.
"How could that be?
  He's *dead,*" Dove says.
"*I'm not so sure?*" he says.
He goes down to wash.
  Salmon is there with his knife.
    The second Wolf brother *floats* down the river.
The third Wolf brother comes back.
"I *smell* Salmon," he says.
"How could that be?
  He's dead," Dove says.
"*I'm not so sure?*" he says.
He goes to wash.
  Salmon is there.
    The knife is pulled.
      The Wolf brother *floats down the river.*
The fourth Wolf brother comes back.

"I *smell* Salmon," he says.

"How could that be?

 He's dead," Dove says.

"*I'm not so sure*?" he says.

He goes to wash.

 Salmon is there.

  The fourth Wolf brother *floats down the river.*

The fifth brother,

 the *youngest* brother,

  comes back from the hunt.

"I *smell* Salmon," he says.

"How could that be?

 He's dead," says the wife of Salmon.

"*I'm not so sure*?" he says.

He goes down to the river to wash after the hunt.

 Salmon is there…

  "Soon the human people will come to this place.

   When the people come,

    they'll find you gone from this country;

     you'll be in the timber country;

      you'll be the first gray wolf,

       (reintroduced in 1995!);

        Wolf *teach them this*," Salmon says.

Salmon takes Dove to the river.

 They care for each other very much.

  She particularly loves his *handsome red head.*

"We'll part from each other for now.

 But each spring you sing your song for me,

  cry for me.

   When I hear your song,

    your cry,

     I'll come up the river.

      We'll be together then," Salmon says.

"Soon the human people will come to this place.

 And when the people come,

  they'll hear you *crying* in the spring.

'The salmon must be coming!' they'll say.
        Dove *teach them this*," Salmon says.
So listen carefully for the cry of Dove,
    the Salmon will *soon be here.*
Salmon always goes up the river,
    because Salmon *always goes up river*!
And by the way,
    even today,
        look closely,
            all salmon have the arrow-point markings,
                just like the one Rattlesnake shot into Salmon's head.
There, the trail ends.

◆   ◆   ◆

Traveling in Agnes Vanderburg's stories? In the act of *re-telling*, a lake is *made* blue? From *singing* a song, a *re-telling* a story, the bones of Salmon are *resuscitated* and *come alive*? The *Awakkuléeshe*? A burnt face *made* as a new-born child's face? When you tell the story, you've got to go inside and *become* the Coyote? Story as *living* being? The sky *falling*? Then there was *dasshússua*? *Swirling* with Coyote? And now perhaps a bit of *resuscitating* from the printed page? From flesh once putrefied firm, the bones brought back to life, a story *swirling* and *supple*. Story as a *pedagogy*…and story perpetuated as a *perpetuation* of the world! I accepted these assertions on face value, patient, trusting my teachers, but still all a great mystery!

As an ethnographer, seeking to re-tell the stories of others, how would I enter and travel within the homes of others, of my teachers—ethically, effectively, and properly? What best practices would help guide me? What best practices would guide me in how I do my research, how I disseminate that research to my colleagues and to the general public, and how I teach that research to my students in the classroom? Entering the homes of others, of my hosts, of receiving from them such wondrous gifts, and just how would I reciprocate?

That woke me up!

Hnleq'ntsutn
"sweat house"

Traveling the Stories of Others— A Professional Protocol

During the fall of 1989 I was having lunch at a café on the Coeur d'Alene Reservation, introducing myself and a potential research project to the Schitsu'umsh elder, Cliff SiJohn. As we had not really visited much before then, I was attempting to build up my credibility, referring to what I felt had been some great research done with the Crow of Montana over the previous fifteen years. But as I continued, it was evident from Cliff's body language that what I was saying didn't seem to hold much weight for him. As I presented my case, Cliff suddenly stopped me, and looking to the south, asked, "Remember seeing that Sweat House, that *Hnleq'ntsutn*? It's like my culture. You can sit back here, in the comfort of this café, talk about it, view it from afar…or you can get off your seat and go inside. As the *elder pours* the water, pouring it just right…he'll lead the way. Can you be *attentive*…listen with your *heart*? Can you *feel* the intense heat, *feel* the sweat pouring out from within…can you *see* into the darkness, *see* from the inside of that darkness and look out beyond it? And when it passes to you, when it's your turn to pray aloud, what are you *going to do*, what are you *going to say*? It's not until you go inside that you really can experience my culture, really come to know who we are." (For descriptions and discussion

A Crow Sweat Lodge, the "Little Lodge." Boulder, Colorado. *Frey 1979*

of the Sweat House/Lodge rituals, see Frey 1987:14–16 and Frey and the Schitsu'umsh 2001:221–28).

It was *déjà vu*, as I immediately flashed back some fifteen years, to June 1974, a warm and very pleasant afternoon, seated with Allen Old Horn. He turned to me and said, "*You see* that tin shed?…it's kinda like our way of life…you can sit back here and talk about it…but *not* really understand…it's not til you go *inside…listen… feel it*…feel the damp…see it from the *inside* looking out…that you really know what it's all about…you've *gotta go inside*. When you leave that tin shed, what are *you going to do* with what you've been given? How might you *help others*?" Despite a history that was soon revealed to me of the adversarial relations between Apsáalooke and Schitsu'umsh (and hence getting off on the wrong foot with Cliff), I was struck by how Cliff spoke of the "Sweat House" in a manner almost identical with that of Allen's "Tin Shed." Both Cliff and Allen would pose the most essential of questions to me before I could pose any to them.

◆ ◆ ◆

"Remember seeing that Sweat House?" … "*You see* that tin shed?"
As I began my interviews with Allen, and years later with Cliff, each could have chosen to terminate the conversation with me right then and there, got up and walked away, and not pointed the way into his Tin Shed or Sweat House. But instead both men re-directed the questioning back to me. Allen and Cliff were asking if I'd be a good guest in their homes. Would I honor and respect the hospitality of my hosts in a manner I would expect from any guest in my home? And had I even been granted permission to enter in the first place?

In researching, in writing and publishing, and in teaching about the lives of others, shouldn't it first begin with us, with being honest with ourselves? In re-directing the questions, were not Allen and Cliff asking of me, what were my intentions? Why have I sought to learn about and then re-tell their stories? Given the hegemony these communities have experienced, what they asked is whether I was acting from a position of economic, social, and political power and privilege. From the start, they asked what I intended to do with that which was entrusted to me. And as a guest in the home of another, would I honor the wishes, authority, and sovereignty of my host? My positioning will certainly affect the host community, as well as my research and teaching. I must acknowledge and take responsibility for my Euro-American heritage and all of the privilege it garners relative to an indigenous community. Can I consciously, with deliberation, re-position myself to some degree and attempt to act in a spirit of equitable collaboration and partnership with my host? It all begins with reflection and honesty. These are ethical questions that vary from those formally asked by researchers' academic Human Assurances Committees and Institutional Review Boards.

As we reflect, we need to understand the status of the stories themselves. Allen and Cliff would remind us that there are the ethical and legal issues associated with *baaéechichiwaau* (retelling one's own). Fundamental to those ethical and legal issues is the inherent, as well as treaty-based, federally-recognized sovereign status of the American Indian—our hosts—and the resulting cultural property rights around the stories. Allen and Cliff were protecting their cultural resources by challenging my intentions. Who has the right to access and then re-tell their stories? Allen and Cliff would hold that the indigenous communities are the "owners" of their knowledge, an assertion of tribal sovereignty, and not the Euro-American academy, nor its individual scholars.

The indigenous communities I've had the opportunity to work with typically have research protocols, formally codified in writing or through customary practice, that must be followed if a researcher seeks entry into their Tin Sheds. Such protocols have guided my own research, from seeking to collaborate and gaining approval for a research topic, to conducting informed consent research in partnership with tribal programs and individuals, through to the completion of that research, adhering to a final review of the materials acquired and their proposed dissemination, by the appropriate cultural resources program, culture committee, and tribal council (Frey and the Schitsu'umsh 2001:286–88).

The "Sqigwts.Org" research project between the Coeur d'Alene Tribe and the University of Idaho, which sought to apply indigenous knowledge coupled with scientific knowledge to address climate change, was initiated and completed using a best-practices research protocol. It included a legal agreement developed by tribal and university attorneys that protected the intellectual property and traditional knowledge, while providing an avenue for collaborative research. At the start of the project and as the research unfolded, any "culturally sensitive" information was identified and labeled by the project principal investigators, Leanne Campbell (the tribe's Historic Preservation Manager) and myself. Each month the project's research was reviewed by the tribe's Natural Resources and Cultural Committee. Only after a thorough review by the tribe was the project's cultural content approved for public dissemination. On September 9, 2015, the Resolution approving the project was issued by the Coeur d'Alene Tribal Council. Virtually all of the collaborative research I've been involved with has resulted in a formal Tribal Council Resolution, specifying the terms of sharing the research, with the ownership tribally acknowledged.

In the cultural property review and approval process—a review of what can be the most cherished and revered traditions and practices, of what elders sometimes refer to as "the Old Ways" or "Heart Knowledge"—the evaluative criteria applied is critical. It is insightful to compare the evaluative criteria typically used by cultural committees and tribal councils with the criteria standardized in social science ethnography, as each is directed at completely different audiences, and each is premised on differing epistemological principles. The key standards that I've encountered, either implicitly or explicitly used and deemed important by indigenous host reviewers, relate to what some elders call "Heart Knowledge." This entails criteria such as "trustworthiness," involving qualities of credibility, dependability, and confirmability, and most importantly, "authenticity," involving the inclusion and acknowledgement of the multiplicity of the elder and collaborator "voices" relied upon and conveyed in the research that seeks to reflect their "original expression" and "genuine representation." In addition, I've found that my collaborators and various culture committees typically consider "appropriateness" as critical to this evaluative process. There is a vast amount of cultural knowledge and many practices that are not meant, for various reasons, to be shared outside a family or tribal community. These forms of evaluative criteria should be differentiated from measures used to evaluate the merit of what academic peer-reviewers and book and journal publishers deem research data, or what elders sometime refer to as "Head Knowledge." Head Knowledge measures include "reliability," using a systematic and standardized method that assess the ability to repeat the observations, data collection, and findings of someone else's study; "internal validity," the ability to correspond the theoretical description of the data with the actual data collected; and "external validity," the ability to apply and generalize the results of one study to other studies. These are measures all premised on an application of the scientific method. Given the sources from which the stories emanate and the audiences to whom the stories are intended to be shared, I have sought to navigate and apply, with some degree of competency, both sets of criteria. I have found it important to know how to travel the varied spokes of the Wheel.

Above all else, *baaéechichiwaau* is the granting by others the right to re-tell their stories. I have been honored, and hold the responsibility close to my heart, that so many great stories originating with my teachers, such as Tom Yellowtail's Burnt Face and Rock Medicine Wheel, Lawrence Aripa's Four Smokes, Lucy Finley's Blue Jay, Allen Old Horn's Tin Shed, and Cliff SiJohn's Sweat House and Swirling Coyote, were "granted" to me by my teachers for the purpose of re-telling. Following in line with *baaéechichiwaau,* those stories others shared with me, distinct from those I've personally experienced, are only re-told here by permission, a "privilege granted by others." Acknowledging the cultural property rights of the sovereign tribes I've worked with, any materials that could be designated as "culturally sensitive information" of the story landscapes of others, for example, that relate to the Sundance or Jump Dance, have not been shared in this essay without first having been reviewed and approved by the appropriate tribal members, cultural review committees, and/or tribal councils. Accordingly, some stories I've experienced or that were shared with me, are meant to be kept with the family or elder, and are not included here. In the instances of overtly personal stories involving myself, such as those of my healing journey with cancer (Frey, Yellowtail, and SiJohn 2008), in conversation with Cliff, we deemed these stories in essence *basbaaaliíchiwé,* my own stories distinct from those of others. As a former chair of the Coeur d'Alene Culture Committee, Cliff didn't feel these stories needed review by the committee. Nevertheless, they were subject to a deliberate and honest introspection by Cliff and myself for their authenticity and appropriateness to share. In all instances, the stories are to be cared for with respect.

"In the café sharing lunch" ... **"As the elder poured just right"** ... **"We sat together...under the shade of an old cottonwood."** With Allen and Cliff at my side, we did get off that bench together, as they guided the way through the interior of the Tin Shed and Sweat House. Without a guide it is easy to stumble and get lost. Research, publication, and teaching should entail developing collaborative partnership with our hosts (Frey and the Sch_itsu'umsh 2001:269).

It has been my practice that from the beginning of a proposed research project, to sit down with, preferably over a meal, and invite the potential hosts to participate in a conversation. It might even commence with an elder's prayer. I'd seek to effectively collaborate in the development of the key topics of research and the research design itself from the start. The most relevant research questions and the best research designs are informed with the help of your hosts. As co-researchers, our hosts can conduct some of the best interviews. When disseminating research, at a conference or through a publication, we seek to do so collaboratively, as co-authors with our hosts. A course based in part or in full upon our host's knowledge is best team-taught. How research is designed, what and how questions are posed, how and what is observed in the field, and how that research is then disseminated and taught are all rendered more meaningful and insightful with our host as a co-researcher, co-writer, and co-teacher.

◆ ◆ ◆

The old man would heat up the rocks on a pretty regular basis. After the fire had died down and the rocks were red hot, with his pitch fork he'd place them in the Sweat Lodge. Then he'd enter with a bucket of warmed water, and close the door and say his prayers during each of "four quarters," the four segments of the Sweat Bath.

Now on some of those occasions, a few non-Indian fellows, young and curious, would show up, just on a little hill, not far from the lodge. They'd look on as the old man prepared the Sweat. Just before going in, he'd invite the boys down to join him, take a Sweat together. But once invited, they'd take off.

Now on this one occasion, the old man told the boys that when he was finished Sweating, he'd place some more hot rocks in the pit and they could take their own Sweat, by themselves. They liked that idea.

So once the old man had completed his prayers and placed some fresh hot rocks in the lodge, the boys came down and took their Sweat. Once the boys were inside, with the bucket of water and hot rocks, the old man lowered the lodge door and began to walk off. As he did, it got pretty hot inside there, and one of the boys asked the others, "what do we do when it gets too hot in here?" So they poured the water on the rocks, to cool them down. And there was an immediate loud cry, as the boys left that Lodge in record time! The old man left with a laugh on his face.

That was a Sweat those boys wouldn't soon forget. It's good to have someone who knows how to guide you in the Sweat. (Re-told from a story heard on the Flathead Reservation, circa 1980).

◆ ◆ ◆

A powerful illustration of just how research can be completely trans-formed and rendered that much more meaningful when grounded in an Indigenous perspective, done collaboratively with Native hosts, is the Life-Long Learning Online (L3) project. Funded by the National Aeronautics and Space Administration from 2000 to 2003, the grant sought to celebrate the bicentennial of the Lewis and Clark's Corps of Discovery expedition in conjunction with NASA's exploration of Mars. As a faculty member at the University of Idaho, I was to reach out to the area tribes, to ask if they were interested in participating. Of course for the tribes, Lewis and Clark represented anything but a moment of celebration, but the Coeur d'Alene Tribe, Confederated Tribes of Warm Springs, and Nez Perce Tribe chose to partner on their terms, telling it from their perspective.

After cultural property rights agreements were established, giving each tribe full ownership and control over content, representatives from the tribes began correcting the official account that had been erroneously established in the written journals of Lewis and Clark. There was a rich oral heritage, kept alive through the generations, which challenged many of the events as characterized by the written accounts. And equally important, each of the tribes refused to be defined in terms of a Lewis and Clark "discovery" and asserted their sovereignty. Each tribe used the project to tell their story in their own manner, dealing with a range of topics, from tribal sovereignty, health care, natural resources and gaming, to language, oral traditions, arts and dance, to the landscape and the seasonal round, to contact history and, of course, the expedition itself.

Each of the L3 tribal partners approached what they wished to share publicly a little differently. The Niimíipuu, for example, chose to limit information on places and sites of cultural importance, as well as information on spiritual practices and ways. On the other hand, having just completed an elaborate Geographical Information System (GIS) Names-Place Project, the Schitsu'umsh wanted to share their extensive knowledge of how and where they had interacted with their landscape. In this collaborative project, it was my co-researchers who were able to identify the best interviewees, who in many instances did the best interviews, knew and asked the best questions, and who already had garnered the trust of the interviewees. On many occasions I was relegated to the role of holding the video camera very still while taping their interviews. I would then edit, upload, and stream the interviews on the Internet module. My role in this project was in part that of a "culture broker," facilitating the negotiation and mediation between the interests of the funding agency and university, and that of the tribes. I am pleased to have assisted my hosts in realizing their desired intentions and allowing their voices to be conveyed through the L3 modules without them

THE SCHITSU'UMSH (COEUR D'ALENE)
LIFELONG LEARNING ONLINE MODULE

To see the results of the Lifelong Learning Online, L3, project, visit www.lib.uidaho.edu/digital/L3/Sites/ShowOneSiteSiteID50.html. There you will find rich images, background texts, and almost six hours of video interviews, stories, songs, and language recordings.

being hindered and compromised, while at the same time gratified that the final product met the expectations of the NASA funders. In the Niimíipuu L3 project, twenty-seven interviews were conducted by my co-researchers, while I did nine interviews. In the Schitsu'umsh project, twelve interviews were conducted by my co-researchers, while I did eleven. And in the Warm Springs, Wasco, and Paiute project, twenty-two interviews were conducted by my co-researchers, while I did ten interviews.

These sorts of collaborative relationships are only built with great care, upon mutual trust and respect. I'd enter these relationships with complete sincerity and honesty, with no hidden agendas, no ulterior motives. The elders know what's in the heart. When I met Cliff SiJohn at the café on the Coeur d'Alene Reservation, what mattered most to him were not the experiences I brought to this proposed project, but what was in my heart. Would I bring a personal honesty and integrity to the various relationships that I sought to develop with the Schitsu'umsh? Could I be trusted as a "collaborative partner" with what was about to be shared? By 2000, we had ten years of built up trust and respect.

"Go *inside...listen*" ... "Be *attentive,* listen with your *heart.*" As I traveled the territory of the Sweat House I sought to position myself as a child, as if swaddled in the blanket of our hosts. I sought to listen and grow under the tutelage and guidance of Tom, Cliff, and the other elders, and be attentive to their oral narratives. Their "textbooks" were etched in the rock and soil of their particular landscapes. This is place-bound knowledge gained through participatory, experiential learning, through *stmi'sm* "being attentive," within a broad family context. Allen, Tom, and Cliff recognized that if I were to learn about their worlds I would need to do so using a distinctly different style of learning and in a distinctly different type of classroom. It was as a child that I sought to conduct my field research, in interviewing and participant observations; it was as a child I sought to structure into my classroom pedagogy for my students.

To help begin to appreciate this approach of traveling the Tin Shed, let's consider more fully one example of this participatory, experiential indigenous learning style anchored in a particular landscape. For the Apsáalooke, from early times, a child's learning occurred entirely within the purview of the watchful eyes and guided hands of an extensive network of matrilineally-related family members (Frey 1987:40–57). Among the members were *basahké*—mothers, all older women of one's mother's clan; *biilápxe*—fathers and "clan uncles," all men of one's father's mother's clan; *basbía*—sisters, all women of one's own generation within one's clan; *biiké*—elder brothers, all older men of one's clan; and one's siblings—*bakúpe*. The child is *baakáate*—"my child," always in relationship with some other kinsmen. Learning transpired not in isolation, as an individual learner, but through the dynamic of kinship-based interconnections, each member with his or her own responsibilities to the child, and the child to them.

The *biilápxe*, fathers and clan uncles, for example, provided prayer and perhaps an Indian Name, offering protection and guidance. And when a deed of note occurred, the *biilápxe* would sing praise songs for the one being honored. In this network of interrelationships the child learned early the pivotal role of reciprocity and of sharing. One's accomplishments were as much the culmination of his or her efforts, as of the contributions made by the various members of the family. Accordingly, when that deed was publicly announced by a *biilápxe* and a praise song sung at a community gathering or ceremony, it would be accompanied by an *ammaakée*, "giveaway," in which gifts were given to all those who had helped make this achievement possible, acknowledging their contributions. And by extension, the child learned of the quintessential value placed in reciprocity between one's kinsmen and of the pervasive practice of sharing with all the peoples, especially those in need.

From the time of being tightly swaddled in the blanket of a beaded cradleboard, through early adulthood, the *baakáate* were present at and engaged in all the activities as that of the adults—root digging with *basahké*, ritual Sweating with *biiké* or *bakúpe*, traveling to a council meeting with *biilápxe*. These were place-bound activities, specific to a particular landscape along the Bighorn and Yellowstone rivers, etched with the adventures and misadventures of the Animal First Peoples, who brought forth this landscape and endowed it with story. It was Coyote's story that took place along that bend in the river, atop that particular hill, in this grove of trees, with each story offering its own critical teaching. As the child engaged the landscape with family members he or she also engaged Coyote and his lessons. In addition to the Apsáalooke, this notion that Indigenous knowledge is place-bound knowledge is well documented, as in Keith Basso's insightful work with the Western Apache (1996), and as I have witnessed with the Niimíipuu, Schitsu'umsh, and Warm Springs and Wasco.

It is within this setting that experiential, engaged learning occurred—the *baakáate* closely (and sometimes not so closely) watching and listening, being "attentive," active listeners and participants, and attempting to at first mimic and then emulate what their parents and grandparents did. Cultivated in the child is an attentiveness, an empathic competency. A village of elders guide with gentle encouragement and deliberate example, informed by a rich covering of oral traditions—spoken, worn and danced, sung, and re-told—all of which were anchored in their particular landscape of rock formations, hills and peaks, and riverbeds, etched with the deeds of Coyote and the other First Peoples.

Of particular importance to this learning style were the *miyp* guiding the young, the "teachings from all things," ranging from overarching moral and ethical codes, to practical utilitarian skills relating to hunting and gathering, to kinship roles and responsibilities, to strategies for interacting with others, from cultural identity to techniques for digging camas. As reflected in Niimíipuu terms, essential teachings would include an ethic of sharing and helping others, *téek'e*, "to give and share [food with others]," along with being *tuk'ukín* (honest), *qa'ánin'* (respectful), and humble and *talxtálx* (modest) with others. Also taught is an ethic of competition and strategic planning in the face of an adversary, *'iceyé·ye*, of being a trickster Coyote and showing *cikaw'íiswit* (bravery). Through the *miyp*, what it means to be Schi̱tsu'umsh, Niimíipuu, or Apsáalooke and the necessary skills to successfully engage that life and all its Peoples—Animal, Plant, Human, and Spirit, are discovered.

Many of these teachings would be revealed as the narrative oral traditions were heard and experienced. The stories such as those of Coyote and Burnt Face were richly layered with essential *miyp* "teachings," that come alive as a "person" when told. It was important for the youth to be, as best they could, an active listener and engage the stories from within, discovering what might be revealed to him or her uniquely. As the young person grew with experiences each year, upon hearing the same story something new would be learned. The stories provided an affective tone to life, as well as the didactic frame for life.

In addition to the story narratives, engaging in the other oral traditions was just as essential. Primary among these oral traditions was the spoken language itself, with all its particular semantic and syntactic significances. Other vital oral traditions included the donning of the richly designed beaded dance regalia and then dancing to the heart beat of the drum, and learning and singing the songs of those dances. And there were the songs of prayer for the hunt of the deer and gathering of camas, for morning and evening, for welcoming and honoring, for healing, for a wake at a funeral, and so many more ceremonies and occasions, all providing opportunities to discover the *miyp* embedded within. In these acts of using the oral traditions, these languages, that all the kinsmen of the landscape—the Plant, Animal, and Spirit Peoples—are engaged, exchanges made, and gifts received. There were no institutional schools in which formal, standardized, competitively-based instruction within age-based grade levels segregated children from the rhythms of family and camp life, from their particular homeland and varied kinsmen.

While I've identified and isolated particular *miyp* teachings for this discussion, it does not reflect the traditional ways this body of knowledge and practice would be disseminated to each new generation. These are teachings indigenously disseminated to the youth while experientially engaged in the oral traditions, participating in storytelling, dancing, digging camas, or salmon fishing, and being asked to be "attentive" and "discover" the *miyp* teachings, or what the Niimíipuu call *tamálwit*, "the law," for themselves, all under the guidance of elders. By artificially identifying *miyp* and *tamálwit* teachings as I have here, I am seeking to provide a sort of shorthand means through which the non-Indigenous might become more appreciative and understanding of Niimíipuu and Schitsu'umsh traditions. Whenever we create these artificially identified and isolated teachings, be it for an academic lecture or journal article, or even a casual conversation with a friend, we must be cautious not to decontextualize *miyp* and *tamálwit* knowledge and practices to such a level that their indigenous-based integrity and authenticity are lost.

◆ ◆ ◆

The following vignette, a bit of creative nonfiction, is a composite of various student comments I've received over the last few years regarding my undergraduate/graduate-level Plateau Indians course, arranged here to provide a glimpse into my teaching pedagogy, from a student perspective.

I'd heard about the class from a friend, and tried to avoid it as long as I could. All kinds of "group projects," field trips, and then there was having to memorize a story and tell it in front of others! All my group projects in the past just didn't work out, as I did most of the work and others slid by. It would take a lot of my time. It was a different sort of class.

Frey started the very first class session by telling the Coeur d'Alene story of "Rabbit and Jack Rabbit." "Interesting." I hadn't thought of seeing Tekoa Mountain and the lands all around us full of stories. And Frey told the story in a way that held my interest; I got into it.

Frey organized us into family groups, four to five members in each, with a graduate student or two as the "headman" or "headwoman." Each family took on either a Coeur d'Alene or Nez Perce place-name—*q'emiln*, for Post Falls, Idaho, or *léepwey*, for Lapwai, Idaho. We researched the oral traditions and meaning of our place-name. Frey gave us an essay on Plateau family and kinship structure, and the roles of each kinsperson, asking us to try to assume those roles as best we could in our own "class family." Each of us were "siblings" with the others, and "children" within the class. Each of us would have to depend on and help each other, as we were graded not as individuals, but how we did as a group.

Instead of written exams, Frey had us participate in oral "in-the-round recitations." We prepped together, and at the meeting, responded to his questions. It was different trying to verbally respond instead of writing it out. We had to listen carefully to the questions. It became more of a dialogue, a kind of learning moment for each of us.

We took three, day-long field trips to the Coeur d'Alene and Nez Perce Reservations, a couple of hours drive from campus, and got to visit with elders and tribal council members, with cultural and natural resources, fisheries, and health care personnel. On one trip, under the direction of an elder, we dug "water potatoes," a traditional root, with tribal school kids, in the marshy areas of Lake Coeur d'Alene. We got muddy and it was cold and rainy, but we listened to some great stories by the elders, laughed with the kids, and that was an experience I won't forget! On each trip, our "families" made or gathered small gifts—jars of jam or honey, small hand-made painted pictures—to give to each of our hosts. It felt good to give to an elder, it kind of surprised them when we did.

Frey had each of us select a traditional story, one that could be shared, one that was written alongside its native language, and we had to "re-member it, and not memorize it." After Frey's presentations on storytelling, and his re-telling of the "Salmon Always Goes Up River" story, the assignment began making more sense. We were feeling pretty comfortable with each other by now and it was actually not too difficult to re-tell the story in front of my family members. In telling the stories we experienced something in each story we hadn't previously seen. We weren't supposed to analyze them, but just reflect on the storytelling experience and what insights we had into the story.

Throughout the semester Frey brought in guest speakers—an elder or cultural resource person. I loved their storytelling.

Then there was the "participatory paper" assignment. We were to select a day-in-the-life, an event, an activity, a season within the seasonal-round, for any time period—pre-contact, historic, or contemporary—and research everything we could on its cultural meaning, kinship, material culture, social and ecological relations, ceremonial association, etc. Then the hard part: we had to come up with a "believable storyline and set of characters" as if we were there, as if each of us were one of the characters! We had to write a narrative of "creative nonfiction," as Frey told us he did with a Sibiriak story. We could use imagery or any means we could come up with to tell the story. Frey kept saying, "There is a relationship between 'what' you are trying to convey and 'how' you do it."

I'd become pretty good at writing research papers, but this? The hardest part was putting myself into someone else's shoes. But we tried as best we could. But in trying, I think I did get a little farther into the Tin Shed, and I realized a few things about myself. It took everyone's help to make this work, and also in the process we found out that each of us had something special and different to contribute. One was a good artist and drew some great images to complement the text. Another had some poetic skills, and put the words of the story to verse. I was a good researcher, and added background context to much of the story. Each of us assumed a different role and this story, too, came alive in a way no other class project had done before.

It was a very different sort of class. I really got a deeper appreciation of the Indian peoples of the Plateau, their history and culture, something I know I will always remember. We didn't get lectures, we got experiences. We weren't individuals, we were part of a family. We wrote and read, but we also spoke and listened. We had to participate. Frey was right, if we're to learn about the Indian peoples, from their perspectives, there is a huge relationship between "what" we are trying to learn (the content of the class), and "how" we go about doing the learning (the learning activities we did). It was the only way that we could begin to appreciate the *miyp* and *tamálwit* knowledge, and begin to travel into the Sweat Lodge. It had to be a different sort of class.

And as we learned when discussing storytelling and kinship, and as we experienced throughout the various learning activities of the course, to make it all work we needed what Frey called the "competency of empathy." I really had to listen if I was to see from someone else's perspective. It really came in handy in attempting to work with my family members. And to be attentive to the stories of our guest speakers and the elders on the field trips, and even in telling my own story, empathy was needed. It was indeed a juicy huckleberry.

◆ ◆ ◆

"*See* into the darkness, *see* from the inside and look out." … "Go inside…see it from the *inside* looking out." Allen and Cliff were certainly aware of so many others who had imposed their own perspectives on their Indian ways of life, misrepresenting and distorting them. If I was to venture into the Sweat House, the Tin Shed, Allen and Cliff wanted to be certain I attempted to do so seeing from the "*inside* looking out," attempting to gain an Apsáalooke or Schit̲-su'umsh perspective. Allen and Cliff were seeking to re-orient the premise and assumptions upon which many of my initial questions were posed, allowing me to better see their world as they did.

In attempting to see from the perspective of our host do we not need to first acknowledge our own perspectives? As Allen had redirected the questioning back to me while seated on the wooden bench, should we not ask ourselves what we bring into the Tin Shed? Just whose "culture" are we attempting to research, and then disseminate in our writings and in our classrooms—that of another, or to some extent a colonized extension of our own? Once we are cognizant of our own biases and preconceptions, we are better able not to let those perspectives blind us from or distort the views of those we seek to understand.

As I travel the Tin Shed, I attempt to position myself as a child swaddled in the blanket of my host—to grow under the tutelage of my host. While this goal may ultimately be elusive—when can we ever really see through the eyes of someone else—what is the alternative? I would offer that it is the only viable goal.

In an attempt to "see from the *inside* looking out," I needed to conceptually frame and organize the research questions, the resulting ethnographic text, and the classroom content using indigenous categories and terminology. So often we present the story of American Indian society configured within a Euro-American, materialist orientation. From this perspective, the prime movers and key causal factors driving the organization of a society are understood as its ecological relationship with the environment and the economic system, which in turn spawns the nature of the social order, with the religious institutions and "mythology" functioning to maintain the entire system. From a Schitsu'umsh perspective, for example, this orientation when applied to them must be turned on its head. As the world was created by the *Amotqn*, "one who sits at the head peak," considered the "father" to all his children and the Animal First Peoples, such as Coyote and Chief Child of the Yellowroot, it is from the spiritual—as expressed and perpetuated in the rich assemblage of oral traditions—that the material world is brought forth. Book chapter headings such as "economy," "social order," "religion" and "mythology" are replaced with "Preparing the World," "Receiving the Gifts," and "Sharing the Gifts" (Frey and the Schitsu'umsh 2001:271).

Instead of a world ripe with "natural resources," denoting commodities of monetary and utilitarian value, it is a world embedded with "gifts" from the Animal First Peoples—the camas, deer, and water, as well as *miyp*, moral and practical "teachings," and *suumesh*, spiritual power—all of which are to be shared freely among kinsmen, and with those in need (Frey and the Schitsu'umsh 2001:269–72). Along with "natural resources," such analytical constructs as "beliefs," "culture," "history," and "worldview," which have their origins outside the Sweat House and Tin Shed, should be clarified and adjusted if incorporated into the theoretical framing of the text (Frey and the Schitsu'umsh 2001:269–72, 297–98). Many of these terms could even be replaced, as in the Schitsu'umsh example, "culture" with their term for "our ways of life in the world"—*hnkhwelkhwlnet*—suggesting a much more experiential-defined, as opposed to ideological-based construct. All the indigenous content that would have been included in a traditional ethnographic manuscript or college course, reflecting such topics as technology, material culture, family and kinship, religion, mythology, etc. could be retained, but only after that content had been critically reconfigured and renamed to better reflect a Sweat House and Tin Shed perspective.

An insightful example of indigenizing a conceptual framing is expressed in the seasonal round. While the Gregorian calendar has become a standard internationally accepted means of dividing time and the seasons of the year, based upon the movement of the earth relative to the sun, it contrasts with the Indigenous seasonal round and manner of conceptualizing time. As in the example of the Niimíipuu experience, time is embedded in their seasonal round, *Niimíipuum 'inmiiwit*. But instead of anchoring that cycle with celestial relations, the calendar is based upon direct relations with the *qémes* (camas), léewliks (salmon or any fish), *'ímes* (deer), and *cemíitx* (huckleberries). Time, with its seventeen months embedded within six seasons of their yearly round, as one elder noted, is associated with the local seasonal changes in weather and availability of particular plants and fish. What is called *Pik'unmaayqáal*, "fish go downriver and salmon to ocean," is that time of the year when the *léewliks* journey to the Pacific Ocean, often associated with Gregorian month of September. But given seasonal and local patterns of rain or drought *Pik'unmaayqáal* may or may not correspond to September. While *'Apa'áal*, "season of *'apá*" (cous cake), can parallel the month of May, if local weather patterns vary, it may not. As the Niimíipuu calendar is intimately linked with local weather patterns, the temporal dynamics of human cultural behavior—the time to fish, to gather, to hunt—is thus regulated by relationships with specific animal, fish, and plant populations, each in interaction with an ever-changing idiosyncratic landscape. Niimíipuu time and its corresponding cultural way of life are not regulated by a calendar based on what, by comparison, seems an arbitrary and detached pattern of standardized seasons. The Niimíipuu are attentive and adjust to a "relative," the *qém'es*, time emanating out of a dynamic landscape, and not anchored to an abstract timetable.

Attempting to see from the inside looking out had direct bearing on how I would re-tell the stories, how I would re-tell that which was so cherished and shared with me, how I would *baaéechichiwaau*. It was indeed a special kind of text that I was attempting to construct, this transitory intersection of participants.

Publication can be very problematic. How does the text of a publication acknowledge and be informed by an indigenous learning style? How does the text acknowledge and be informed by an indigenous perspective? How is an oral-based learning and knowledge system to be effectively conveyed through a literacy-based format? For many elders, the very act of writing down oral traditions or even the words of an interview can only drain the stories and the words of their life. For others in the Native communities, however, the value of preserving for future generations the knowledge and oral traditions of their elders in a written format outweighs any possible harm putting those words into print might bring.

Tin Shed/Sweat Lodge texts ultimately emanate out of and are conveyed through the *oral* tradition. I was reminded of the dynamics and implications of orality itself, of the "voices" of story, song, and dance, of the special kind of text, as I attempted to access and disseminate Heart Knowledge (Frey, Aripa, and Yellowtail 1995:141–58; Frey 2004). And for my discussion here, I'd like to use as a point of reference and illustration the dynamic entailed in the narrative oral traditions, within the context of the spoken native languages.

As was discussed previously, the contrast between literacy and orality could not be more revealing. The shift is from viewing stories as explanations about and descriptions of the world, as predictors of reality or suspenders of disbelief about reality, to experiencing the stories as the world itself, as intensifiers of what is most real. The shift is from understanding a reality separate from yourself as described through the eyes of a scientist or novelist, to experiencing the unfolding of a story with its raconteur in concert with you and the other engaged listener-participants as co-facilitators, as co-creators of that transitory intersection. The shift is from compartmentalized cubicles to dynamic amalgamation. To slightly rephrase Meister Eckhart (1260–1327), the influential Christian mystic-theologian, and Ananda Coomaraswamy (1877–1947), the eminent scholar of Buddhist and Hindu philosophy, both of whom asserted while contrasting European and Asian aesthetic traditions—the shift is from viewing every artist (and by extension, every author and scientist) as a special kind of person, to experiencing every person, each of us, as a special kind of artist (Coomaraswamy 1934:64).

It is indeed a specific kind of text I attempted to construct, an intersection of participant orality-based "voices," each contributing to the co-creation of a series of transitory effervescent events. Accordingly, with Heart Knowledge as my goal I would seek to construct written texts, these symbolic clusterings, which experientially engage readers, audiences, students. I seek to convey the orality dynamic in my publications, incorporating a poetic oral-nuanced format and inviting the reader to participate in the "discovery" of the *miyp* embedded within the pages of the text. The Cuban-American anthropologist Ruth Behar (2007) offers a very persuasive position regarding ethnographic writing that goes beyond conventional formal writing, of "blurring the genres," to bring "art" to ethnography and include poetry, drama, memoir, fiction, and creative nonfiction. This blurred ethnography can bring insights into and humanize the human condition not obtained through formal conventions.

With Heart Knowledge as my goal, I seek to employ a pedagogical delivery of these written texts that would transform the formal classroom of the academy into the classroom of the elders, filled with the experiences of relationships involving stories, landscapes, and hosts, embedded with the *miyp* and bones of the Animal First Peoples. I sought in my classrooms, transformed with an indigenous learning style, to disseminate the oral tradition through experiential activities, through storytelling itself and in-the-round recitations, by engaging the elders in "their classrooms," through field trips—events of converging voices. In essence, I sought to re-tell the indigenous oral traditions, be they on any number of topics and expressed in any number of narrative, aesthetic, social, ecological, or political "story text" forms.

As in any indigenous storytelling experience, the resulting text, be it a publication or a classroom presentation, is the experiential transitory confluence of the voices of my hosts, as well as myself, as ethnographer/teacher, and of the audience of readers and students, with my hosts certainly the predominating voices, infused with the bones of their stories (Frey and the Schitsu'umsh 2001:285–86). A story, after all, is only brought to life when all are in the canoe of the storytelling session—the raconteur and participating listeners—each equally helping paddle up the "river," with the storyteller guiding paddlers to keep the canoe on course.

In an attempt to convey elements of oral nuance through a written publication, in putting the spoken word to print, one consideration entails presenting oral-based texts in a poetic style, noting intonation, pauses, cadence, and even the hand gesturing and facial expressions of the elder as recorded during an interview or storytelling session (Frey, Aripa, and Yellowtail 1995:20–24; Frey and the Schitsu'umsh 2001:126–27, 188–204, 279–82; Frey 2004:161–62). The resulting "script" can better express the rhythm, pacing, and context of an interview or storytelling, which are so critical to the oral-nuanced meaning. In turn, I ask those who engage these written texts to do so not as a reader, but to have another read the stories aloud to them, so they can experience something a little closer to the original oral-nuanced storytelling (Frey, Aripa, and Yellowtail 1995:20–24). I owe much to the pioneering work of Dell Hymes (1981) and Dennis Tedlock (1972) for first introducing me to the "poetic" in oral tradition. In attempting this sort of poetic-style formatting in some of my publications it's been gratifying to hear from family members of both Lawrence Aripa (Schitsu'umsh) and Tom Yellowtail (Apsáalooke) that upon reading their respective transcribed stories, they "could hear his voice speaking to them."

The following text is an example of an oral-nuanced transcription of a segment from Tom Yellowtail's re-telling of "The Little People" recorded in the summer of 1993. Notice Tom's use of repetition and pacing, with frequent pauses, as indicated by commas and a series of dot ellipses, depending on length of the pauses. His stressed words are indicated in italic type. A few of his hand and face gestures are also identified in parentheses. Note the importance Tom places on the location of this story.

◆ ◆ ◆

We talk about the Little People...,
  that are among the mountains.,
    in fact...my own medicine..come from the..Little People that
    I call on....
And..this one time.,
  not too long ago.,
    possibly I would say..about fifteen years ago when this
    happened..,
  on our present day..buffalo pasture
    on..the south of the Big Horn Canyon..,
      what they call the Yellowtail Dam..., [Tom points]
  branches of canyons that run into the..main Big Horn Canyon
  are the Black Canyon.,
    the Bull Elk Canyon., [continues to point]
    and so forth that lead into it.
And in that area is.,
  where our buffalo pasture is..*now*..,
    comprising a big area.,
      of some near thirty thousand acres.,
    there where our tribal buffalo herds..are being kept.
They have natural..canyons that comprise *high walls,* [Tom motions
  with hands to sky]
  that *not..not very much* fencing has been done to close up this..
  wide space
    comprising around twenty-five to thirty thousand acres.,
      where our tribal herd of buffalo are being kept *today*..
And..some fifteen years ago..the buffalo warden..,
  a man...,

a clan brother of mine.,
who comes to visit me.,
josh with me.,
because that's our..general..custom,
according to our Indian ways,
that we josh each other.,
whenever we meet.,
not meaning anything *real*
but we josh.,
make jokes.,
and so forth.
And...this..buffalo warden at that time who is Frank..He Does It..,
who *lives*..in the Big Horn valley,
his home is on the Big Horn valley,
close to..the present day..Fort Smith....
And..he had this job of being the buffalo warden,
so he *stays up there*..
There is a cabin up there
which we call "hunter's cabin"..
And it's a place provided by the..tribe.,
for the buffalo warden to live in..,
its a..log cabin,
a barn,
corrals,
a good spring close by..
And..the areas..for camping is very..nice
around near that..cabin
where the buffalo warden stays..
And he stays up there,
has his saddle horses to ride around with.,
looking over the buffalo herds..,
check the..fence lines,
and so forth..
And he lives and stays there.,
all alone...

And..*this..one night,*
>   when he rode during the day
>>   and come back and put his horse away.,
>>>   in the barn.,
>>>>   corral.,
>>>>>   for the night.,
>   he retired.,
>>   nightfall had come..
He come into his cabin,
>   and prepared himself a little..supper..
>>   And..after he ate.,
>>>   had his supper,
>   he laid down on his bed,
>>   had his lights..his lights on,
>>>   and..reading magazines.,
>>>>   old newspapers,
>>>>>   and so forth.
He was laying on his bed.,
>   *all alone...,*
>>   he's baching it up there (a bachelor)
>   *he's all alone...,*
>>   *nobody near...*
And while he's..laying there.,
>   silent,
>>   reading..by his..lights...
And..all at once he heard a *little noise*?, [Tom has a questioning
expression on his face and looks off to his porch]
>   out on his porch,
>>   porch like this that's out here.. [Tom points to his own porch]
He heard a *little noise*..out there..,
>   thinking
>>   "*Somebody's* coming?" [Tom whispers]
He's listen! [whispering]
Pretty soon...there is a *knock* on his door.., [Tom pats his hands
together]

a *knock*...on his door..
And he says,
  "*Hay, hay, come on in*, [in a loud, welcoming voice]
    come in!" [Tom motions with hand to come in]
The door opened..,
  and in walked *four little men*..., [Tom holds out four fingers]
    standing about three and a half..four feet...*high*,
      that's..the height of the Little People..,
        a grown man..,
  he maybe a hundred year old man.,
    only..standing about three and a half feet high
      or so..,
Little People just like a little.. a little..tiny child..,
  is what they are.,
    that's the size of them.
Yet..they are powerful...,
  the strength of a giant.., [in a strong voice]
    is what those Little People.,
      as *little as they are....*
They have the *medicine..*,
  they have the *strength..*,
    so they take care of things..
But...they come to the buffalo warden to do them a favor...

(Courtesy of University of Oklahoma Press.)

◆ ◆ ◆

I've attempted in several of my published works, both print and elec-
tronic/internet, to format the texts in a manner that encourages the
reader to explore and discover for himself or herself the embedded
meanings within (Frey, Aripa, and Yellowtail 1995:173–75; Frey and
the Schitsu'umsh 2001:279–82). As with my classroom students,
readers are asked to take on an active, heuristic role as they engage
the texts—a learning resulting from discoveries made by the reader
or student. The elders have insisted that the discovery process is

essential to the storytelling experience (Frey and the Schitsu'umsh 2001:282). As noted, traditional storytellers typically do not add specific, Aesop-like, moral commentaries to the beginning or end of their stories, inviting each listener to discover the lessons and *miyp* teachings in the story that are uniquely meaningful to him or her (Frey, Aripa, and Yellowtail 1995:174–75). As the stories are so richly layered with multiple meanings, to offer but a single lesson may serve to close off other possible lessons that might be of value to the range of diverse listeners. Other than identifying some broad literary motifs or underlying teachings, to help contextualize and anchor the texts for readers (what I will call "signposts"), I've sought to minimize analysis of the stories. For that matter, I've tried to refrain from overtly interpreting any of the knowledge and experience emanating out of the Tin Shed. In this regard, I've sought to present ethnography in the Boasian tradition, free from theory-laden, nomothetic assertions.

I've also incorporated the use of short story "vignettes" that would be placed within the appropriate chapters and sections of a book's text, similar to those used in this essay. The vignettes are comprised of narrative oral traditions, first-person participant-observations of social scenes, or particularly poignant segments from transcribed interviews, all without commentary or overt interpretation (though it is acknowledged, that in the acts of identifying and isolating such vignettes, and of placing them in a particular location within the manuscript, implicit, albeit partial, interpretations are made). In peppering the manuscript with such vignettes, the many "voices" of the elders can be presented less filtered, and the reader asked to do the work of making the connections and "discoveries" within and between the many meanings embedded within the narrative vignettes.

This style of constructed text is not always acknowledged as viable in the academic community. I clearly remember my first attempt at publishing a short essay on the Apsáalooke Sundance with an extensive use of isolated and seemingly randomly placed vignettes augmented with more formal interpretive analytical text. The submitted essay was rejected, the journal's reviewers dismissing it as incoherent, and one reviewer characterizing the writing of its author as that of a schizophrenic! I have nevertheless persevered, certainly refining the style, and have found publication platforms on which I can juggle multiple voices and challenge the readers to engage the text and make discoveries, to "connect the dots."

In "If All These Great Stories Were Told, Great Stories Will Come," a narrative that chronicled my first healing journey with cancer, Cliff and I deliberately sought to identify and distinguish some of the many voices in this text (Frey, Yellowtail, and SiJohn, 2008). We also sought to overtly acknowledge the essay's collaborative, equitable co-authorship. This essay is perhaps the best expression of the vignette style, a montage of interwoven voices. As one voice, we have the edited segments of Tom's contributions that were based upon a 1993 audio-recorded transcription of an interview we had done, and a conversation that followed on the use of an oral-nuanced format. Central to the essay was a re-telling of Burnt Face, another voice itself. Another voice is that of Cliff derived from transcript segments of an interview we did together in 1997, and from a 2006 recorded conversation specifically intended for the essay. To better give a sense of the dynamic rhythm in Tom and Cliff's words and thus convey their "voices" we italicized their voiced inflections and stresses, and added a series of dot ellipses to approximate pause durations, from brief (two dot) to longer (three dot and four dot) gaps in their speech. Both Tom and Cliff's texts were further differentiated from mine as they had indented margins and a smaller font size, yet were distinguishable from each other by style, topics, and embedded identifiers in the previous paragraphs. Each paragraph demarcation reflected a critical and coherent segment of content and message selected for the presentation, resulting in an article made up of a storyline of alternating sequential yet associated paragraph texts from each of the three authors. Within Tom's story there were thus conveyed his voice and the voices of Burnt Face and of the Little People, while within Cliff's narrative there was his voice, along with those of Coyote, Eagle, Chipmunk, and Cedar, among other Animal First Peoples. And along with my voice were those of my son and of *Bishée*, Buffalo. We also asked the reader to contribute his or her own voice; to appreciate a little more the power of storytelling, we asked the reader to become a listener, having someone else read the text aloud to him or her. As we suggested in the essay, "a great story is to be experienced as it is told," the listener transformed into a participant voice within the unfolding story. Each time the text is engaged, "If All These Great Stories Were Told…" offers an entrance to an assemblage of potential voices at any one moment, interacting with one another, as an unfolding event.

In publishing the cherished stories of the elders, I have sought, in most of my publications, to acknowledge co-authorship of the texts. In collaboration we are the co-genitors of the text, the re-tellers of the stories, stories anchored in the experiential heritage of the elders. While this admission may seem an obvious conclusion given the cultural property rights of indigenous communities, this is not always the case in the academy and with its publishers. The publisher of "If All These Great Stories Were Told…," a co-authored essay for a proposed book chapter, questioned its co-authorship, assuming that the Native individuals must surely be understood as the "subjects" of the essay and of my research. The publisher even requested from me the signed "informed consent forms" for Tom and Cliff, if they were to be included in the legal documentation of the essay. However the book's editor, Suzanne Crawford O'Brien, came to our rescue, insisting on a shared authorship role for Cliff SiJohn, Tom Yellowtail, and myself (Frey, Yellowtail, and SiJohn 2008:185–205).

As an alternative to the written word and as a means to convey orality-based knowledge, it is worth considering the digital world of the internet, DVDs, and other possibilities. Streaming oral traditions and interviews as told by elders over the internet or on a DVD can render the voices of the elders more immediate, vibrant, and authentic. While certainly not a substitute for a living encounter, their voices are not mediated through a literacy-based media that can inadvertently distort, nor through a writer that can unintentionally misrepresent. In addition, the interface of a web-page module or DVD can offer the user a non-lineal, non-progressive experience. Instead of beginning at an introduction and step-by-step culminating in a book's conclusion, subject to an author's intended agenda, the user can experience a "web," navigating about to various topics and presentations, exploring that which is relevant and meaningful to him or her—a sort of self-paced, individualized instruction, which is typical of an indigenous learning style. The learner takes on some of the instructional responsibility for the learning.

In 2001 I was presenting the completed web module of the extensive Niimíipuu Life-Long Learning Online Internet-based project, L3, to the Nez Perce Circle of Elders for their review. We had over four hours of streaming-video interviews with thirty-three elders and cultural consultants. I can remember my own anxiety as I was beginning to present the project to these elders, the tribe's cultural committee. But soon into my formal talk, my apprehension was replaced by an excitement in the air and the approval on the faces of these grandmothers, the tribal elders. Upon seeing and hearing their own voices and the voices of other relatives presented so clearly and untrammeled through this media they quickly became intrigued and a bit enamored with the experience. I overheard several comment to each other that they wanted to have their granddaughters show them how to access the new world of the "Web"!

The immediacy of the spoken voice and the active role of the learner were elements both brought to bear in one of my graduate student's thesis project. In "Voices that Soar with the Eagles," Jennifer Gatzke elected to present her research on a contemporary, all-women's drum group among the Schitsu'umsh not through an established written thesis, but through the agency of a DVD (2008). Her interviewees had their voices fully presented, unedited by an editor or shortened in length, nor mediated through a written script. Most critically, the particular sounds of the drum beat and voices of this all-women's drum group, so unusual in powwow country but supported by tribal elders, could also be better described and appreciated. Users of the

DVD could then move about the rich and diverse content and topics with the ease allowed by a computer mouse and guided by his or her own intentions to explore. The Coeur d'Alene Tribe fully endorsed and approved the project, while the University of Idaho's Graduate School and Library were less enthusiastic—a reluctance stemming from the issue of the "permanency" of this emerging digital format compared with the written page. The university finally accepted Jennifer's DVD thesis, though only after it was also accompanied by a shortened written version of the thesis. The power of the written word! It is ironic that such a technological-based media can hold promise for the delivery of a very organically-based knowledge. See Frey and the Nez Perce (2001), Frey and the Schitsu'umsh (2002), and Frey and the Confederated Tribes of Warm Springs (2003) for an example of my internet-formatted publications.

But I was still in search of a more authentic and effective means to convey the voices of the storytelling elders. How to address the challenges of presenting the content of an orality-based tradition via a literacy-based format? What format could possibly replicate that transitory intersection of those participating, and do so within a specific place-based landscape? While much closer, the non-interactive digital means thus far explored still did not effectively align the "what" and the "how." Could there be no substitute for the face-to-face encounter? Would there yet be a new, emerging communication format for an alignment of "what" is conveyed, the content of the story, with the "how" it is conveyed, the means of doing so?

"And when it is your turn to pray aloud, what are you *going to do*, what are you *going to say*?" … "What are *you going to do* with what you've been given?" Our host-guides would insist that we "give back," seek to bring comfort and support to others, a collaborative endeavor in the pursuit of application. Allen and Cliff knew all too well of the many who had come only to take.

As a collaborative effort and given cultural property rights, I have sought in my research, publication, and teaching of my hosts' knowledge to ultimately serve the wishes of the host's community, as defined by our host. Inevitably asked on a tribal research permit application is the question: "How will this project benefit the Tribe?" Or as when Cliff SiJohn had spoken in my classes—"as a student in this class...*what will you do* with the knowledge gained?...how will it be used...to *help others?*"

One of the foundational teachings I've found shared throughout Indian country is encapsulated in the Niimíipuu term, *téeke*, "to give and share [food with others]" or Apsáalooke term *ammaakée*, "giveaway." As expressed among the Schitsu'umsh, an "ethic of sharing" with those in need, without expectation of reciprocity, is the dynamic that binds all the members of the extended family together (Frey and the Schitsu'umsh 2001:10). As my host has so generously shared with me, I ask how I will "give back" to help others, through my research, publication, and teaching. In my efforts at collaborative research, publication, and teaching, I ask how I will support my host as an equal sovereign partner. What is termed "pure research" has its vital role in the academy and for the public good. But when research involves a reliance on knowledge from an indigenous community, I believe it must be done in concert with that community, bowing to the wishes of the host regarding the manner in which that research is to be used and applied.

While I was being guided by my Indian collaborators to do research that would benefit their tribes, to help others in need, I was also being encouraged to do so by my dissertation chair at the University of Colorado, Deward Walker, whose passion to help others introduced me to a professional life as an "applied anthropologist." For examples of my applied, collaborative research I would mention the following two exemplary projects.

My first ethnographic field work was at the invitation of the Crow Tribe after completing my master's degree in anthropology at Colorado State University in 1974. There was a lack of good communication between the well-intentioned Indian Health Service (IHS) physicians and their Apsáalooke patients; the physicians were skilled medically but lacked Apsáalooke cultural competencies and understandings. Working with elders such as Tom and Susie Yellowtail, Allen Old Horn, Joseph Medicine Crow, and members of the Old Coyote and Real Bird families, and with Father Randolph Graczyk, I researched and we put together an introductory paper on traditional Apsáalooke understandings of health care and illness, and the larger cultural context. The paper was presented to the Crow IHS staff and subsequently used by the physicians to help them to better understand, communicate with, and provide health care for their patients. The following year, under the auspices of Sister Karen Watembach, I did research on male roles, social relations, and dynamics to help provide better counseling services through the Catholic Church. The results of this 1974 and 1975 research provided the impetus for my 1979 University of Colorado doctoral dissertation. After a thorough review by and approval from each interviewee, this research led to the 1987 publication of my book *The World of the Crow: As Driftwood Lodges.*

In 1996, as a faculty member with Lewis-Clark State College, I was approached by Alfred Nomee, director of the Coeur d'Alene Tribe's Department of Natural Resources, and asked to assist the tribe in a Natural Resources Damage Assessment (NRDA). With over a hundred years of Silver Valley mining in the Coeur d'Alene River watershed, the entire river-lake ecosystem adjacent to it and on the reservation had been subjected to high levels of heavy-metal pollutants, especially lead. An ethnographic baseline study was needed to show how the Schitsu'umsh had defined and interacted with their landscape of water, plants, and animals prior to the arrival of Euro-Americans, and given the mining impact, how those relationships had continued or changed into the present.

Brought to bear were five years of previous participant observation and interview research, and with the initiation of the NRDA, three additional years of collaborative research. Over twenty elders, representing thirteen different families, participated in in-depth interviews specifically related to the NRDA. To better reflect the Schitsu'umsh perspective, the organization of the report followed their ontological indigenous conceptualization of the world, starting with their creation stories involving the Creator and Animal Peoples who prepared the world for the coming of Human Peoples. It was followed by an encapsulation of the essential food, teaching lessons, and spirit "gifts" embedded in the landscape and needed by the Schitsu'umsh. The report concluded with how those gifts were shared among all the peoples, Animal and Human, to sustain the world. A complete ethnography was offered, though organized in a manner not typically done in an ethnographic report: with the primary causal chain starting with ecology, technology, and subsistence practices, followed by social, political, and religious orders, and with mythology justifying it all. In the Schitsu'umsh instance, it all starts with story. Before submission to the Coeur d'Alene Tribal Council for review and possible approval, the completed draft report was first reviewed by each interviewee, by the Coeur d'Alene Tribe's Culture Committee, and because they were respected for their opinions, by the Spokane Tribe's Cultural Committee, with all reviews resulting in unanimous approval that the cultural content could be publically disseminated. Upon the request of the Tribal Council, this project led to the publication of *Landscape Traveled by Coyote and Crane: The World of the Schitsu'umsh* (Frey and the Schitsu'umsh 2001).

◆ ◆ ◆

Traveling in Agnes Vanderburg's stories? From *singing* a song, *retelling* a story, the bones are *resuscitated* and *come alive*? *Swirling* with Coyote? I accepted these assertions on face value, patient, trusting my teachers, but still all a great mystery!

With "best practices" to help guide my way into the Tin Shed and Sweat House, just *who* was this "ethnographer" I called myself? What professional competencies and skills would I need and should have to effectively and properly travel within homes of others, of my hosts, and re-tell their most cherished stories?

Stmi'sm "listening" and *'Itsk'u'lm* "doing"

Traveling the Stories of Others—
On Being an Ethnographer

One of his *biilápxe*, a "clan uncle," is singing a "praise song" for a "clan son," as they ride through the huge tipi encampment in this Crow Fair Dance Parade. There are over a hundred riders; they and their horses are in full beaded regalia in traditional Apsáalooke floral and geometric patterns and colors. The clan son had just returned from active duty, serving his family and country in the armed forces with pride and distinction. Throughout his life, whenever an achievement of note had occurred—a birthday, a graduation, service to others—one of his *biilápxe,* a man of his father's mother's clan, in a strong voice and with deliberate words, would convey this young man's deeds and honors to family and friends, to the entire community. The inexperienced young man should never speak for himself; he should never boast in any way about himself. The deeds are best conveyed through an elder's voice, one experienced in the use of words.

Following the procession, an *ammaakée* ceremony, a public giveaway, is held. The *biilápxe* listens attentively as the young man re-tells his deed. Then, in front of the many gathered, the *biilápxe* re-tells the young man's experience. Next, piled-high Pendleton blankets and other assembled gifts are distributed to other *biilápxe* and to the many family members gathered. As a public "thank you," it is a subtle but deliberate acknowledgment that an individual's accomplishments are only the result of the efforts made by so many others. Perhaps it is a *biilápxe*, who in a Medicine Bundle ceremony, had provided an Indian Name that nurtured and protected the young man. Certainly in the prayers during a Sweat Bath or the Sunday Mass many clan uncles sent words out to the Creator that sought to look after and guide this clan son. In the *biilápxe's* act of re-telling the young man's story, there is the hope that others might be served, helped in some way to navigate a challenge in their lives or the life of a loved one, a huckleberry offered. And the stories swirl about. (Re-told from experiences in the mid-1970s; also in Frey 1987:40–57.)

◆ ◆ ◆

At early junctures in my unfolding career, it seemed most fitting that I would have the opportunity to orient my own ethnographic research techniques, writing styles, and teaching methods based upon men and women who, in essence, were "indigenous ethnographers." Allen, Tom and Susie, and Cliff had carefully listened to the stories and witnessed the great deeds of their elders, and then, in turn, re-told those cherished stories, with authenticity and appropriateness, to a large and potentially diverse audience, to me and, through me, to you. They had practiced *baaéechichiwaau*, "re-telling one's own." They had *stmi'sm* "listened" and were retaining the *miyp* bones, and they were *'itsk'u'lm* "doing" and resuscitating the bones with flesh, keeping the stories alive. How remarkably similar are the *biilápxe* and the ethnographers with *'me'y'mi'y'm*. Each cares deeply for the stories, and for those they are attributed to and for those who hear them. It is instructive to note the confluence of the "indigenous" as brought forth in this essay with a variety of Native scholars who articulate indigenous methodologies. Consider the important works of such Native scholars as Karletta Chief, et al. (2014), Margaret Kovach (1999), Linda Tuhiwai Smith (2012), and Shawn Wilson (2008). The voices of the elders find multiple paths for the sharing.

I must acknowledge that my own *stmi'sm*, "listening," and *'itsk'u'lm*, "doing," also has kinship with the tradition of Boasian ethnography, in reference to the work of Franz Boas (1858–1942). German-born and educated in physics, his doctorate dealt with researching the color of ocean water in the arctic, which brought Boas to the Central Eskimo and later the tribes of the Northwest Coast. Boas' scientific training would help focus his research on the empirical details of a society. Boas reacted against the "grandiose armchair theories and theorists" of his day, many of whom were overtly racist. He challenged the notions of "nomothetic universal laws," "environmental, geographic or economic determinism," as well as the use of the "comparative method." Boas stressed the need for intensive and long-term field work, grounding research in a particular history and its description, anchored in the language of the people. He also stressed doing collaboratively-oriented research, as he did successfully with George Hunt (1854–1933), a Tlingit. Considered the father of American anthropology, Boas' legacy can be seen in the works of his many students, among them Alfred Kroeber, Robert Lowie, Edward Sapir, Alexander Goldenweiser, Melville Herskovits, Leslie Spier, Clark Wissler, Paul Radin, Ruth Bunzel, Ruth Benedict, E. Adamson Hoebel, and Elsie Claws Parson. Boas trained the first American Indian anthropologist, William Jones, of the Fox nation. The "sins" of our ancestors can bring us angst, but we must recognize and address them. Some anthropologists sold human skulls, parting souls from subjects, as the American Indian was objectified in the name of science. Nevertheless, I acknowledge myself of mixed parenting, in part a progeny, albeit a distant cousin, of this Boasian extended family. It is from this Boasian lineage that I was led to Clifford Geertz and his use of "thick description" and religious symbols (1973), which is certainly embedded in my research and writing styles. This essay's vignettes have affinity with Geertz's classic "Balinese Cockfight" narrative (1973:412–53). We share in a desire to provide detailed, thick descriptions of social events and their contexts that don't objectify our hosts, but bring an immediacy to them through a retelling of a "participant observation" in which the researcher is embedded in the unfolding story. It is a description that can at once humanize others, while rendering their unique behaviors more meaningful. It is a description that gains "access to the conceptual world in which our subjects live so that we can, in some extended sense of the term, converse with them," a description that at its "heart" is an "interpretation" (1973:24, 18). As the offspring of a mixed marriage, perhaps I have some advantage when attempting to travel and bridge multiple spokes?

Questions arise. What is the role of a university in training ethnographers to do work with tribes? What is the role of a university faculty member in doing ethnography for tribes? Who is to "don the regalia" of an ethnographer and travel into the Tin Shed, conducting research on what is held most cherished—Heart Knowledge?

As seen in the Life-Long Learning Online (L3) projects, tribal-member co-researchers were more than capable of telling their own tribal stories. During the L3 projects, from 2001 through 2003, the Nez Perce Tribe and the Confederated Tribes of Warm Springs had their own Cultural Resources Offices, with their own tribal ethnographers. The Coeur d'Alene Tribe had yet to establish their program, despite staffing some comparably trained personnel in their GIS and language programs. Hence many of the Niimíipuu (Nez Perce), and the Warm Springs, Wasco, and Paiute L3 interviews were conducted by tribally-enrolled ethnographers, while I held the video camera. In 1996, soon after I had been asked to assist the Coeur d'Alene Tribe with their Natural Resources Damage Assessment, I was visiting with Chairman Ernie Stensgar. He relayed to me a question asked of him by another tribal member, "why are we hiring a non-Indian to do this sort of work for us?" Chairman Stensgar's response was something to the effect, "if we had an ethnographer on staff with the tribe, we'd have him do it, but we don't." The Coeur d'Alene Tribe has since established its own Cultural Resource Management

Program, later renamed the Historic Preservation Program, with a Schitsu'umsh director, and Schitsu'umsh and Euro-American staff, all trained in historic preservation, ethnography, archaeology, and linguistics. The director, Leanne Campbell, was the co-principal investigator in the "Sqigwts.org" project of 2015.

The word "ethnographer," whether applied to a tribal or university faculty member, derives from the Greek "ethnos" referring to a people, and "graphein" meaning to record in a written format. An ethnographer is someone skilled in gathering, recording, preserving, and disseminating a people's story of themselves, for the purpose of informing and benefitting, for addressing a specific need, or just for the greater good. In its distilled yet inclusive definition, "one who seeks to appreciate the stories of others, and then to re-tell them, with permission, for the benefit of others—a descriptive account that seeks to give back."

The university can be a place that prepares ethnographers to work with tribes, especially when coursework is co-taught and student research is done in collaboration with tribal hosts. There are many capable of donning the ethnographer's regalia. We come back to where we began and the critical issue first posed by Allen and Cliff—*"you see* that tin shed?" While a university's Institutional Review Board (IRB) can consider the ethics of doing ethnography, who is to be trusted to re-tell the cherished stories is a decision only the caretakers of those stories can make. Whether the skilled ethnographer is an enrolled member of the tribe, an employee of the Tribe, university or not, who dons the regalia and is permitted to travel the territory of the Tin Shed is a question to be ultimately answered only by a sovereign tribe. As ethnographers seeking to re-tell the stories of others, don't we need to be granted the right to *baaéechichiwaau*?

If I were to travel the territory of the spoke—indeed the many spokes of the Apsáalooke, the Schitsu'umsh, and other indigenous peoples of this land, and those beyond—as a student, as a teacher, I'd need to attempt to gain some level of competency to don the regalia as an ethnographer. In reflection, is not "ethnography" something we all seek, regardless of our particular disciplinary upbringing—to appreciate the stories of others and retell them for the benefit of others? These could be stories of the past, engaged by an archaeologist or historian. These could be stories of our neighbors, engaged by a sociologist or journalist. Are we not all ethnographers?

Following Cliff and Allen's lessons from the Sweat House and Tin Shed, I learned that the ethnographer's competence involves first obtaining permission from my host and then of traveling in collaboration, with the host as guide, and always attempting to see from his perspective. This is a competence predicated on acquiring the language of our host, and of being as if a child, swaddled in the fabric of his indigenous blanket—skilled in our application of sampling techniques, obtaining informed consent, semi-structured interviewing, and participant-engagements, skilled in coding and interpreting the gathered research—all in concert with our host. This is a competence predicated on adapting research design and methods, research-legitimizing criteria, publication format, and classroom pedagogy to an indigenous learning style—to the place-bound, experiential knowledge, the *miyp* of the oral traditions and the power of the spoken word. This is a competence that seeks to mediate an unbridled literacy with a nuanced orality, and render the stories accessible, welcoming to all. This is a competence that seeks to give back to those we serve, and to all in need. This is a competence that shares with strangers only that which the indigenous community elects to publicly share. In seeking this competency I've come to realize the rich and vibrant terrain that is the unique indigenous landscape.

The ethnographer's regalia is remarkably similar to that worn by a contemporary powwow clown! Certainly devoid of spiritual qualities that can be imbued in the powwow clown, the ethnographer is nevertheless like the clown with its own distinctive albeit ambiguous regalia, often a combination of styles, Indian as well as Euro-American, fused in an amusing if not contrary fashion. While clearly standing out from the crowd, standing out as unique, the clown is begrudgingly accorded a place within the Grand Entry and on the dance floor, a place within an interdependent whole. And while dancing, the clown/ethnographer provides a translation, an interpretive yet comic pantomime of the other dancers—the fancy, the traditional, and the many styles about, all for the benefit of the on-lookers in the bleachers and chairs that surround the dance floor. And you know where I'm going with this: both clown and ethnographer can be made to look the fool! We should never take ourselves too seriously, or be too self-assured, too Coyote. Paul Stoller (2009), with a wealth of personal experiences and theoretical extrapolations from the discipline of anthropology, insightfully wrestles with the positioning of ethnographers, as someone between cultures and realities, between the experiences of scientists and sorcerers, between universal rationalists and relativists, as someone like a Sufi master, pursuant of "embodied rationality."

I had this role and lesson wonderfully re-iterated during a pow-wow Cliff SiJohn was emceeing a few years back. It was a pretty well-attended dance, mostly Indian families, but a few non-Indians as well, with several drums providing song. As with most powwows, various dances were highlighted, including Men's Traditional, Fancy, and Grass, along with Women's Traditional, Jingle, and Shawl—with plenty of intertribal dances for all to partake. Then Cliff announced on his PA system, "I'd like "Rodney Frey...*professor* from the University of Idaho, an *anthropologist*, and I'd like...," naming other specific white males in attendance, "and all the non-Indian men" to go out onto the dance floor. Surprised, we reluctantly did so, some twelve or so of us. On the floor we were greeted by several women, who loaned us their bright, fringed dance shawls. Most of these women then sat back down in the chairs that surrounded the dance arena, but a few women remained on the floor, as judges. Then Cliff gave the signal to a drum to begin the song and we were told to dance, dance the Women's Shawl Dance! You could imagine, or maybe not, but the laughter started almost immediately, continuing until the drum beat ceased. It seemed like forever, awkward, trying to move with the beat, legs and arms going every which way, the shawl with a mind of its own. A clown in another form. What a way to learn and what a way to bring a good laugh to everyone, and what a reminder to oneself!

As ethnographers on the dance floors of others, of all competencies needed to be able to don the regalia of the many diverse and unique spokes, one competency in particular stands out. I am convinced that Tom and Lucy, and Allen and Cliff, welcomed me in and guided me through their homes, in large part because I exhibited a certain quality. I believe we played, explored, and discovered, and laughed, wept, and cared through our "empathy" for each other, through *snukwnkhwtskhwts'mi'ls*.

Is not empathy a prerequisite for entry, and a necessary condition for communicating and engaging within and outside the Sweat Lodges/Tin Sheds? Is not empathy the quality that facilities the communication of a *biilápxe* as he sings his praise songs for a clan son? Is not empathy the quality that facilitates indigenous communications with plants and animals, as in a prayer or song shared with Camas or Deer? Is not empathy that quality that ultimately serves to enable human and spirit peoples to commune with one another, be it with the Little People as a face is made as a child's, or as Coyote swirls around and a lake is *made* blue? As ethnographers, if we are to begin to appreciate these indigenous social, ecological, and spiritual relationships, we should also appreciate the dynamic that binds them. And just maybe, in successfully acquiring the languages and traveling the diverse spokes of the Wheel, revealed will be a language or two of our shared humanity, of the hub?

When teaching the ways of Plateau Indians, I have sought to offer my students a classroom infused with an indigenous pedagogy, rich with teaching methods that are family-based as opposed to solely individual-based, experiential and place-based as opposed to solely analytical-based, orality-based as opposed to solely literacy-based. I sought to swaddle my students in the fabric of an indigenous blanket and nourish them with Heart Knowledge, so they could begin to appreciate and engage the regalia of the Plateau People's spoke, while reflecting on possible hub languages.

When teaching anthropological research methods, I have sought to offer my students some level of competency to be able to don the regalia of both head and heart spokes, of both positivist and constructionist/indigenous research design, methods and interpretations; of both empirical (validity and reliability) and post-modern/indigenous (authenticity, trustworthiness, and appropriateness) criteria for legitimizing research, of both scientific (formal) and aesthetic (narrative) forms and styles of writing. I have sought to provide an opportunity for my students to gain a competency in dancing the spokes of our human diversity, while reflecting on possible hub languages.

Ethnography: Humanities Style. Attempting to understand, articulate, and convey another culture's knowledge is always fraught with challenge. To attempt to do so with indigenous knowledge and practices, predicated on ontological, pedagogical, and epistemological anchorings distinct from that of the general American public, necessitates caution and deliberate considerations. As an ethnographer conducting research, writing monographs, and teaching courses, while attempting to travel with one foot on the spoke of the Sweat Lodge and the other planted on the spoke of the academy, I've always felt more comfortable wearing my collegiate shoe in the style of the humanities. More than in other academic disciplines, the humanities have offered a style that has facilitated travel over the many diverse spokes, while also allowing me to explore other possible hub languages. More than other disciplines, I've found the humanities to offer a means to more fully engage and articulate the indigenous, providing a language to bridge cultural divides. And I am reminded of the words of Alfred Kroeber, a founding father of the discipline: "Anthropology is the most humanistic of the sciences and the most scientific of the humanities," and bridges academic divides as well.

The humanities certainly share goals with other academic disciplines, such as the natural and social sciences, and with the arts; for example, the goal of seeking to understand and appreciate the human condition, in all its rich expression in time and place. What distinguishes the humanities from other disciplines is not so much its content and subject—a creative playwright, a behavioral psychologist, and a humanities professor could each be dealing with the same subject (for example, Native American identity)—but its methodology.

The humanities belong to what the Idaho Humanities Council identifies as "interpretative disciplines." These disciplines include cultural anthropology/ethnography, communications studies, cultural studies (such as American Studies, American Indian Studies, international studies, religious studies, and women's studies); they include the languages, law, literature, history, philosophy; and they include the reflection and theory in creative writing, in the performing arts of music, dance, and theatre, and in the visual arts of painting, sculpting, and architecture.

While not a black-and-white distinction, the approach of the humanities disciplines is typically distinguished from the positivist and empirical methodologies of the natural and social science disciplines, and from the creative and imaginative endeavors of the arts. The social sciences have provided powerful analytical tools that challenge misrepresentation, bias, and prejudice. The arts can pierce the heart with unsurpassed and memorable imagery and insight into the human condition. Humanities methods can include hermeneutics, literary criticism, phenomenology, and in the discipline of ethnography, thick description. Influential in my own research, writing, and teaching are such exemplary scholars as N. Scott Momaday and his discussion on the power of words and story, Keith Basso and Mircea Eliade and their treatise on the power of story and place, and Owen Barfield and his homage to the power of transitory participation and creativity.

What distinguishes the humanities from other disciplines is its style, method, and scope. For my purposes here, let me identify four essential components of what for me defines the humanities. They include an "integrative" approach to the human experience (distinct from a segmented, reductionist approach), a "narrative" style of communications (distinct from a more formal, impersonal, objective style), an "interpretative method" (distinct from a social scientific analytical method), and a focus on revealing "wisdom" (distinct from "knowledge" per se). It is an approach well positioned to better reveal the meaning of the indigenous in ways otherwise unavailable. Let me briefly elaborate.

Integrative. With its breadth of interrelated disciplinary lenses, of communication, comparative religion, ethnography, history, linguistics, literature, performing arts, and philosophy, for example, the humanities can distinctly spotlight the integrated content of the cultural landscapes of the indigenous. The cohesive oral traditions of the indigenous are expressed through such varied forms as narrative creation stories, songs, powwow regalia, spoken language, kinship relationships, subsistence and ritual practices, and ways of knowing and doing.

Interpretive. The humanities uniquely offer an interpretive style. To interpret seeks to render something meaningful and understandable, serving to inform, enlighten, instruct. Likely first expressed in the fourteenth-century Middle English, "interpret" is derived from the Latin, *interpretārī*—"someone who serves as an agent, a negotiator." Hence, to interpret seeks to (1) generate new knowledge, rendering something meaningful, be it culturally or historically distinct, be it something more immediate but veiled in some fashion. But to interpret also seeks to (2) render that knowledge accessible, applicable, relevant, that is, to link and integrate, to negotiate between what is known and the one seeking to know, between known and knower. To interpret, I would suggest, entails rendering knowledge empathic, of projecting the seeker into the known, of placing you into the shoes of another…of projecting the listener into the story as a participant with others.

Narrative. To interpret relies upon various forms of "storytelling" as a means to effectively engage audiences and bring them into the story as "participants," bringing an intimacy to the negotiation, be it a Sibiriak or Salmon story. The humanities and indigenous communication are allied in reliance on figurative language and narrative, on non-verbal gestures and cues, on comprehensive story within which "teachings" are revealed, in a manner not found in the social sciences. Social science strives to fragment narrative into reductionist patterns of discrete simplicity and redundancy often for statistical analysis. Through story, the humanities strives to render the whole, more than the sum of its parts, and render the depth of interwoven heart and mind. With its narrative familiarity, to interpret allows each the opportunity to think about and reflect more deeply upon what is too often veiled in our daily lives.

Wisdom. The Idaho Humanities Council goes on to state that "through [the] study [of the humanities it seeks to] yield wisdom." As written in the 1965 National Foundation on the Arts and Humanities Congressional Act, which established the National Endowment for the Humanities and all the state councils, "Democracy demands wisdom and vision in its citizens." Wisdom is that deep understanding that goes beyond knowing, to thicken and extend our understandings, to apply, to engage that knowledge in civic life, both locally and globally, to address the challenges faced by humanity. To interpret is to reflect upon fundamental questions of ethics, purpose, and meaning, to explore our "mega-stories," to go deep down to the bones to get to the big picture, and in so doing possibly reveal wisdom. As interpretive reflection, wisdom is an application of knowledge to inform judgement. Among its many definitional attributes, "wisdom" entails the appreciation of the intersection of the particular and universal, the spokes and the hub; in this instance, linking the diverse of the indigenous with the shared in our common humanity. The confluence of the humanities and the indigenous is as a mirror through which we can see and reflect upon the diversity and ubiquitous, the unique and the universal, within ourselves and our humanity, and apply those reflections to our lives.

In his 2007 keynote address, Gary Williams, in his role of Distinguished Humanities Professor at the University of Idaho, emphasized that the humanities are "a way of thinking about and responding to the world—tools we use to examine and make sense of the human experience in general and our individual experiences in particular.

The humanities enable us to reflect upon our lives and ask fundamental questions of value, purpose, and meaning in a rigorous and systematic way." As the 1965 Congressional Act stressed, the term "humanities" pays "particular attention to our diverse heritage, traditions, and history and to the relevance of the humanities to the current conditions of national life" to both the particular and diverse, as well as to the national and "shared in common."

With this understanding of the interpretative, integrative, narrative, and wisdom-seeking nature of the humanities, the humanities are particularly well suited for our travels on the many spokes, traveling the Sweat Lodge of Heart Knowledge or, for example, traveling the STEM disciplines—science, technology, engineering, and math—of Head Knowledge. For all its formality, science can be framed and understood as a mega-story. In interpreting and reflecting, and in

Turning of the Wheel: A Humanities Exploration

During 2011–12, I was honored with the Distinguished Humanities Professorship, the second awarded by the College of Letters, Arts and Social Sciences at the University of Idaho. I organized a program entitled, "Turning of the Wheel: the Interplay between the Unique and Universal—a Humanities Exploration," a year-long series of events, talks, performances, and exhibits featuring University of Idaho faculty and graduate students. Each explored the meaning of the unique spokes and universal hub from within his or her own disciplinary perspective. We sought to discover and celebrate the distinct languages of the many spokes, while also exploring the possible shared languages of our common humanity. It was a rich and insightful endeavor for all. To experience the various "Turning of the Wheel" talks and performances, including the story of how Tom Yellowtail's Rock Medicine Wheel informed my thinking on the humanities, please visit www.lib.uidaho.edu/digital/turning.

the re-telling of the indigenous and STEM stories, we can more fully render them accessible and applicable, and to integrate them more fully into our lives. The humanities, with its affiliation with empathy and storytelling, might just also offer another dialect of the Wheel's spokes, a means for traversing the material and imaginative, the head and the heart in our lives, of traveling the varied spokes of the many strangers amongst us. We can always take a lesson or two from Tom, and strive to balance the Wheel, maintaining the integrity of the varied spokes, while striving to find the shared hub.

Bumps in the Road. In reflection on the last four decades of my ethnographic research, the numerous professional rewards far, far outweigh any frustrations. There were the many successful collaborative team efforts. A unanimous vote of approval by cultural committees and a tribal council or two. That first publication. The joy on the faces of students upon graduation. The faces of students as I re-tell the story of Burnt Face or Salmon, and they become participants and begin to swirl in the story. The "aha moments," when the dots get connected. And above all, being entrusted with what is held most cherished by someone and asked to pass it onto someone else, to help another.

But entry into the Tin Shed can also bring close calls and challenges. As my ties with certain families strengthened, so too could their rivals became my rivals. As I was becoming associated with this or that elder or family, my professional reputation could become tainted through the lenses of social schisms between families. As my ties strengthened with the elders, their grandchildren might feel slighted and express jealousy. To some, I represented Euro-American intrusion, and became a target for pent-up frustrations by those with open hegemonic wounds. It is easy to get caught between sibling rivals. Even with the best of intentions, with the best of guides, the best of adopted grandparents and brothers, the journey is not always a smooth road. The bumps can leave you uncertain, off balance. How to deal with a person who states that she hates you? I don't remember covering that topic in my undergraduate research methods. There were close calls and challenges along the way.

There will always be schisms and divides in any community, between families, that you might get caught up in. The unanticipated encounters we face as ethnographers in the field require some degree of finesse and quick action that limits harm to one's self and to members of the host community. Seek to equip yourself as best you can in order to navigate the unexpected within the Tin Shed. What might be some of the pre-existing social dynamics of the community? How might your presence in the community, perceived or otherwise in varied ways, affect that dynamic? Have I acknowledged my white, male Euro-American privilege as new relations are initiated? The bumps will occur. Sometimes you just cannot take it too personally. As a close elder advised me in one such circumstance, "Rodney, you just have to let it go." While watching for the bumps, we should also be receptive to possible insights that might await, revealing a dynamic otherwise hidden. With frustration can come reward.

◆ ◆ ◆

Working in collaboration with members of the Cultural Resource Office and Tribal Museum on a council-approved research project, a particular elder had been selected for interviews. I spent time with him, and built trust. In several interviews, he provided insights into topics relevant to the project, insights not nearly as well articulated by other interviewees. After compilation of the research, to the satisfaction of team members, we went before the Cultural Committee. They reviewed the project with intention. Upon conferring, they approved the project, but strongly opposed inclusion of any information obtained by the elder endorsed by project team members. "We don't want him representing our tribe!" A history of intra-family rivalry was exposed, and the valuable information of this elder was deleted from the project. I always felt remorse when I later interacted with that elder, who had shared with me from his heart.

◆ ◆ ◆

During a Crow Fair in the mid-seventies, I was invited into the tipi camp of someone I knew, but not well, a prominent man in the community. I soon realized he'd been drinking and was pretty intoxicated, but only after he had invited me into his tipi for a talk. His talk soon turned belligerent, as he wanted to "beat the crap out of me." It was only when his sons came to my rescue and escorted me from his camp that I left without a blow struck. His intense rivalry with the Yellowtail family meant I too was a target of his enmity.

◆ ◆ ◆

Even at a cultural committee meeting, having known and worked with its members and other elders for over twenty years, I have been caught off guard. The collaborative research project, with tribal members as co-principal investigators, had already been unanimously approved by this committee and the tribal council the year before. The committee members themselves had selected the plant around which the research would be conducted. Months later, as the project was nearing completion, from a committee member came words accusing me of endangering a tribal treasure, words emotionally conveyed. "Rodney, if you study this plant it will be taken from us by non-Indians, they'll come and take it, just as they had taken our huckleberries. They're not up on the mountains anymore. I want to continue to go down there, get them and taste them." Frustrated, the committee member walked out of the meeting. It is absolutely true that by identifying specific locations of culturally important plants or sites, they can be exploited by an unscrupulous public, and that has happened far too often. The claim of the committee member had merit. But such identifiers were consciously not included in this project. In a final review, the culture committee approved the project, absent a vote.

The action left me a confused and saddened, as this elder had been one of my dear teachers. We'd always greeted each other with warm hugs. Had laughed, shared, and prayed together. At the time, something had changed. Another form of mystery. But time can heal a wound, as we've again become friends.

◆ ◆ ◆

I had just finished with a wonderful interview in Pryor, a rather isolated community on the west side of the Crow Reservation, and was on the long drive back home to Wyola, a drive on a highway few traveled. Some miles into the drive I saw a little distance ahead of me a pickup truck parked along the shoulder of the road, with several folks standing about beside it. As I approached I could see they had a flat tire and seemed to be having trouble changing it. Being the Good Samaritan, of course I stopped and offered to help. The men were Northern Cheyenne, and, I soon realized, all inebriated. Some were less concerned about the flat tire than they were with shooting erratically at some illusive target out in the field with their rifle. And they all were boasting of soon "getting some Crow!" Not a good idea to have stopped. I never changed a tire so quickly and was soon on my way, never offering to identify my destination or involvement with the Apsáalooke.

◆ ◆ ◆

I had been involved with a tribally sponsored, ethnographic research project for over two years, combining interviews with participant observations and library archival manuscripts. An ad hoc committee of elders was convened to review the assembled materials. One elder was concerned about the "questionable character" of one of my interviewees and asked that his contribution be removed. As a result, the entire research was rejected.

I caught my breath and started in again. I asked the concerned elder for an interview, and she offered some great insights. A few months later the ad hoc committee again reviewed my research, this time approving it, without deletion of the materials from the elder with the "questionable character." Soon after the tribally designated cultural committee reviewed my research, endorsing it unanimously.

But that led to another moment of great anxiety. I had now to have the entire research reviewed by the Spokane Tribe's Cultural Committee. The tribe I was working for had tremendous respect for the wisdom held by Spokane elders. But these elders had not been part of my research design and interviewing. I had not previously worked with any of these elders in any context; I knew no one. I even had to bring along a map to find my way to Wellpinit, Washington, where the tribe's headquarters was located. At the meeting I remember being met with a gracious welcome, as my pacing heart began to settle down. The members of the committee reviewed the manuscript, discussing it at length. The Spokane fully validated the Coeur d'Alene research. And in a final review by the Coeur d'Alene Tribal Council, the research was approved as "authentic" and for public dissemination.

◆ ◆ ◆

One year in the mid-1970s, while residing with Tom and Susie Yellowtail, they took off for a planned trip to Wisconsin and asked if I'd take charge of the household in their absence. "Look after the place while we're gone; sleep in our bedroom." I was still relatively new to the family, and a few of the grandkids were far less accepting. One night, well after midnight, I got a collect call, asking if I'd accept charges. Half asleep, I automatically replied, "No," and hung up. Sometime later I heard the brakes of a car screech and car doors bang shut, with many steps marching to the front door. They had been out for a night of partying. Before I knew it, some of the boys, with knives in hand, were ready to "do business." They were angry in so many ways with me. Perhaps paramount was a feeling that this "white boy" had supplanted the affections of their grandparents. Perhaps having had too much to drink also exacerbated the situation. In our little homestead, near Wyola, far out into the countryside, I never before spoke with such calm and reassurance, addressing their frustrations head on, and, in the process, eventually disarming their intentions. I understood their frustration, dug deep, and stood my ground. Over time, we've since become close family.

◆ ◆ ◆

Traveling in Agnes Vanderburg's stories? From *singing* a song, *re-telling* a story, the bones are *resuscitated* and *come alive*? *Swirling* with Coyote? I accepted these assertions on face value, patient, trusting my teachers, but still all a great mystery! As an ethnographer, with "best practices" to help guide my way into the Tin Shed and Sweat House, even with (or because of) a few bumps in the road, I had a sense of who I was professionally, anchored in the humanities.

But I was more than the ethnographer's clown regalia I wore. My particular Tin Shed and Sweat House entry also became a deeply personal journey, a spiritual journey, tapping into the intimacy of my core humanity. At that core is a Sundance journey. At that core are also the special ethical considerations of someone not of a community participating so intimately in that community.

Ashkísshe
"representation lodge"

___

Traveling the Stories of the Sundance—
A Personal Journey

Coyote is traveling along one day, over there.
    He hears some *strange* singing and whistling.
There, he approaches an *old buffalo skull*,
    the sounds get *louder*.
        He still does not recognize the songs.
He stands over the skull,
    the singing is coming from *beneath it*.
Coyote turns the skull over
    right there are mice holding a Sundance!
        They are *dancing* and *singing*,
            blowing these *tiny little whistles*.
    They are doing exactly what you'd see in the Sundance.
Coyote likes it so much that he wants to *jump in*,
    dance *alongside* these mice.
He's about to do that,
    the mice *yell* at him,
        "*Stop*, you're *too big*.
            You won't fit in our Dance."
It is from the mice that Coyote learns of the Sundance,
    he travels about, over there
        teaches it to the Human people.
There, the trail ends.

(Re-told as originally conveyed at a Crow Sundance by "Old Man John" Trehero, the powerful Shoshone medicine man who passed on his "medicines" to Tom Yellowtail; also in Frey 1987:37.)

◆ ◆ ◆

A most unexpected, unanticipated fork in the road. As we drove home under the dark-winter night's sky, I felt the love I had for my year-old son, yet felt such helplessness with his motionless body in our arms. This twenty-five-year-old father reached out to the most tangible expression of spirituality I'd yet experienced. The summer before, at my second Sundance, observing into it from its door, something radiated out from the Lodge, from the Dancers…and I fell to my knees, tears flowing. As we drove to the hospital that night, I offered a prayer and pledge. Not long after I found myself on a lone hilltop, Eagle-feather fan in hand, fasting from food and water, far from the urban, white middle-class world I usually traveled. And then, in the depth of the night a visitor appeared…an *Awakkuléeshe*. Upon coming down from the hill, I took a Sweat, re-told the story, and received an invitation. So began my Sundancing. The road was made possible only under the guidance of Tom and Susie Yellowtail, and with the continuing support of the family.

◆ ◆ ◆

I have interspersed the following text with a series of Sundance story vignettes, some involving myself and some involving others, yet all defining me. Several of the stories came out of my University of Colorado dissertation research with the Apsáalooke, dating back to the mid- to late-1970s, which also become the basis for my first book, *The World of the Crow: As Driftwood Lodges*. Other vignettes are of events I have experienced since then. Some are narrative accounts, for example that of Coyote and the Mice, while other accounts are of story manifested in ceremonial deeds and actions. All illustrate some of the contours deep within the Tin Shed's landscape, stories that swirled around me and through me. This is my Apsáalooke Sundance story—*basbaaaliíchiwé*.

◆ ◆ ◆

Last winter, with its leaves off, the towering cottonwood's two great branches were revealed, its fork clearly visible. Two days before this July Sundance, after offering a prayer, it was cut from its roots, trimmed of most of its limbs and leaves, except the foliage on the tips of its two huge forks, and transported many miles to this plateau site. After a prayer, including the Song of the Tree, it was then raised from the ground with ropes and poles and precise coordinated effort, and placed in its four-foot hole, the earth firmly packed around it. It now serves as the Center Pole for the Sundance Lodge, the *Ashkísshe*. With its twelve lodgepole pine rafters extending from the forked posts of its perimeter, their tips left green with foliage, crisscrossing at the Tree's fork, the Big Lodge is enclosed by a thick wall of cottonwood brush, its open door aligned with the rising of the morning Sun. One meaning of *Ashkísshe* is "representation lodge," it is a replication of the larger world, the cosmic order. As Tom Yellowtail explained, in the structure of the Big Lodge and movement of its dancers are reflected the image of the Medicine Wheel, with its rock spokes and hub. On the Tree are mounted an Eagle and a Buffalo head, as the hundred or so men and women dancers blow their Eagle-bone whistles in unison, and charge the Center Pole, dancing back, and charging again and dancing back, accompanied by the beat of the drum and voices of the singers at the door. Through the Tree, blessings came and with Eagle-feather fans in hand, dancers administered "doctoring" to those in need.

It is a particularly hot day. The dancers enter the Lodge vowing to give of themselves for a beloved one in need, to go without food and water for the three days of the Sundance, all expecting to suffer, it's part of the prayer, but there is one among the dancers who is suffering too much. He's in his sixties, and suffered a stroke sometime before. Old Man John Trehero, with his Eagle-feather fan in hand, makes his way out to the Center Pole and begins to pray to his spirit Medicine Fathers and to the Creator, focusing his attentions and his Feathers on one of the Tree's trimmed knots. Moments later from that knot a few drops emerge and then a small stream of water flows. A cup is filled and a little of the Tree's Water is given to the one in need, and to many other dancers that hot July day. Through the Tree the *baaxpée,* "spiritual power" flowed, nourishing many. (Re-told from experiences at a Sundance; also in Frey 1987:138–40.)

◆ ◆ ◆

I began my Sundancing prayers for Matt that summer of 1976. Those prayers would continue through the years to come. It is the expectation that if you pledged to go in and "blow the Whistle," you'd have to do so for four separate Dances. I did two such sets, completing my eighth Dance in 1996. I am so indebted to Tom and Susie for inviting and welcoming me into the Dance, guiding me through it, and supporting me along the way. They provided two beautiful dance skirts, and a most cherished gift: an Eagle-bone whistle, with its fluffy plume, and two Eagle plumes to hold in each hand as I danced. It was Lucy Real Bird who made a most exquisite beaded-belt, with a floral design in Crow colors, blues and white, for me to wear while dancing. In that perfect belt, Lucy had beaded in a flaw, as a reminder of our need for humility.

Some years I just couldn't make it over for the Sundance, given a job or family commitment. Other years, when I didn't go in and "blow the Whistle," I still traveled over, camped and assisted family and friends from outside the Lodge. Those who don't dance them-selves might make financial contributions to those sponsoring and "running" the Dance, or help to gather and distribute cattails, "man sage," and mint to the Dancers. Poles for the "starting gates" to help brace the Dancers on the second and third days would be located, cut, and pealed of their bark, and firmly anchored within the Lodge. In the camp, helpers prepared meals, made grocery runs to Billings or Sheridan, always picking up a half dozen bags of ice for the camp coolers. Some joked that it was easier to go in and Dance than stay in camp and work from the outside the Lodge. And then there was the summer of 2011 that I had the honor and privilege to support Matt in his first "blowing of the Whistle." All ways to give back, if just a little.

When Tom was the Sundance Chief, running the Dances for their Apsáalooke sponsors, I'd come along with Tom and Susie and help out as best I could, though being quite a novice. At the Dance location, be it near Pryor, Lodge Grass, or Wyola, we'd set up camp early, a couple of days before the Dance started. I'd go out with the sponsor's family and others, locate the lodgepole pine stand, often at a great distance from the Dance site, and cut down the twelve long overhead poles needed to assemble the Lodge. The day before the Dance, we'd go out to cut down the Tree identified by the sponsor and bring it back to the site of the Dance. During the months leading up to the Sundance, four Medicine Dances were held as a preparatory prayer. The fourth of the Medicine Dances would be held the evening before "going in." Then the day of the Sundance, I'd lend a hand in building the Lodge, which took much of the day, even with a crew of twenty to thirty men. That evening the dancers assembled, typically numbering over a hundred men and women, with Eagle-bone whistles and bedrolls nearby, with the Drum and its singers on hand at the Lodge's door, and the three- sometimes four-day Sundance would begin. The sounds of songs and whistles filled the air, as the dancers went the next days without food and water, a small gift to demonstrate their sincerity, a gift to offer to the Creator. Each dancer had made a vow to give of themselves, typically so someone loved, in need, ill, troubled, could be helped.

Throughout extended summers of the 1970s, and even during a winter or two, I lived with Tom and Susie, residing in a fixed-up, well-insulated wooden shed, with an oversized coal-fired furnace, near their Wyola home. While a divorce separated me from my former wife, she and I alternated care for our son Matt who stayed in Colorado. A warmth radiated from within the Wyola shed, as the cold winter's snow fell outside. We ate together, travelled to Sheridan or Billings together to shop, shared in and listened to stories, old and new. We laughed and cried together. In our frequent Sweats, we prayed together, opening and sharing our hearts. Tom was known for his "long, hot Sweats," as his prayers to the Creator were so deliberate, including all who needed help. Throughout the year, as a respected *akbaalíak*, Tom held "Prayer Meetings" at his home and in the homes of others, during which his Medicine Bundle was opened and its contents smudged. Accompanied by the Drum and Sundance songs, healing prayers were bestowed on someone in need, a person ill, or perhaps challenged in some manner. Tom would pat the patient with his Eagle-feather fan, focusing on the area of the illness. Then he would pull back the fan, and with it the affliction, which he tossed to the east, "gone with the wind." Tom and Susie's lives were filled with Sundance songs and stories, year-round.

I got to know the entire Yellowtail family, extending to such folks as Leonard and Regina Bends and Leonard's sister Ada Bends, Alvin Howe, Marshall Left Hand, Joe Medicine Crow and his daughter Diane, John Pretty On Top, Jerome White Hip, Bill and Maggie Yellowtail, Father Randolph, and the Old Coyote, Old Horn and Real Bird families, among so many others, who would become so essential to my unfolding story. I was honored to be a part of their lives. Like a child, a sponge, I tried to listen and watch, absorb as best I could, everything that unfolded, events and actions so unfamiliar, all with respect and humility, asking few questions, as I wasn't even sure how to phrase my inquiries. But I'd also step up, join in, and assist as best I could. As my personal journey took me deeper into the Sundance Lodge, I also continued deeper into the ethnography of the Tin Shed and Sweat House, certainly each informing and toning the other, each in fact interwoven inseparably. Having been welcomed into the warmth of their wooden shed, my early adult formative years were fed and nurtured by Tom and Susie's steady hands.

I'd been dancing for a couple of years, when one day Susie, at the kitchen table with cigarette in hand, turned to Tom and me and said, "Rod needs an Indian Name." If I were to continue my Sundancing prayers, I would need a name to identify not just my physical being, but my spirit, my heart, as I, in prayer, sought to communicate with those around me and with *Akbaatatdía,* "the one who made everything," the Creator. I needed to acknowledge and be acknowledged in a manner appropriate for prayer and for "blowing the Whistle."

◆ ◆ ◆

We gathered that evening in the living room of their Wyola home and had a little Prayer Meeting. A small fire had been built outside and hot coals carried in with an old iron skillet. The lights were dimmed. At the center of the floor lay a buffalo robe, with Tom seated to the west of it, facing east. From a small brown trunk he carefully brought out and laid with purpose his Medicine Bundle, the tangible representations of his particular spiritual gifts. Among them were a tray of dirt that anchored the leather effigy of an Elk, an Otter skin, a mirror, and an Eagle-feather fan, each in turn smudged in the smoke of the sweet cedar sprinkled on the coals. These were among the gifts that had been passed to Tom from Old Man John Trehero. And we looked on in silence.

Tom rose, arms outstretched, eyes closed, holding his Eagle-feather fan, and began his prayer, his words spoken so gently in his Apsáalooke language. A cigarette was lit and held in raised hand, and as the smoke ascended so too did the words ascend to the Creator. A song was sung, one that you'd hear at the Sundance. He asked if I'd join him, facing east, to the side of the bundle, with Tom immediately at my back. Susie placed more cedar onto the coals. His prayer continued, as he patted me with his Fan, on my head, along the sides of my body and my legs. And I felt something I'd never experienced before, hard for me to put into words, but the best I could do was to describe it as a pulsating, cooling warmth that penetrated my skin and went deep. Then Tom spoke the word, *Maakuuxshiichíilish*, though I can't recall catching it at the time in the stream of his Apsáalooke-spoken prayer.

After the bundle items were again smudged and wrapped securely in the trunk, the living room lights were turned on. We visited over a meal and the name was reiterated and discussed. *Maakuuxshiichíilish* meant "seeking to help others," though Tom said it was a difficult word to easily translate. It was a name that Tom felt particularly fit me, that would help guide my actions as well as protect me on my journey. That evening Tom and Susie "adopted" me into their Yellowtail family, as a member of the Whistling Water clan, and I soon addressed them as "Grandpa" and "Grandma." It was a kinship and a name that encumbered great expectation and responsibilities, and great potentiality, if respected. (Re-told as experienced during a medicine bundle opening in 1977; also in Frey 1987:135–37.)

◆ ◆ ◆

We had a good road trip together, Rob Moran and I. Our destination was Fort Washakie on the Wind River Reservation in Wyoming, Rob coming from his home on the Warm Springs Reservation. At Janet and Rayburn Beck's home, as he'd done before, Rob bestowed an Indian Name on another "grandchild." A Sweat had been taken that afternoon and that evening, with Eagle feathers in hand, and cedar and prayer in the air, a young person was given a special name that would help nurture and guide. With laughter now in the air, the naming was followed by exchanges of gifts and a good meal. We all had been joined by years of friendship, family ties, and the Sundance.

Another road trip brought me to Warm Springs, joined by Janet and Rayburn and many, many others. Rob had passed unexpectedly just before Christmas 2007. We began with exchanges of warm hugs and deep sympathy, as some two hundred people gathered in the community's Longhouse for the all-night wake, and then that morning we drove to the cemetery for the burial services. Throughout it all, great words of respect and admiration, of joy and sorrow, recounting this event, re-telling that story, a laugh here and tear there, came forth from family and friends. Back at the Longhouse, I was sitting with Janet and Rayburn at the morning meal as we watched one of their grandchildren running about, as if in a dance, with others. It was an image of youth and exuberance I'd not soon forget. Just then Janet turned to me and said "Rob was to name her. As his brother, it is now your responsibility to give her her Indian Name." A great honor, but entirely unexpected, it was a responsibility I was not sure I was prepared to fulfill.

A year had passed and the many were again assembled for Rob. It was a day of remembrance, of words again shared, along with a giveaway of gifts to help let go and move forward. I had been asked to say some words for the man who was my "brother." At the grave site, from the heart, I spoke of love and deep appreciation for one who unwaveringly gave help to others. As I did, there above us circled an Eagle, the Bird to whom Rob's own Indian Name referred. And just like that, as clear as day, the grandchild's name came to me.

Another road trip in 2008 to Fort Washakie for a Naming ceremony. I'd consulted one of the linguists working at the Crow Language program for the spelling and pronunciation of the name, as Apsáalooke was the language of our Sundance. At the home of Janet and Rayburn the name was bestowed. We also visited on how we would co-sponsor the Sundance next year, with all the preparation it would take. As I so generously had been given by Tom so many years ago, now I had the opportunity to give to another that which would nurture and guide, an Indian Name.

◆ ◆ ◆

He'd arrived from Fort Washakie that spring for a little visit. Tom and Susie always looked forward to having John Trehero stay with them at their Wyola home. This Shoshone Sundance medicine man had passed his many medicines to Tom, and there was always something to talk about. One morning John decided to take a walk, out to the recently plowed fields, not far from the house. As he walked along the barbed-wire fence, an old friend waited, resting his body on a large rock, warmed by the sun. As he approached, John raised his hand and offered a hello. He stopped at the rock, bent over and picked up his friend, Rattlesnake, and John was greeted with a "hiss." They had a little visit that morning.

It's said that few liked dancing alongside Old Man John in the Big Lodge, as he'd always danced with one of his medicines, a live rattlesnake, coiled around his arm. (Re-told from a story conveyed by Tom Yellowtail; also in Frey 1987:60.)

◆ ◆ ◆

It was a good Sundance, the songs sung and the whistles blown with determination. The day was hot. Among those standing at the door of the Lodge was one who was here for the first time. She watched, she understood little and felt even less. Then a dancer took a hard fall. Something had come to the dancer, something about to be received. He lay there on the dance floor and had cattails laid on him by others. He was not to be disturbed. Then she started in, yelling loudly. "He must be hurt, call an ambulance, stop the dancing!" And she kept it up, as loud as ever. "Stop this dancing!" But the one laying there should not be disturbed.

Old Man John got up and went to the Center Pole, with his Eagle-feather fan. Praying before the Tree, John then turned and pointed his Feathers at the one who would not stop disturbing the one laying on the Lodge floor. At that very moment she collapsed, silent. Her friends tried to revive her, saying "it must have been heat stroke." They took her to the cool shade of a near tree, but nothing brought her back. As he cannot use his medicines to harm another, John went to the woman and "touched her up," and the moment he did, she came back. She continued to look on, but didn't say another word all day. (Re-told from experience; also in Frey 1987:64.)

◆ ◆ ◆

It's said that one of the Little People sits in the crotch of the Center Pole, the fork of the Cottonwood, only to be seen when he chooses. The *Awakkuléeshe* were one of Old Man John's medicines.

Tom and Susie traveled to Fort Washakie to have a little visit with Old Man John. When they arrived, it was late into the evening, and all were tired. Traveling in their pickup, with a camper on board, Tom and Susie could get a good sleep before tomorrow's visit. Being deliberate, Tom put the pickup in gear and pulled the break lever. And Tom and Susie bedded down for the night.

After they were well asleep, Tom and Susie awoke with a startle. The pickup was rocking back and forth. Knowing John was a big trickster, Tom yelled out, "Stop it John, stop it!" It stopped, and Tom and Susie fell back asleep. But again they woke to the rocking of the pickup. "Stop it John, we're tired!" The rocking stopped.

In the morning, as Tom and Susie stepped out of their camper and John came out from his home, a surprise greeted them. The pickup was now facing 180 degrees opposite from where Tom had parked it the previous night. And with a big smile on his face, John said, "Oh, the Little People paid you a visit!" They had come during the night, picked up the pickup, and turned it around. They too like to play tricks. (Re-told as conveyed by Tom Yellowtail; also in Frey 1987:69.)

◆ ◆ ◆

One night several days earlier, Tom had a dream. He saw one of his clan nephews driving back from Billings. Stopping along the highway, he got out of his pickup and came to an Eagle. There the Eagle offered him two of his tail feathers. Tom said nothing of his dream to the young man.

The young man was driving home from Billings. As he traveled, something to his right, just off the shoulder of the Interstate, caught his eye. In no hurry, he stopped on the shoulder of the road. But a hill now obstructed his view of what he thought he might have seen. Jumping over the fence and around the hill, there it stood: a live Eagle. He thought it must be hurt, as it just stood there, watching him as he approached. Standing just in front of the Eagle, as it looked up, the young man, not knowing what to make of this, reached down and around to the Eagle's tail feathers. The Eagle continued its gaze upon the young man, not taking flight. It seemed to present his twelve tail feathers to the young man, who pulled the two center feathers, the evenly matched pair, from the Eagle's body. With feathers held in hand, the Eagle then flew off.

Not knowing what to make of this, the young man sought the counsel of one he respected for these sorts of things. When he arrived, Tom greeted him with a smile and relayed the dream he'd had some days ago. Tom kept the two tail feathers a few days to "work" on them, smudging them and preparing them for use in the Big Lodge. A clan nephew now dances with the gift Eagle provided. (Re-told from a story conveyed by Tom Yellowtail; also in Frey 1987:96.)

◆ ◆ ◆

There had already been talk of them in the camps of the Sundance that summer of 2014, as there is often talk about them each summer.

I had come over with Jan, a friend of many years, who had often attended and assisted the dancers from outside. We'd brought several salmon over from Nez Perce country and baked them up for a dinner to serve to some of the folks camping. It was the day before the Dance, and the meal went well, was a hit, as salmon is not often served in buffalo country. While we served over sixty, there was still some salmon left over.

During the night, they were about, walking close to the tents and trailers, awakening some. A gift needed to be made. The next day some of the salmon, broken into flakes, and an assortment of brightly colored seed beads, "sparkly beads," were placed some distance from the camps, near a tree, beside a big gully. They were placed in an orderly fashion, as would be appropriate.

A couple of days later, before leaving for home, we visited the site of the offering. The salmon was gone, as were the beads. There were no animal tracks around. A little prayer was given to the *Awakkuléeshe*—the Little People.

◆ ◆ ◆

I had come to the Sundance that summer in 1978, to complete what would be my first cycle of four, all prayers for my son Matt. During the afternoon, before we would go in that evening, I felt for some reason a bit of trepidation. But after a reassuring conversation with Grandma Susie and then once in the Lodge that first evening, my apprehension was gone. That next morning I began the Sundance dancing hard. I remember feeling oh so comfortable, at ease, and watched over, and I danced hard. I charged the Center Pole, brushing it occasionally with my Eagle plumes, than danced back to my stall, charged again and danced back, and again, with the mounted Eagle, its wings spread, and Buffalo head hung from the Tree's fork. Again and again, dancing to the song and beat of the Drum, with Eagle-bone whistle in mouth and Eagle plumes in hand. As I blew the Whistle I could see my life's liquid spew out into the dry air, dripping from the tip, until there was none. From my angle within the Lodge, the mounted Buffalo head looked down upon me. Continuing for some time, I lost all track of time, and the angle changed. The Buffalo no longer looked down upon me. I was now looking down upon the other dancers and the Lodge, looking down upon my body lying there on the dance floor, covered with the cattails other dancers had laid over it.

And I traveled on. I first found myself in a deep, dark, and rocky canyon. As I looked up into the sky, a hard jagged rock edge bordered the view, and I anticipated seeing something in the sky. There was nothing. Then I was in a dense pine forest, the sharp tips of the trees distinct against the open sky, still searching above, yet seeing nothing. Then I came to an open cottonwood grove, the sky framed by the gentle curves of its leaves. Still the sky was clear. And then I was in the sky itself, floating amongst clouds. All the while I continued to look for something, waiting, but seeing nothing in front of me. Then amongst those fluffy white clouds, as I looked out...there were horns coming out from beside my head? At that moment I realized I was now looking out through the eyes of *Bishée*, the Buffalo! I would not find something out there, distinct from me, as we were indistinguishable, as one. And then, I was back in the Big Lodge, among the other dancers. I would continue my prayers with the Whistle until we all walked out of the Lodge together. (Re-told as experienced in 1978; also in Frey 1987:120–21.)

Following the Dance, with Tom and Old Man John at my side, they had me re-tell my story, my journey, with *Bishée*, to those gathered at our camp. I had collected what I had with me that was of value and personally meaningful, and presented the items to those who had helped me. I had a little giveaway. John Cummins, the sponsor of the Dance, received my Pipe, the bowl of which I had carved from black soapstone and the stem from chokecherry wood. I was told by Tom what items to assemble to be part of my Medicine Bundle, to use when I pray, and was told never to eat the meat of the buffalo—*Bishée,* now my "Medicine Father."

◆ ◆ ◆

Under the watch of each full moon, with my wife Kris joining me, we continue to open my little Medicine Bundle, smudging its contents with sweetgrass, singing the Song of the Tree (the song sung prior to cutting down of the cottonwood and during its raising, and one of the morning songs sung at the Sundance), and offering prayer to *Bishée* and to the Creator. A prayer for family and friends, for students and colleagues, for those challenged and struggling wherever they may be. Grandpa Tom had passed to me the right to pour water and conduct Sweat prayers in the Little Lodge, the Younger Brother of the Big Lodge, the Elder Brother, doing so procedurally following his Sundance way. I continue to do so from my backyard. While no longer dancing in the Big Lodge, I continue to attend the Sundance each year, often with Kris, and occasionally with Matt and his partner Kelly, camping with the Beck and Bends families, renewing with the Yellowtail family and other Sundance family members, assisting from the outside those who were offering prayers on the inside.

Returning to the Big Lodge in 2009, where he had first visited while tightly wrapped in the blanket of a cradleboard in 1975, Matt assisted in co-sponsoring the Sundance and, two years later, began his own Dancing with our Sundance family, giving voice in prayer with the Indian Name Grandpa had bestowed on him years ago, *Awakúikiiaateesh,* "Little Dwarf." Matt as strong as one of the Little People, protected by them. I am so proud of my son.

◆ ◆ ◆

In one of those insightful visits I had with Cliff SiJohn, over a lunch at the Coeur d'Alene Casino, we were talking about the Animal First Peoples, such as Coyote and Wolf. As we went further into the topic, exchanging our thoughts, Cliff asked, "Did you get it? Do you understand that the Animal First Peoples of the creation stories are the same as the Spirit Peoples who might visit you in a dream or on a hill top?" The Niimíipuu (Nez Perce) have a term, *Titwatityáaya,* roughly meaning "Animal First Peoples," that conveys what Cliff meant. The *Bishée,* the *Awakkuléeshe,* are of a landscape, since time immemorial, revealing themselves in stories ancient and contemporary. In Tom's re-telling of Burnt Face and while on a fast for Matt, I swirled with the Little People.

◆ ◆ ◆

In 2016 I was continuing my Sundance prayers. Kris and I were attending the July Dance, four decades after I'd first entered the Lodge and "blew the Whistle" for Matt. As in past years, we were there to help support the dancers and renew with family. But in our camp, around midday, before the Dancers would go in that evening, others had also remembered the decades, and family members gathered to acknowledge and reminisce about my years, catching me by surprise. The gathering was led off by kind words of honor from Leonard Bends, followed by gifts of a beautifully beaded pouch from Janet Beck and a beaded Buffalo-effigy from Heather Kay Binkley, and then they had me pray prior to the noon meal. I humbly thanked all.

At this 2016 Sundance, it was Thomas Yellowtail, the grandson of Tom, who was now a Sundance Chief, officiating and "running" the Dance. There were a few others who also have this responsibility and trace their right to do so to John Trehero. In Thomas's instance, Old Man John's medicines had passed to Tom Yellowtail, then to John Pretty On Top, then to Leonard Bends, and now to the man I viewed standing beside the Center Pole. As a young teenager, I always felt there was something very special about Thomas, aka "Tommy Hawk"—wise before his time. As I looked back those many years, that don't seem so many, but yet fresh and vivid, and now look out and into the Big Lodge, little has changed, all remains fresh. The Lodge and Center Pole, the drum and songs, the whistles and plumes, the beating hearts of the dancers and those blessed at the Pole and the stories that brought them all into the Lodge, were as they were in 1975. As I stood at the door of the Lodge, the same wave of "heart outpouring" swirled and flowed out. The life-giving power and quintessential meaning emanating from *Akbaatatdía* and through the *Ashkísshe* continues to guide, renew, and heal. Anchored to its ancestral bones, bones strong and stable, the perennial Sundance story continues with vitality, its flesh and muscle supple, welcoming the participation of those in prayer.

◆ ◆ ◆

Before departing the Big Lodge story, I'd like to account for what I brought out with me. I'd like to address the critical concern of cultural and spiritual appropriation. The participating in what should not be participated in. The taking of what should not be taken. The wholesale adopting of elements from an indigenous community by someone not of that community without invitation or permission. When and how is it appropriate for a non-Indian to participate in sacred Native American ceremonies? While Allen's Tin Shed and Cliff's Sweat House provided an ethical protocol guiding my professional entry and travels in their homes, there seemed no overt protocol guiding the ethics of my personal spiritual journeys, no elder with a Tin Shed story. Or was there, radiating out from a warmed wooden shed? In retrospect and reflection, and with the kind assistance of Suzanne Crawford O'Brien who identified the importance of this issue for me and the readers of this essay, let me offer words on a protocol that helped guide my interpersonal actions and spiritual participations in the Big Lodge and other sacred places.

In this gray ethical area, I am distinguishing between appropriation and inspiration, between taking from and learning from, between fruits confiscated and huckleberries revealed. It is one thing to learn about Indigenous practices, to even be inspired by them, and subsequently alter one's own views about and actions toward the Indigenous. This is cultural appreciation and the best way to challenge intolerance and prejudice. And it is another thing to appropriate. It is one thing to be moved by a powwow song and drum beat, by the beaded patterns on a dancer's regalia, and by the rhythmic movements of that dancer, and then subsequently compose a piece of music, paint a portrait, or even modify one's own dance step to the music you hear. This is creative artistic expression that can continue the life of the Indigenous inspiration. And it is another thing to appropriate. It is one thing to hear and engage in a narrative oral tradition, and then rely upon that story to help guide you through a dark journey in our own life. Is this not the impetuous for and purpose of *basbaaaliíchiwé*? And it is another thing to appropriate. I would have you consider the ways potential huckleberries are presented, revealed and freely given, distinct from their confiscation, their appropriation. Though in my own instance, I am going deeper than inspiration and appreciation, and the gray is that much more blurred.

I acknowledge that regardless of what I may say here, there will be some who will still accuse me of being a wannabe, and my actions tantamount to spiritual theft. Others might think, "wow, if Frey can do it, so can I," and see my actions as a license for unbridled participation. Most assuredly, the following are my own reflections on when I, a non-Indian, found myself at the door of indigenous spirituality, reflections on my specific experiences. I do not and cannot speak for or as an indigenous person, from his or her shared but ultimately vastly different experiences. One must dig deep, and with honesty and, hopefully, the guiding hand of a trusted indigenous mentor close by, consider the implications and ethical responsibilities of crossing through that door. It all does begin with introspection and honesty. Most assuredly, the path of my own spiritual protocol and the ethical decisions that resulted may differ from that of another. Each must dig deep. This is my particular *basbaaaliíchiwé*.

For me it is a protocol anchored by two key kinship elements—relationship and reciprocity—imbued with Apsáalooke and Schitsu'umsh practices. Blood affiliation is of course of primary importance in Apsáalooke matrilineal, clan-oriented society, but it is not the only family tie acknowledged by the Apsáalooke or by other indigenous communities. Kinship relationships are extended to include adoption and marriage. The adoption might be legally and/or ceremonially acknowledged, as mine was during a Medicine Bundle ceremony in 1977 when an Indian Name was bestowed on me. Or the adoption might be recognized informally, by the community, after a period of close association with and mutual support by members of a particular family. And as transpired in my fourth Sundance, the adoption may even be spiritual in nature, with *Bishée* adopting me, becoming my Medicine Father.

Kinship reciprocity entails the act of giving back. Kinship relationships are initiated, nurtured, and sustained through acts of reciprocity. It is a reciprocity that certainly does no harm to others, but seeks to bring support. For me it all started with giving. First were my two extended summers in service to the Crow Tribe, using my ethnographic skills to help with health care delivery and counseling. Later, my helping took the form of driving to town and getting the groceries, stacking bales of hay, doing the dishes, preparing a Sweat fire, providing words of comfort or a shoulder to cry upon at a time of need, laughing with others at one's own foolishness, praying for the health of a loved one or of a perfect stranger, contributing without expectation of return, contributing without even attribution, contributing in perpetuity.

It is a kinship that provides the permission to enter in the first place, and once in, the protection needed so as not to possibly injure one's self or, especially, someone else. While I can only surmise, in me Tom may have seen a young man who presented himself earnestly, willing to help others, and as a father who was himself hurting. Tom offered to guide me in a fast on a hill to help in the healing. I had not sought it, but following my fast for Matt's health, it was Tom who then invited me to join him and others in continued prayer in the Big Lodge. It began with an open, sincere heart, no agenda, no veiled intention, followed by an invitation. It was an invitation extended, and a guiding hand offered.

There are unfortunately examples of an outsider just showing up, unannounced, without preparations, without local support to assist, and the dilemma faced by the Sundance leaders—letting him or her dance or not? Who would assist her, with cattails, sage, a blanket for the gift of the elder painting her and praying over her, who will guide her in the proper procedures and etiquette, watch out for her so she doesn't harm herself and others? It can be a huge burden imposed on others.

There is the example of a young white man, very athletic and physically fit, just out of high school, who seemed sincere and was granted entry into the Lodge. But he entered alone in the company of many, without an "elder brother" beside him who could have perhaps guided him at a time of need. During the night, something disturbed him deeply and he freaked out, only to be found a great distance away from the Lodge the next morning, disoriented, exhausted, his bare feet full of cactus thorns. There can be physical and spiritual injury. A Sweat or a fast on a hill, without permission, without supervision, can bring harm to one's self and to others.

It is never ultimately an issue of skin color or ethnicity. As a Crow "brother," an experienced Sundancer, once remarked in the context of who should be allowed to Dance, "if it was based upon native blood, which leg, which arm would you leave outside the Lodge, as we all have some white blood flowing through our veins." I vividly remember the 1996 Dance and the criteria established by the sponsor on who can "go in," a prerogative granted to him. As we lined up, I felt pretty conspicuous, one of only two non-Indians about to enter the Big Lodge. There always seemed to be a handful of white participants. I had not known beforehand, but family members publicly announced that Pierre Chesnel and I, "grandsons" of Tom Yellowtail, were to be allowed into this "Indian-only" Dance. Pierre had showed up at Wyola about the same time I did in 1974, though each of us via very different routes. He had arrived from France only a short time before, hitchhiking his way across the country, his English barely intelligible. Pierre and I became grandsons, and he continues to join the family to blow the Whistle in the Big Lodge each year. Adoption can transcend the differences of racial, ethnic, or national boundaries, affirming the possibility of a shared humanity.

When traveling the cultural and spiritual landscapes of others with such intimacy, the kinship of relationship and reciprocity certainly blur the lines of professional and personal, as the very category of "others" itself fades. But in this blurring, the ethical responsibilities associated with *basbaaaliíchiwé* are elevated. From inception, share your name and speak your story from the heart, a humble honest heart. Reveal your humanity. Seek to serve others. Be respectful, attentive, and patient. Listen. Adopt only *after* an invitation, *with* permission. Until then, you are but a guest. In speaking from the heart, as Cliff advised, "you'll have clean hands." Then, come what may. Kinship conception is in the hands of others. Adopt only after adoption. And even then, with diligence, continue listening, asking permission, as adoption can always be revoked. With introspection and reflection, do as your "grandmother and grandfather" would do. Perhaps it is ultimately an issue of sincerity—of offering your heart *and* of others opening theirs.

◆ ◆ ◆

Traveling in Agnes Vandenberg's stories? A burnt face *made* as a new-born child's face? Story as a *living* being? From the bones, life *resuscitated. Dasshússua? Swirling* with Coyote? Now, deeper yet into the Tin Shed, and its warmed wooden shed and Big Lodge, with family and Sundance stories all about. *Swirling* with *Bishée*? A perennial ceremony as story, its bones *stable*, its flesh *supple*. With the tremendous ethical responsibilities entailed with such a personal journey by a non-Indian? I accepted these assertions on face value, patient, trusting my teachers, but now even more a *great mystery!*

And yet I asked, had some of the dots yet to be connected? Dots yet not even revealed? Had I listened, and experienced well enough? Been attentive? *Felt* the damp, *felt* the heat? Is what I had experienced as most *real* part of a larger, cogent body of knowledge and practice, a bigger story that can help connect the dots?

And I awoke with such a desire.

Hnkhwelkhwlnet
"our ways of life in the world"

Heart Knowing—The Structure
and Dynamics of Story

He came to the IHS Hospital at Crow Agency seeking a cure. But left with a treatment. His diabetes was diagnosed as serious. His doctor strongly advised him to watch his diet, to exercise regularly, and told him he'd need to take the insulin injections. A tough regimen under any circumstances. He'd heard that Tom had a "Brew," and thought he should look into it as well. So he paid him a visit. Tom was more than willing to assist anyway he could. He told the diabetic that he should offer prayers to the *Akbaatatdía* each evening, and handing him a milk gallon container of his Brew, told him to take a cup full a day. Tom asked nothing in return.

Some time passed and it was time for a checkup at the hospital. Blood work was run, weight and prescription records checked. The man's weight was unchanged, and the insulin prescriptions were left unfilled. But his blood sugar levels were normal; there were no symptoms of diabetes. The physician was entirely amazed with the condition of his patient. His curiosity prompted him to ask his patient what he had done to get such results, and he learned of Tom and his Brew.

Calling Tom up, the doctor asked if they could visit. Tom was always up for a good visit. The physician was most courteous, as he asked Tom about his "brew." Tom understood what he was being asked, as he was himself versed in the language of the biomedical world, given that this wife, Susie had spent much of her life as a nurse in the hospital. "We should have the bush the brew is made from identified and analyzed in a chemical laboratory, to discover its medicinal properties," said the physician. "That way we could mass produce it. Sell it more widely, to more people. We'll need to patent it too, put it under our names. You could receive royalties." Tom listened, courteously.

Tom responded by saying, "The Brew isn't mine to sell…I don't own it…I couldn't make the decision by myself…it belongs to my Medicine Fathers…only they could make the decision." He said, "I don't charge for my healing…don't ask for money." Tom went on to say, "The Brew isn't just the plant…it is the spirit in it…it only works when we offer prayer." (Re-told from an interview with Tom Yellowtail circa 1975; also in Frey 1987:73–74.)

◆ ◆ ◆

In both of their stories, Allen's Tin Shed and Cliff's Sweat House, we're told, "you've gotta go *inside…feel it…*feel the damp" and "*feel* the intense heat, *feel* the sweat pouring out from within." And what was it that I needed to "feel," and feel distinct from what I was experiencing while seated under the shade of that cottonwood on the wooden bench, while in the comfort of the café? As I came to know and work with Allen and Cliff, and Tom, and many other elders, I saw how they recognized that there were differing ways of knowing, of doing, of experiencing the world. Cliff referred to it as "Heart Knowledge," in contrast with "Head Knowledge." I was asked to "feel" something from the "heart." It is embodied in the Schitsu'umsh term, *hnkhwelkhwlnet*, "our ways of life in the world," in the experiences of water emerging from a Center Pole, of swirling with Coyote, and of the *Awakkuléeshe* paying a visit. It is at the heart of the structure and dynamic of the indigenous story. I am certain that Allen and Cliff were asking, could I begin to move off that well-worn bench of familiarity and upbringing, and move into the unknown of the Tin Shed? Could I begin to see, to listen, to feel, to experience that which is within? Connect the dots in previously unimagined ways? What huckleberries would be needed to be picked here? Seeking to navigate the interior of the Sweat House, without stumbling, without getting lost, has certainly been among my greatest of challenges.

I first sought to put words to what Cliff was referring to as Head and Heart Knowledge in a little book entitled, *Eye Juggling: A Workbook for Clarifying and Interpreting Values* (Frey, American University Press 1994). It was an early novice attempt on my part to identify many of the key ontological premises of what I called "Glass Pane" and "Looking Glass" worldviews, i.e., Head and Heart ways of knowing and doing. As a values clarification workbook I developed while teaching a seminar at Lewis-Clark State College in the mid-nineties, *Eye Juggling* presented the student with a collection of what I called "story texts," a series of narratives that were infused with either Glass Pane or Looking Glass principles. The student was asked to engage the texts, "eye juggle," and attempt to interpret the underlying teachings (Frey 1994:33). Most of the Glass Pane stories emanated out of the European experience, starting with Pythagoras and Descartes, expressive of secular, scientific ways of knowing, and reflective of an underlying duality separating inner self from the outer world, each separated by a thick glass pane. The Looking Glass stories came out of indigenous cultures, starting with Coyote and Burnt Face, reflective of a spiritual monism, in which the inner is a replication of the outer, each a reflection of the other as if through a looking glass. I was exploring the internal landscapes of two incredibly powerful but contrasting mega-stories.

I suspect part of the Head and Heart knowledge dichotomy is a function of contact history, of the collision of two worlds and the elders' desire to contrast much of their way as distinct from that of the Euro-American. Nevertheless, I don't believe Tom and Cliff are suggesting that Head Knowledge is exclusively the domain of European-based epistemology and Heart Knowledge is synonymous only with American Indian ways of knowing and doing. Certainly spiritual Heart Knowledge is expressed in forms of European-based thought and experience, for instance. And the American Indian has always been an astute empirical observer of the physical landscape, rendering precise calculations of the workings of the seasons in interaction with animal and plant life. A very efficient, pragmatic-based technology was successfully applied to the pre-contact lives of indigenous people.

I do believe both Tom and Cliff would argue that it is inappropriate to attempt to offer an analytical, empirical-based understanding of Heart Knowledge, for something that can only be felt and experienced through the Heart—something which often defies words. Isn't it true that "how" we attempt to access the "what" of something directly colors our lenses of that "what"? Wouldn't using the Head Knowledge "how" to access Heart Knowledge "what" only cloud the Heart with Head, distorting it? I offer words here that will hopefully help lead us to threshold of the "felt," so we can be receptive to the "experienced through the Heart."

Head Knowledge. Sometimes you have to travel far from your destination to be able to travel your destination. As I grew in an understanding and appreciation of *hnkhwelkhwlnet*, Heart Knowledge, the greater the rift formed with Head Knowledge, each in juxtaposition with the other, each highlighting the landscape contours of the other. It was a growing realization that Cliff and Allen anchored their understanding of Head Knowledge well into a scientific way of knowing, a scientific worldview, though not exclusively so, and without using the word "science" to refer to this mega-story. Please allow me to venture down this path, as it will help shine a clearer light on the nature of *hnkhwelkhwlnet*.

The etymology of the word "science" is from the Latin sciō "I can, know, understand," which in turn, derives from the Proto-Indo-European *skey- "to split, to dissect." Its contemporary meanings and applications have had a long evolution, beginning with the contributions of such European philosophers and observers of nature as Pythagoras (580–497 BCE), Aristotle (384–322 BCE), René Descartes (1596–1650), and John Locke (1632–1704), along with others. These are the godfathers of science. While much more nuanced than suggested here, science as a discipline of study, expressed in the "scientific method," is ultimately premised on two quintessential sets of ontological (what is considered real) and epistemological (how we come to know what is real) principles, Aristotelian materialism and Cartesian dualism. To illustrate the influence of four pivotal contributors of the many philosophers who were instrumental to the development of science, let's start with a glimpse into the story of Pythagoras.

◆ ◆ ◆

Walking past the village blacksmith's shop, the pleasant ring of hammers striking an anvil catches your attention. It is music in harmony. Going into the shop, you find that the lower notes that you hear are produced by heavy hammers, while the higher notes are caused by lighter hammers striking on the anvil. As you've observed from the strings of a musical instrument, the objects creating the sounds can be broken down into discrete, mathematical units. Each of these units, when paired with another that has been divided into exact parts of two, three, or four, will produce a harmonious sound. A string is stretched tight and plucked. A sound, a note, is heard. A second string, exactly half as long as the first, is stretched alongside the first and plucked. The sound of the note is an octave above the first note. A third string, exactly one third as long as the first, is stretched and plucked. The sound is a fifth above the first. It's all harmony to your ears. But when the second and third strings are shortened or lengthened, if only slightly, the plucked sound is discordant. The world of sound is governed by a universal and all-pervading mathematics, numbers in balance and harmony.

You are Pythagoras (580–497 BCE), and what you assert for the world of sound you assert for all of the world. The world of shapes and forms are governed by a harmony of exact numbers. Knowledge of this fundamental relationship between the world of space and mathematics leads you, Pythagoras, to a critical discovery.

◆ ◆ ◆

Let us replicate in our own experience what Pythagoras discovered in the sixth century BCE. We'll begin with the assumption that gravity is vertical and that horizontal stands at a right angle to it. The conjunction of the vertical and the horizontal fixes a right angle. Following Pythagoras, this basic spatial relationship is to

Pythagoras, in the center with the book, teaching music, in Raphael's fresco, "The School of Athens" 1508–11. *Wikimedia Commons*

be found throughout all of nature. From this assumption a most important observation and subsequent application can be made. An experiment will demonstrate.

Take a right angle and cut it out from a piece of paper in the form of a triangle. Lay it down on another piece of paper, and with the side opposite the right angle facing out, move it down and sideways four times. As the triangle is moved, place the sides of the right angle against each other. Draw a line completely around the sides of the triangle. After moving the right angle four times, the triangle should rest at its original starting place. A square is formed if the hypotenuse of the right angle is kept on the outside as it is moved, i.e., a square of the hypotenuse. Only a right angle can do this.

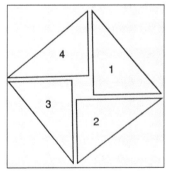

Square of the hypotenuse.

Because of the right angle, two other squares can be formed from the movement of the same triangle. On the same piece of paper that the previous square was drawn, place the hypotenuse of the triangle against the outside of the square. Draw a line along the sides of the right angle. Now place the triangle on the outside of the adjacent side

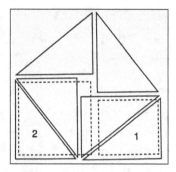

Squares of the other two sides.

of the square, again with the hypotenuse against the square. Draw around the sides of the right angle of the tri-angle. Each of the two sides of the right angle should mark out each of two separate squares, though each smaller than the original square.

From this experiment and with these observations, a general theorem can be stated for every triangle that contains a right angle: the square on the hypotenuse is equal to the square on one of the other sides plus the square of the other. This is true, if and only if, the angle they contain is a right angle. Of course, this is the Pythagorean theorem, i.e., a right angle is the square of the hypotenuse equal to the sum of the squares on the other two sides.

The test of the theorem offers proof of its validity. If a triangle is 5 inches by 4 inches by 3 inches, for instance, is it a right angle? Five inches is the hypotenuse and squared it is 25. Four inches squared is 16, and three inches squared is 9. The sum of these two squares is equal to the square of the hypotenuse, i.e., 25. The triangle contains a right angle, and our theorem has validity based upon this test.

$$a^2 + b^2 = c^2$$

For Pythagoras, the world of space is governed by exact numbers. Within nature and throughout the cosmos, numbers organize the forms, structures, and dimensions of all being into a *harmonium*, "harmony." As with the music of a properly stringed instrument, the parts of the cosmos "vibrate" in harmony.

This is not to suggest that all is in harmony. Much of the physical world as well as our own bodies are discordant and unbalanced. In fact, as understood by the Greeks, the soul is condemned to a cycle of purgings in Hades and rebirths as a prisoner of the physical body. It is for this reason that Pythagoras abstained from consuming the meat of an animal. The soul of a relative could be within.

But as pure mathematical patterns are apprehended through observation and disciplined mediation by humanity, humanity can then apply these universal principles to bring order to the world and thereby redeem the self and the soul. Once harmony between one's soul and the cosmos is obtained, the soul ceases the cycles of reincarnation into varied material forms and becomes forever part of the singular divine cosmos.

While the sacred connotation of numbers has been discarded over the centuries, the monumental significance of Pythagoras's discovery of the relationship of discrete numbers to the patterns of the world continues to reverberate. As was subsequently echoed by Galileo and, later, Jacob Bronowski (1973), a contemporary philosopher of science, "the language of nature is mathematics." With this fundamental knowledge of the structure and workings of the world, geometry and physics became a science. The Doric temple of Parthenon and the Sears Building in Chicago could be built. A man could walk on the moon. With this knowledge our modern world came into being.

Aristotle. From his detailed observations made off the island of Lesbos and other areas in the Aegean Sea, Aristotle recorded some of the most accurate and early descriptions of aquatic life, including the catfish, angler-fish, paper nautilus, and octopus. He was among the first to classify fish distinct from the mammalian species. While discredited until its rediscovery in the nineteenth century, his account of the hectocotylus arm of the octopus was two thousand years ahead of its time. While searching for "universal forms" like his teacher, Aristotle diverged from Plato (427–347 BCE) in locating

Plato (left) and Aristotle (right), from Raphael's "The School of Athens." Aristotle gestures to the earth, representing his belief in knowledge through empirical observation and experience, while Plato gestures to the heavens, representing his belief in the Forms. *Wikimedia Commons*

the universal in the particular concrete entities existing in the observable natural world. Plato had argued that universals existed as Forms or "ideas," distinct from particular material things, as models or archetypes of those objects. As illustrated in Plato's allegory of the cave, our protagonist, while chained within the cave, understands that which is directly observable and reflected on its walls to be what is real. But upon being freed from the chains and encountering the bright sun outside the cave, what had been thought to be reality is now revealed to be a mere reflection, an illusion, derived of the sun's light and the Forms casting shadows on the walls. The great truth of the Forms is realized. On the other hand, Aristotle insisted that universal Forms were encapsulated intrinsically within the tangible. If a universal could not be predicated in an object, argued Aristotle, as for example observed in an octopus, surely it could not exist. Forms remain the unconditional basis for all overt phenomena, accessible through the observable, in essence, what are to be found on the walls of the cave. Aristotle's approach to universals and the particulars, his methodology, implies an ascent from particular phenomena to the knowledge of their ultimate attributes and Forms, an inductive approach. Plato stressed the opposite approach to methodology, a descent from a priori knowledge of universal Forms to a contemplation of particular imitations of these, in essence a deductive approach.

While Aristotle's "natural philosophy" certainly included rigorous philosophical-based inquiry as well as politics and poetry and other fine arts, it also was the critical first step toward becoming what we would refer to as material reductionism and John Locke's (1632–1704) inductive empiricism and, in this sense, anticipating the scientific method of today. Among his many works that have had such an impact on Western civilization, his *Nicomanchean Ethics* is widely considered one of the most important historical philosophical works, influencing a range of subsequent thinkers such as Thomas Aquinas (1225–1274) and the development of Christianity, Niccolò Machiavelli (1469–1527) and the foundations of modern political science, and Francis Bacon (1561–1626) and Thomas Hobbes (1588–1679) and the beginnings of modernity itself.

Descartes. René Descartes (1596-1650) adds another plot or two to our story, approaching what is knowable from quite a different stance than that of Aristotle and John Locke. Yet these are contributions to our story that are not only complementary, but essential to the overall story of science, as we have come to know it today. This French philosopher starts with the assertion that we as humans have ultimate knowledge of our own existence because we are thinking beings—*cogito ergo sum*—"I think, therefore I am." The foundation of knowledge consists of a set of first, "self-evident" *a priori* principles. The mind is not an empty cabinet, a "blank slate," but filled with universal, though not readily knowable, principles. For Descartes, access to these first principles is not based on "the fluctuating testimony of the senses" (empiricism), nor is it contingent on the "blundering constructions of imagination" (aesthetic or spiritual awareness). He distrusted sensory evidence as much as he avoided any undisciplined flirtations of thought. The first principles are those anchored on "conception which an unclouded and attentive mind gives," on conception "wholly freed from doubt," principles derived from clear and logical thought. One can even begin with a set of assumptions that are only hypothetically true, all of which need not be verified by observation, need not exist in fact. They need only be

Portrait of Descartes, after ca. 1649–1700. Frans Hals, 1648. *Wikimedia Commons*

hypothetically correct. Keeping to our oceanic examples, one can hypothesize that a shark is a fish structured for rapid, agile swimming. This assertion need not be proved empirically. From these first principles, other truths can be deduced by a meticulous application of logical rules and axioms. Mathematically rigorous formulas can be applied in order to arrive at conclusions. If one designs a human submergible as a "shark," it logically follows that the submarine would likewise be rapid and agile. Knowledge is not so much what corresponds to experience, as it is a coherency within and among their principles and deduced statements. And so the deductive and rational methods are born, their strength and legitimacy residing in their ability to objectively think about the natural world and deduce statements of truth about that world. Descartes published his approach to knowledge in 1637 in *Discourse on Method*.

René Descartes made another important contribution to the unfolding story of science. Descartes reasoned that if the mind is capable of clear, objective thinking, then it cannot ultimately be reducible to the influences of the material world. "Mind" and "matter" are the basic constituents of the universe. The defining characteristic of "matter" is extension and movement, i.e., the possession of dimension such as time or space. The defining characteristic of "mind" is thought, i.e., the activity of thinking. Regardless of the way "matter" is extended, e.g., straight or curved, it must be extended. Regardless of the way "mind" thinks, e.g., abstracting or imagining, it must think. Each is absolutely different from the other, requiring nothing but itself to exist. Neither has the properties of the other, nor is causal of the other, and neither is reducible to the other, yet all in the universe is reducible to one or the other, to either "mind" or "matter." Cartesian Dualism thus adheres to the understanding that the natural world of "matter" is independent of the "mind," and, conversely, that the "mind" is independent of the "natural world." Objectivity is possible. The Proto-Indo-European *skey- "to split, to dissect" is realized. The world of the "other" and of "man" himself

has become "objects," for study, in which independent ideas and symbolic representations of them are possible— scientific hypothesis and theory. The "science of man" was ushered forth.

Locke. The English philosopher, John Locke (1632–1704), stated in *Essay Concerning Human Understanding*, that the mind is as a "white paper, void of all characters, without ideas," like an "empty cabinet," as yet unfurnished. The mind is

Portrait of John Locke by
Godfrey Kneller, 1697
Wikimedia Commons

tabula rasa, a blank slate. The material to furnish the cabinet is the knowledge that comes from experience. For Locke, all knowledge is founded on observation, through the senses. And so is founded the empirical method, i.e., "relating to experience." Knowledge is the precise correspondence between what is observed by the human senses and what exists in the natural world. The world Locke is referring to is the natural world of what would be defined as physics, chemistry, biology, psychology, and sociology. It is a world that exists independent of the mind, with its own structures and governed by its own processes, all of which can be discovered through rigorous observation.

The empiricist begins with observations of the natural world. These observations must be controlled, objective, verifiable, and replicable. Subjectivity and affectivity must be kept out. The observations are based on those senses that can be controlled and objective, i.e., sight, sound, smell, touch, and taste. The empiricist then forms a hypothesis that attempts to account for the observations. The process is called induction, i.e., reasoning from a limited number of observations to a conclusion or hypothesis. From the hypothesis, testing begins. Deliberate, systematic experimentation and extensive observation now occur to discover if the hypothesis is indeed correct or needs revision. The hypothesis is tested. The attempt is to verify what was originally observed. Replication is the criteria for verification. If a reasonable verification results, the empiricist then ventures a prediction of what will be discovered under similar natural circumstances. The strength and legitimacy of the empirical method is its ability to predict what occurs in the natural world.

The evolving story of science continues with other great men and their contributions, such as that of Galileo Galilei (1564–1642). Following the lead of Pythagoras and looking into the heavens, Galileo placed an emphasis on observable, quantifiable variables and their relationships, a reality of discrete numerically based chunks, i.e., statistics—"the language of nature is numbers." Continuing the story of rigorous observations, Isaac Newton (1642–1727) sought to establish universal generalizations—"laws" to describe, explain, predict and ultimately control the natural world—the "laws of motion." As the unfolding narrative sought to bring maximum benefit to human welfare, Francis Bacon (1561–1626) and his utilitarianism articulated a science that ultimately holds the keys to unlocking the power of mankind over nature. Collectively all these stories bring forth the scientific method, of a duality that separates us from nature so that we can understand it, predict it, and ultimately control nature. Of "pure" and "applied" sciences, seeking to improve our comprehension of the subatomic and astronomic, and advance the condition of human health and wellbeing. Science is thus most often associated with rational-deductive and empirical-inductive modes of thought, all premised on certain ontological principles, such as the mind/body dualism and objectification, material reductionism, and quantification of that material (Frey 1994:95–104, 123–26, 162–68). Acknowledging other avenues of development and expression, much of science can be seen as operating within the broad sweep of what is known as the "positivist paradigm."

When asked "what is real and knowable through the Head," Cliff and Allen would declare that it's to be discovered outside the Sweat House, outside the Tin Shed, viewed from a café's window, from a wooden bench. Reality is ultimately understood as separate and apart from the viewer, as if viewed from behind a great "glass pane." It is a tangible world made up of discrete, quantifiable material "objects" interacting together with a great regularity and order through lineal time, devoid of any spiritual animation or significance. It is a world made knowable and verifiable through deductive and inductive tests of logic and empirical observation, and of experimentation, all of which can be measured in terms of reliability and validity (Frey 1994:95–104). While traveling outside the Tin Shed, systematic analysis of dependent and independent variables, anticipatory predictions of cause and effect, explanations, axioms and theories of things are proposed, and experiments and manipulations of the physical world can all be attempted and made. This is knowledge of explanations, axioms, and theories of things and their forces. The classical Western scientific method results.

As I've come to understand and apply the "scientific method," it provides for:

1. a systematic approach (the process is shared and replicable in the scientific community),
2. that utilizes logical reasoning (deductive methods, i.e., logical reasoning from a premise and logical reasoning from the "facts"), and rigorous and standardized empiricism (inductive method, i.e., keen observations of the "facts"),
3. to investigate specific independent and dependent variables (the cause of something; the effect from something) and their relationships with one another (focusing on standardized, quantifiable variables; often statistics),
4. in order to establish generalizations (that can be compared with other studies, that can offer substantiated predictions),
5. that are held to standardized tests of validity and reliability (i.e., acknowledging various forms of validity, that the facts support the findings; reliability refers to the procedures and

conclusions being able to be independently replicable in another study),

6. all of which is framed in a tone of organized skepticism (nothing is accepted on faith, everything questioned).

Co-evolving outside the Sweat House, outside the Tin Shed, is another essential narrative, the social and cultural construct of the "autonomous individual." It becomes the foundation for the articulation of political rights and freedoms, of economic consumption and production, of the diagnosis and treatment of illness, of educational assessment, of athletic achievement, of the pivotal component even within the family, of the stimulus for and attribution of technological and scientific discovery and innovation, as well as of spiritual salvation, of the Euro-American ideal of "rugged individualism." And between these individuals there prevails a relationship of maximizing one's gains and minimizing one's losses, in Euro-American history expressed as the economic system of "capitalism." It is a world differentiated not only by binary oppositions, but also hierarchies. The human species is understood as sitting in a very privileged position, unique with its intelligence and volition, above all other species, as the "caretaker" of its garden, "whose purpose is to benefit the caretaker" (Frey 1994:164).

Heart Knowledge. Arriving at our destination, "Heart Knowledge" is often associated with participatory modes of action, all premised on very different epistemological and ontological attributes and principles from those of Head Knowledge. These are the principles that in their totality the Niimíipuu call *tamálwit*, "the law" and embedded in what the Schitsu'umsh call *hnkhwelkhwlnet*, "our ways of life in the world," and individually referred to as the *miyp*, "teachings from all things." Another, altogether distinct mega-story.

◆ ◆ ◆

In the summer of 1974 on the Crow Reservation, with Tom, Susie, Allen, and so many others, were so many swirling stories. Consider the word *ashammalíaxxiia*. Literally meaning "driftwood lodges," it is the term the Apsáalooke use to refer to a clan, each made up of numerous matrilineally related families (such as the Whistling Water clan)—an appropriate metaphor for the bonding of relatives. On the Yellowstone River the water is high and fast with the spring runoff. Pieces of dislodged driftwood are seen bashed against a rock, over there, or submerged under a current, right here. Individual lodges don't do well against the strong force of that river. But over there on the other side of the bank, there are those that are withstanding the river's destructive force. There, lodged together, next to the bank, are numerous pieces of driftwood, each lodge, each tipi intermingled with the other, each interdependent on the other, each together withstanding the river's power. And so it is with a clan of driftwood members, each interlinked, each interdependent, and the whole withstanding any force, any enemies that would seek their demise. While apropos for social relationships, *ashammalíaxxiia* is extended to apply to relationships with all peoples, be they animal and plant, ancestor and spirit. *Ashammalíaxxiia* characterize the relationship of the many individual entities of the phenomenal world, as interconnected, a home of human, animal, and spirit kinfolk, each in participation with the others, each supported by the others, each a *biilápxe*, a clan uncle to the others. (Re-told from interviews and experiences from the mid-1970s; also in Frey 1987:3–7, 40, 154–176.)

◆ ◆ ◆

Over the years of engaging with elders and their stories, certain *hnkhwelkhwlnet* attributes and principles were revealed to me. Among them is the unity of interrelational existence, of holism and monism, as expressed in the procession of dancers at a powwow's Grand Entry, in the spokes and hub of Tom's Medicine Wheel, in the Apsáalooke concept *ashammalíaxxiia*, "driftwood lodges," in the Niimíipuu term *yéeye*, "family," and by extension kinship with all the "peoples," or in the Schitsu'umsh terms *uchnek'we'*, literally "we are all relatives/we are all one," and *chnis-teem-ilqwes*, "I am your relative, I am part of all peoples—human, plant, animal, fish" (Frey, Aripa, and Yellowtail 1995:40–41; Frey and the Schitsu'umsh 2001:10, 183). Kinship throughout; no dualism.

The interrelationships are characterized by an equality among all entities, as expressed in the Schitsu'umsh term *unshat'qn* "eye-to-eye," seeing all beings as equals, be they human, animal, plant, rock, or spirit (Frey, Aripa, and Yellowtail 1995:41–42). No one dominates another.

Reciprocity transpires between these relations, as reflected in the Niimíipuu term *téek'e,* "to give and share [food with others]" and implied in the Schitsu'umsh term *pute-nts,* "respect." The sharing with one another securing the sustaining of the relationships.

These are relationships imbued with the transcendent and the animating spiritual nature of reality, expressed in the Schitsu'umsh phrase *snqhepiwes,* "where the spirit lives, from horizon to horizon" (Frey, Aripa, and Yellowtail 1995:42–43) and the Niimíipuu term *hewléexhewlex,* "spirit," the animating manifestation of which is the Apsáalooke term *baaxpée,* the Niimíipuu *wéeyekin,* or the Schitsu'umsh *suumesh,* all three referring to "spiritual force" or "Indian medicine" (Frey 1987:59–63; Frey and the Schitsu'umsh 2001:9, 176–80). An animating spirit alive throughout.

This is the story of an omnipresent Creator—*Akbaatatdía,* "the one who made everything" (Apsáalooke), the *Amotqn,* "one who sits at the head mountain" (Schitsu'umsh), the *Hanyaw'áat* (Niimíipuu), the ultimate source of the teachings. This is a story of a multitude of Peoples, kinsmen—human, animal, plant, rock and spirit, both of the present and the past—the ancestors and the Animal First Peoples of creation time, the *Titwatityáaya* (Niimíipuu), the people of the oral traditions, the mediating link between the Creator and the humans. This is the story of Coyote and Salmon, Rabbit and Jack Rabbit, Chief Child of the Yellowroot and Burnt Face, not as the Godfathers but the Guardians of the Oral Traditions. It is they, sent by the Creator, as extensions of the Creator, who prepare the world for the coming of the human peoples, overcoming "man-eaters" and other monsters, and inundating the landscape with gifts—the varied foods, tools and shelter, the *miyp* teachings and the *baaxpée* animating life-force—what the human peoples will need to prosper. This is the story of deer, camas, and salmon who are brothers to the hunter, root digger, or fisherman, offering themselves up voluntarily when given gifts of respect and song, and then of only offering their flesh when it is shared with those in need. These are brothers never to be taken by asserting one's self over them, never to be taken for one's sole use and appetite, never to be taken without the consent of the kinsmen (Frey and the Schitsu'umsh 2001:204–11).

◆ ◆ ◆

He had sung his hunting songs, a prayer to a brother he now sought. The terrain is tough going at times, steep and rocky, and thick with foliage and downed trees. But he has to be on his toes, quiet, for he is being tested. His brother will only come out of the thicket if he is up to the task, had showed his skills as well as respect in song and in his heart. And there, just beyond that row of trees, in an open flat, a *ts'i*, a deer has emerged. He aims his rifle and fires a shot. As he cuts into the flesh of his brother, he continues his song. Attentive to the hunter's need, his brother has allowed his flesh, his meat, to be taken that day, but only by his consent so that others are fed and nourished. No other deer would be hunted this day, as that is all the meat the family needs. (Re-told from an interview in 1996; also in Frey and the Schitsu'umsh 2001:164–72.)

◆ ◆ ◆

When asked "what is real and knowable through the Heart" Cliff and Allen would insist that it's revealed while traveling within the Sweat House, within the Tin Shed. Phenomenal reality is ultimately experienced as the transitory intersection of all those participating, an event of converging relations, always in the making, anchored to place-based oral traditions, the *miyp* teachings. *Hnkhwelkhwlnet* is an event made real by those participating, their relationships with each other guided and rendered meaningful by the oral traditions of a specific landscape (Frey and the Schitsu'umsh 2001:262, 286; Frey and Campbell 2015).

The "vital act" is the "act of participation." Those participating are thus inclusive of human, animal, plant, rock, and spiritual Peoples, both of the present and the past—the ancestors and the First Peoples—all in temporal and spatial kinship with one another; no glass pane separations. As an indigenous form of knowledge, *hnkhwelkhwlnet* cannot be fully understood if it is isolated and separated from the behavioral practices within which it finds expression. Thought and intellect are integrated with felt experience; no mind/body dualism. Consider that *hnkhwelkhwlnet* refers to "our ways of life," i.e., ways of being, of existing, and not ways of knowing, per se. Knowledge is accessed through and interwoven with experiential participation with others, and as such, it is praxis-actualized collective knowledge. Reality is the ever-unfolding action, an ephemeral event, always in the making, an *Ashkísshe* of transitory dancers; reality is not reducible to discrete, quantifiable material objects.

The world is unified through kinship, imbued with spirit. It is a world precipitated and animated by the spiritual, with its animation and volition shared equally within all Peoples (Frey 1994:169–76; Frey and the Schitsu'umsh 2001:10). While traveling within the Sweat House/the Tin Shed, perennial meanings are revealed and spiritual animation channeled, permeating and renewing all the relations and lives of the world. This is knowledge of relationships and their meanings. Conversely, knowledge has existence in the interlinking relationships of the many participants; it is experiential, it is collective knowledge.

◆ ◆ ◆

Over the years I've had the honor of attending several of Cliff's Schitsu'umsh family Jump Dances. At one of those first Jump Dances, knowing of my relationship with Tom Yellowtail and the Sundance, as well as with the University of Idaho, he made the point of introducing me as, "Rodney Frey, a Crow Sundancer," not as an "anthropologist," an identifier that carried certain baggage, appropriate as the butt of a joke at a powwow, but inappropriate in this place of heart-felt prayer and spiritual swirling. In the days running up to his Jump Dance, Cliff often made a point of asking if I'd bring some of my students, and on a few occasions I did. Upon arriving, we'd enter the Longhouse-Community Center and in counter-clockwise fashion, I'd have each student introduce him or herself to all those already assembled. Standing with his wife Lori, Cliff would extend a warm hand and embrace each student, saying, "Welcome home, we're with family." In the Jump Dance we shared in kinship and prayer, at this place, in this timelessness, if only momentarily. The academy with its concrete silos were left outside. (Re-told from experiences during the 1990s through 2011 on the Coeur d'Alene Reservation.)

◆ ◆ ◆

Intimacy, not estrangement, characterizes the intersection of *hnkhwelkhwlnet* relationships. An affinity embodies *biilápxe* and clan son, *ts'i* and hunter, and *Bishée* and Sundancer associations. This is an intimacy only brought about by the capacity of *snuk-wnkhwtskhwts'mi'ls*, a deep listening to and appreciation of the other. The *biilápxe* are aware of the needs of a clan son, the *ts'i* attentive of the respect shown by a hunter, and a young Sundancer sees through the eyes of *Bishée*. None are strangers to the others.

As a confluence of those participating, *hnkhwelkhwlnet* is necessarily "place-bound knowledge," intertwined with the specific physical and spiritual members who at the moment are inhabiting a particular landscape. Consider that the term *hnkhwelkhwlnet* refers to "our ways of life *in* the world," i.e., the many participants are not "apart from," but "a part of" a place, *in* the world. In the instance of Schitsu'umsh *hnkhwelkhwlnet*, its *miyp* oral traditions stem from and are only meaningful when linked to a lake called *Chatqéle'*, Lake Coeur d'Alene, and of the deeds and adventures of such Animal First Peoples as *Sp'ukhwenichelt*, Chief Child of the Yellowroot. The landscape is a "textbook" interwoven with story ripe for re-telling. I recall the many trips we took to Sheridan, Wyoming, for groceries, as Grandpa Tom would point to a particular hill as it came into view, then a riverbed, now an open plain, each with its own story, each re-told as we drove the landscape. And he'd look up, toward the Big Horn Mountains. Among the assembled rocks perched high atop those mountains were the stories of the Wheel and Burnt Face. To travel a landscape is to engage its story; to re-tell a story is to travel its landscape. Landscape and story are indivisibly one.

As oral tradition, *hnkhwelkhwlnet* is knowledge and practice disseminated from generation to generation, since time immemorial, in orality-based forms of communications, such as spoken language, story narratives, songs, dance regalia, and even in the perennial acts of gathering *sqigwts* with one's elders. *Hnkhwelkhwlnet* is infused with the *miyp* teachings, awaiting *chetche'in'nts*, their revealing. What is experienced as real is thus an experiential stream of ongoing events made up of human, plant, animal, and spiritual participants, their relationships with each other aligned with the core teachings anchored to a specific landscape.

◆ ◆ ◆

Alone, Old Man John gone up into the mountains. He came to a large cave opening, and looked inside. There emerged the *Awakkuléeshe*, the Little People. They asked him to look closely, into the depth of the cave. As he did, he could see two passages. Down one passage there were great things we desire, riches of all sorts, but the passage ended abruptly. Down the other, without any of the treasures, but the passage seemed not to end, going beyond what he could see. They asked him to make a choice, which passage would be his? John Trehero lived a very long life, seeming without end. A life not filled with material wealth but of greater rewards, becoming a powerful healer, a medicine man, touching the lives of others, with the *Awakkuléeshe* close at hand. (Re-told as heard from Tom Yellowtail circa late-1970s.)

◆ ◆ ◆

While the tightly-bonded interrelationships of *ashammalíaxxiia* might have us assume a world of predetermined actions, with each participant—human, animal, spirit—lodged so firmly with others as to preclude independent volition, John's "cave" would suggest otherwise. At each junction in life, one's actions are imbued with the responsibility of adhering to the *miyp* teachings as best he or she can. Or one might choose actions other than the teachings of the elders. Burnt Face could have chosen to remain ostracized. Allen and Cliff could have stopped our conversations and walked off. Upon facing my own greatest challenge, a choice would be required. Could I connect the dots and select the course of action Tom and Cliff and others had shown me? *Hnkhwelkhwlnet* is about taking responsibility for one's decisions.

◆ ◆ ◆

The off-reservation bar has never been a good place to settle a dispute. The disagreement soon breaks out into a fight, a gun is pulled and a young man lays there bleeding with two bullets close to his heart. He is rushed to the Indian Health Service Hospital at Crow Agency, but the doctors there want to bring in a specialist from Billings before doing the surgery. The parents are told their son, so close to death, has to wait. While the nurses are away from his bedside, Old Man John, called in by the parents, goes in and prays to his Medicine Fathers for help. *Baaxpée* is called upon. Just before departing and with care, John places the powder of a particular medicine root in the open wounds. The nurses soon return to change the blood-soaked bandages, and when they pull the sheets back, lying there are the two bullets, right beside the young man, "they came out the same way they had gone in." X-rays are taken and there were no bullets, and as soon as he regained his strength, the young man was discharged. (Re-told from an interview with Tom Yellowtail, circa 1975; also in Frey 1987:127.)

◆ ◆ ◆

The Rainbow. Sometimes it takes that special experience, an "aha moment," to wake us up. As I have done with my students, now with you, to help us get off the wooden bench and begin an appreciation of Heart Knowledge, of *hnkhwelkhwlnet*, of an existence not of discrete objects but of events and relationships, let's re-imagine an experience that they, you, and I all have had—re-imagine a rainbow. After considering what it takes to create that rainbow experience, then let's extend it to the experience of digging *sqha'wlutqhwe'*, also known as camas or *Camassia quamash*. I owe the following "aha moment," and this teaching moment to a source far from the Tin Shed, to the British philosopher Owen Barfield, who first articulated the possibility of another view of a "rainbow" (and of the notion of "original participation") in his book *Saving the Appearances: The Study of Idolatry* (1965:15). He had planted the seed that not long after sprouted.

While returning home to Colorado after completing a summer of ethnographic work for the Apsáalooke during the late 1970s, the following occurred. I had just come out of the downpour as I sped south on the Interstate Highway. Except for the sun's radiance from the west, the sky remained dark blue. Then I saw it, bright and clear, not more than a quarter mile to the east. With all its vivid colors, the rainbow emerged from the ground, arced, and re-entered. It was a perfect rainbow. And I thought, what a perfect ending to a great summer.

But the perfect rainbow had something else to offer that afternoon. As I continued south, the rainbow seemed to move with me. I passed a wooded area, then a deep coulee, now a ranch house; at each site the rainbow touched down and moved across. I slowed my car to sneak a picture with the camera; the arc of color slowed as well. I sped up; it sped up. A hill rose a few hundred feet from the car; the rainbow touched down so close that I could almost run my fingers through its vibrant colors. I soon realized that this was my own special rainbow.

Did others see my rainbow traveling south with me, even as many other drivers traveled north? No one else would indeed see it as I saw it. Others who traveled that highway may also have seen a rainbow, even at the very same moment I saw mine, but theirs' were not mine. It was a gift to me alone. And I raised my right hand from the steering wheel and gave thanks, *ahó*.

◆ ◆ ◆

It took some time to locate, but there, between the gravel road and plowed field, is a patch of the blue-flowering plants. As we approach, the elder takes out some tobacco and places it beside the first of many plants she soon would be digging with her *pitse'*—digging stick. Bending over and in a deliberate but quiet voice, she addresses the *Amotqn*—the Creator—and the *sqha'wlutqhwe'*—the camas. She asks them for permission to dig into the earth and pull out the small bulbs from these plants; she tells of the family's desire to use these roots, to cook them to provide nutrition in body and spirit for others who will be attending her family's Jump Dance this coming winter. And as the steel *pitse'* pierces the soil, opening the plant's roots to air and light and an elder's hand, she pulls the camas out and replaces it with an offering of tobacco. Each of us continues throughout the afternoon, with a *pitse'* in hand and a growing bag of camas, gathering only what we will need. The camas will provide for the needs of many others. When *sqha'wlutqhwe'* is annually dug in this manner, it reciprocates by producing larger tubers when compared to *Camassia quamash* left in the wild, without human and spirit interaction. (Re-told from experience in 1996; also in Frey and the Schitsu'umsh 2001:155–64.)

◆ ◆ ◆

Re-imagine the last time you experienced an arc of richly-varied, vivid color, rising out from the ground, reaching into the sky, and then arching back down into the earth. What were the elements, if you will, the participants, and their relationship with each other, which allowed the phenomena you might call a rainbow to come into existence? Certainly moisture, the water molecules suspended in the sky, with light from the sun reflecting off those tiny droplets.

What else? You, i.e., your physical ability, was required to visually perceive the light interacting with the moisture.

And what else? You again, i.e., your cognitive ability, was required to mentally recognize, conceive, and conceptualize that the inter-action of yourself, with the suspended moisture in the sky, relative to the sun's light hitting those molecules, was indeed meaningful. You needed a word, an ideational construct.

Anything else? How about a certain place, for a certain time. Your rainbow only had existence where these interacting elements aligned in a particular relationship with each other, i.e., you had to be at a place, on a landscape, in a particular angle relative to the light and the moisture, in alignment with each other, for a particular moment.

Your rainbow only had existence when these participants come together, aligned if only momentarily, as an unfolding event. The phenomena we call a rainbow has existence as a transitory intersection of those participating, anchored to a particular place, interjected by you with a particular construct infused with certain meaning. We interject, have a word, a concept for these interactions that imbues the experience with semantic significance. We have, in essence, a *miyp* for it. Let's note here, that for indigenous peoples, with place-bound oral traditions emanating from the Creator and Animal First Peoples, the essential additive are the *miyp*-aligned words of the place-based story. Hence the understanding to be discussed presently, "stories make the world."

And of course, the moment when all these particular participants—mist, light, you, and others, place, all in relationship—disengage from one another—so too does this event disconnect in the sky. The rainbow no longer has existence.

The focus of *hnkhwelkhwlnet* is not so much on the participants, as discrete and concrete objects, as it is on their temporally aligned relationships with each other. Would a rainbow have existence if any one of these relational participants were missing? The rainbow is not reducible to the solitary qualities of its empirical, physical properties; Aristotelian materialism does not flourish in this reality. The rainbow does not have existence autonomous from human participation; Descartes' Cartesian Dualism does not estrange "body" from "mind" in this reality; no separation of behavioral action from knowledge. The rainbow has existence not as a distinct physical object in the sky, nor reducible to its ideational configuration, but as an unfolding event of the many in relationship with each other.

Now consider, how similar is the reality of experiencing the rainbow to that of digging *sqha'wlutqhwe*? For the Schitsu'umsh, *sqha'wlutqhwe*' has existence only when aligned in a strong reciprocal relation as "kinsmen" (Schitsu'umsh and Frey 2001:6, 154–55,

172). For the human kinsmen, there is a responsibility for acquiring a vast level of knowledge and teachings, of *miyp*, including a keen awareness of the seasonal cycles and unique weather patterns that effect location and timing of the digging, as well as the obligation for certain acts of prayer and respect during and after the digging. Before the *pitse'* (digging stick) pierces and loosens the earth around the camas tuber, a prayer to *Amo̲tqn* and the *sqha'wlutqhwe'* is given, asking permission to gather the tubers, asking if we could gather his fruits. A small gift of tobacco might also be offered. Only that amount of camas needed by the family would be dug, never more. For its part, the *sqha'wlutqhwe'* reciprocates,

Flowering camas, with a bee. *Frey 1996*

responding with its own gifts of nutrition, feeding the body and the spirit of human kinsmen. Camas, when annually dug in this Schi̲tsu'umsh manner, responds by producing larger tubers when compared to camas left in the "wild," void of human interaction. Once dug and prepared, the human also has the responsibility of sharing the camas with those in need, and of not hoarding it for one's self.

Are not both the raindrops and fibrous bulbs of *Camassia quamash* made up of similar elemental, constituent physical properties, just simply arranged differently, perhaps most distinguished in that one set of properties is on a much slower temporal scale—a slow growing plant? If a rainbow is the result of our interaction and particular relationship with raindrops and sunlight, would it not follow that a "*sqha'wlutqhwe'*" is also the result of our experiential interaction and particular relationship with a relatively hard, fibrous growth, the result of our physical and conceptual interactions with it? Consider that *hnkhwelkhwlnet* refers to "our ways of life in the world," i.e., the many participants are a part of a connection with the many others, in a particular place, and not apart from them, separate from that place. For the Schitsu'umsh, this particular physical interaction entails the behavioral acts of prayer, the acts of digging, the acts of cleaning and storing, the acts of sharing the *sqha'wlutqhwe'* with those in need, with the elders and children, and the acts of consuming and providing nutrition and health. It entails acts with both physical and spiritual others, with a brother, and with the Creator, though the event is not reducible to either the physical or spiritual. The conceptual interaction with the fibrous growth anchors the event with the *miyp* that guides the behavioral acts and renders the interactions meaningful, though the event is not reducible to the ideational. The entirety of this unfolding event of the many relationships is *hnkhwelkhwlnet.*

◆ ◆ ◆

Even anthropologists can co-create reality. As a graduate student I remember being introduced to four classic ethnographies that illustrate precisely the importance of identifying one's name in the text one researches and writes (Frey 1994:37–38). When life in a Mexican village was described by the American ethnographer Robert Redfield in his *Tepoztlan, a Mexican Village: A Study of Folk Life* (1930), it was characterized as cooperative and integrated, made up of content, well-adjusted people. We find in Oscar Lewis' *Life in a Mexican Village: Tepoztlan Restudied* (1951), the same village, a few years later, engulfed with tension, schism, pervading fear, envy, and distrust. Had some twenty years brought that much change? Or had Redfield and Lewis, however unwittingly, each brought something of their own respective cultural milieu into their studies? For Redfield, had it been the optimism of an age of prosperity in which "the War to end all wars" had just been fought and a League of Nations established? For Lewis, was it the tension and fear of an age of Cold War—the Bomb about to drop and global conflict about to erupt at any moment?

In 1930, the British anthropologist E. E. Evans-Pritchard initiated what would become the definitive study of the Nuer, an east African

Nilotic people. The first in a series of works, *The Nuer: A Description of the Modes of Livelihood and Political Institutions of a Nilotic People* (1940), quickly became a classic in the field. With the outbreak of World War II, Evans-Pritchard was forced to relinquish his research and return to England. While there, he became a Catholic. With the war concluded, Evans-Pritchard resumed his studies among the Nuer, and in 1956 published *Nuer Religion*. While describing the same people, albeit differing domains within the same culture, in comparing *The Nuer* with *Nuer Religion* it is as if two different writers were at work. In *The Nuer*, it was a humanity defined in terms of the material praxis and functional qualities of its social existence, while in *Nuer Religion*, it was the symbolic and ideational qualities that defined this humanity. Was it his own newly acquired religious sensitivities that allowed Evans-Pritchard to better appreciate Nuer spiritual sensibilities? And in the instances of Redfield and Lewis, could not the times from which each viewed the world have actually helped reveal differing aspects of the same village life in Tepoztlan? As ethnographers, writers, teachers, students, it is so critical we identify who we are, our family lineage, and greet others with our names—acknowledging what we are contributing to the intersection of those participating. It is not just that we need to be open, but also acknowledge and take responsibility for what we are co-creating. Is it not just an issue of reflexivity, but an issue of honesty?

◆ ◆ ◆

A reporter from the *Billings Gazette* showed up to the Sundance, asking to visit with an "official." She wanted to learn about what was going on for the article she was writing. From within the Lodge, Tom turned to me and asked if I'd visit with the reporter. "Me?" I thought to myself, feeling so unqualified. At one of the breaks during the dancing, I went out and visited with her. Perhaps Grandpa Tom thought I could best speak the language of the reporter, negotiate words with her. I attempted to communicate with one who sought to communicate with others, each of us endeavoring, together, to create a story to bridge with others.

◆ ◆ ◆

Acknowledging the grand kinship of the many diverse peoples, the *ashammalíaxxiia* interconnection in the world of *hnkhwelkhwlnet*, attention is paid by the participants to each unfolding momentary interaction, and to the responsibility each has for the unfolding story. One cannot be a passive onlooker, cannot avoid responsibility. And it is a responsibility, adhering to the *miyp*, not to harm, but nurture, to support the others in need. Each is to *stmi'sm*, "listen deeply," with empathy, to the diversity of others, and with your *'itsk'u'lm*, "actions" and words, help co-create that moment. *Hnkhwelkhwlnet* "our ways of life in the world" entails taking responsibility.

Efficacy and Explanation. And you ask, how does it work to produce a desired result? How does water emerge from a knot on a recently cut down cottonwood tree, which had been planted four feet deep into a dry plateau bluff, just as Eagle feathers fan over that knot? A question certainly never asked by Tom or Cliff, or any other elder I've ever worked with. "It just does." But a question asked by one of mixed parenting. A question that for me stems from an ethnographic desire to communicate a response other than a retort reducing it to a simple psychological explanation, such as a self-fulling prophecy. Or, "They just believe it to be true, though we know it's not." But a response affirming the "how it works" predicated on a systematic set of ontological principles, akin to any complex causal enunciation. A response that seeks to negotiate between known and knower, bridge *hnkhwelkhwlnet* with those on the wooden bench, offer an interpretation. All these principles have already been identified in this essay's previous discussion. Now let's connect the dots.

A first shot at the question, as I might share with my students. Given the spiritual animation of and kinship-based unity within this expanded world of the many Peoples, in the human *acts* of re-telling, re-singing, re-dancing the perennial stories of the creation time and place, stories embedded with all their essential *miyp* and *tamálwit* bones, the world as presently engaged is re-created and perpetuated. Now that is a sentence you have to dwell on, but it does put it all together. It is the act of *going* inside, *being* attentive, *saying* the prayer aloud, of *doing*. It is the act of "re-telling one's own," *baaéechichiwaau*, or what the Niimíipuu call *titwatí·sa*, "re-telling my stories." It is aligning that act of re-telling with the perennial bones, and in so doing aligning the act with a life-force. In these experiential acts, now endowed with spiritual vitality, the world is renewed, as the temporal present is rendered one with the Animal First Peoples of creation time and place (Frey, Aripa, and Yellowtail 1995:171–73, 176; Frey and the Schi̱tsu'umsh 2001:197–204, 234, 260–68; Frey 2004:166). As Cliff SiJohn has said, in telling the stories of the Animal First Peoples, "they come *alive…*they *swirl around* you as the Turtle is saying his thing or as the Chipmunk is saying something…they *swirl around* you and you see the *Indian medicine…* this is Chipmunk talking to you…this is Coyote talking to you… all these things *suddenly come alive…*they are just as alive as they were a thousand years ago" (Frey and the Schi̱tsu'umsh 2001:197). In the acts of telling, singing, and dancing, the Human Peoples thus have an essential co-creative role and huge responsibility. Hence the Apsáalooke expression, *dasshússua*, "breaking with the mouth," and the phrase, "stories make the world." That which comes through the mouth, be it spoken or sung, be it an Indian name or a creation story, has the efficacy to bring forth the world. Efficacy, as used here, relates to *how* it works, the structures and dynamics that bring about the *swirling* with Coyote.

In re-telling Coyote's story of the Rock Monster, the *blue* in Lake Coeur d'Alene is perpetuated. In re-telling Burnt Face's story, a scar is removed and a face made new, as a child's…and a cancer abated. In giving voice through a prayer or a song, or through the movement of body and feathers in a dance, Deer or Camas would offer themselves up to kinsmen in need, a name would protect, water could usher forth from a Tree, bullets emerge from a young man's body, and humans transform into Blue Jays. In giving voice through words, songs, and dance, it's never a matter of suspending disbelief while viewing a play about a coyote, but invariably of intensifying what is most real and true, of swirling and talking with Coyote. "The world is made and rendered meaningful in the act of revealing Coyote's story of it" (Frey, Aripa, and Yellowtail 1995:214). In re-telling the stories, the *miyp* are not only passed on to the next generation, but the world itself is perpetuated for that generation. As Cliff would so assuredly affirm, we and the world are the stories we re-tell.

◆ ◆ ◆

During this Jump Dance, "heart talk" and *suumesh* songs are shared by the many gathered at the Longhouse. The Jump Dance is the Coeur d'Alene people's most important annual ceremony, held over two nights, from dusk to dawn, during the height of the winter. As the songs are sung, others join in and jump, dancing to the beat, offering their own prayers. It is during the early morning hours when it happens, those two men had been dancing hard and then they "went out," they "Blue Jayed." They flew to the top rafters of the building and then out into the night, into the mountains like an Animal, no longer human beings. A little later, during the early morning hours the medicine leaders, who know how to take care of them, sing their *suumesh* songs. Those who had Blue Jayed come back in, and they go around the room and doctor the sick and bless the food that will soon be consumed, though never touching any that are gathered around. The Blue Jays are eventually "brought back," made human again. (Re-told from interviews in 1996; also in Frey and the Schitsu'umsh 2001:232–36.)

◆ ◆ ◆

Symbols. Let's take another approach at addressing the question of efficacy and explanation. Let's consider symbols, the elemental unit upon which we communicate and store our knowledge. Symbols can be defined as a specific *unit of reference* that refers to a particular *referent*. The unit of reference can be an object, a behavior, or a sign. The referent can consist of a concept, phenomenon, or process. Simply put, a symbol is something that stands for something else. The phonetic pronunciation, *rān'bō*, a unit of reference, can refer to a vivid arc of color across the sky, a referent.

As symbols define the parameters of and assign the meaning to the phenomenal world of objects and of images, that which symbols refer to is *brought forth* and *created*. The meaning of an object or image does not rest in that object or image alone, but is the result of a complex interaction involving the object or image, human sensory perception, and human mental conception. Conceptualization, in turn, is influenced by the particular cultural and historical paradigms of the specific human who is conceptualizing. We are reminded of the question: what constitutes the phenomenon, rainbow? Certainly the mist of the rain and the light of the sun, physical particles, but also a human perceiving that particular interaction of light and mist, a physical perception, and a human conceiving of that particular interaction, a cognitive category, and assemblage of symbols.

And as we engage the particular symbols emanating out of the Sweat Lodge/Tin Shed, added to this complex interaction of referents, perceptions, and conceptions are spiritual meaning and animation—added are the symbolic clusterings of *miyp* and *tamálwit*. Sweat Lodge referents have the potential to be infused with and be an extension of all that which is spiritually animated and significant, all that which is most real. In being linked to the bones, to what can be called the sacred, what is normally veiled and hidden, spiritual symbols have an ability to reveal what is most real and access what is most powerful—*baaxpée* and *suumesh*. Hence in the Apsáalooke assemblage of verbal symbols, of *dasshússua*, when a name is spoken, a vow stated, a story told, a prayer offered, a song sung, the world is brought forth and made. It is, of course, in this quality that Head and Heart symbols are fundamentally distinguished. As I suggested, the shift is from viewing the oral narratives, the '*me'y'mi'y'm q´esp schint* as explanations about the world, to experiencing the '*me'y'mi'y'm q´esp schint* as the world, continually unfolding as the words are spoken.

I am reminded of the vividly poignant story shared by N. Scott Momaday. He relates how he was working on the closing passages in what would become his Pulitzer Prize-winning *The Way to Rainy Mountain*. Late one night, he was dwelling on an old Kiowa tale and on a time far removed from his own. It was 1833, under a night sky of meteor showers, and he imagined and wrote, so completely, about a "living memory" of an old woman, Ko-sahn. Absorbed in the words, Momaday spoke her name aloud, and there, stepping right out of the language, standing right before him, was the "ancient one-eyed woman." And they commenced a most astonishing conversation!

By extension, the spoken *dasshússua* symbols of the Apsáalooke are not unlike those engraved in and form the character of a painted wooden mask, as donned by a Haudenosaunee (Iroquois) *Face* dancer or a Kwakwaka'wakw (Kwakiutl) *Hamatsa* dancer. And while dancing the story of these Spirit People, the dancer is transformed into the Spirit People, the Schitsu'umsh Jump Dancer into a Blue Jay. The spoken *dasshússua* symbols are not unlike the distinct patterns of sand and color applied by a Diné (Navajo) healer as he lays out a "dry painting" on the floor of a ritual hogan (traditional Diné dwelling), in it embodying the *Yei*, the Holy Ones of the Creation Time, imbued with *Hózhó*, "beauty and harmony." In the ritual act of sitting upon the *Hózhó* symbols, on the dry painting, the *Yei* swirling about and a patient's illness is purged, a healing order is restored. The Apsáalooke Medicine Bundle and its sacred objects are laid out so precisely on the floor, channeling the *baaxpée* from the Creator and Medicine Fathers, through the Eagle-feather fan and into the patient, "a pulsating cooling warmth," pulling out the affliction, then tossing it to the east, with the prevailing winds, with a flick of the feathers.

At this point of our inquiry, I would like to pause a moment and reflect on any insights that the nature of Tin Shed/Sweat Lodge symbols might provide for a better appreciation of their own meaning and efficacy. As you might continue to be asking, among other questions, "Really Frey, how is it that a special cluster of symbols—the words of prayer and the ritual movement of Eagle feathers—can draw water from a tree?" While I have participated in the Sweat Lodge for almost four decades, personally witnessed so many mysteries, so many remarkable transformations and healings, and sat with so many great teachers, I claim no certainty, no firm understanding of the dynamics of this process. I have described for you some of the ontological foundations upon which this world is distinguished from others, and we have considered some of the defining qualities of orality, which will hopefully render the Sweat Lodge landscape a little more accessible. While I know it is true and have experienced it as real, I remain uncertain regarding just how it all works.

Perhaps the desire to resolve this ambiguity is a function of my Head Knowledge mind at work. Worth reflecting upon are the insights offered by Mircea Eliade (1907–1986). He was the renowned interpreter of religious experiences, from the indigenous Australian to the Asian Hindu, from the Ancient Egyptian to the Abrahamic Muslim. Perhaps he can guide us a little farther into the Tin Shed. While a graduate student at the University of Colorado, it was Davíd Carassco who introduced me to Eliade.

Let me offer a glimpse of Eliade's eloquent enunciations. For Eliade, a prolific writer and mentor to numerous scholars, reality and the religious experience start with the sacred. The sacred is understood as having *being* (having existence), as having *power* (the animating force to create the world), and as having *reality* (what is most meaningful), providing a "celestial archetype," emanating from what Eliade calls "supraterrestrial planes." The sacred oscillates in, around, and through two interrelated ubiquitous transcendent spheres of existence: the cosmic center, the *axis mundi,* and the primordial time of the Gods and Heroes, *in illo tempore, ab origine.* The "religious symbols" used in ceremonies and pilgrimages, in the oral narratives and songs, in the dances, regalia, and masks, in the temples and atop mountains are the languages of the sacred, of the Gods and Spirits. These revered symbols are derived from the sacred, their source and inspiration, while also a revelation of it, revealing what is normally veiled and hidden in everyday existence. When humans participate in and use these religious symbols, in their rituals and storytellings, communication is re-established with the *axis mundi*s and *in illo tempore,* and the sacred shines through, its meaning and power, its existence flows forth into the world, materialized, in what Eliade calls a "hierophany." Reality is manifested, derived from the transcendent, reminiscent of Plato's allegory of the cave.

But the use and application of the religious symbols must be deliberate; as Eliade insists, they must be aligned with and parallel to the sacred archetype. The rites of initiation, the world renewal ceremonies, the re-tellings of the creation accounts must repeat the perennial sacred if that sacred is to spew forth and into the lives of the participants. Are not the Sundance Lodge and the behavior of its dances, the *Ashkísshe*, in replication of the cosmic Center as the water flows from the Tree? Are not all the *miyp* and *tamálwit* bones of the primordial Creation included in the re-telling, as the Animal First People swirl about you, Coyote and Chipmunk come alive, talking to you, and the blue in a lake brought forth and per-petuated, a world renewed? At a Jump Dance, aligned with the *axis mundis* and *in illo tempore*, is not Cliff's "welcome home" greeting as much a pronouncement of family inclusion awaiting my graduate students and myself, as anticipatory of a hierophany about to shine through? As words in prayer are offered, as a cup of Brew is taken, or as a medicine root is placed in open wounds, an alignment can bring forth a renewal. Is not each of these intersections of those participating—human, animal, tree, spirit—when aligned with the perennial bones, a hierophany shining through? In response to our uncertainties, is not Eliade worth reflecting upon?

Deconstructing. A little house cleaning. Any pretense of a glass pane separating you as independent from all the other Peoples is shattered (Frey 1994:126–41). Any pretense that the words of a story can simply describe a world out there is vanquished. Any pretense that you can have an "understanding" of, "explanation" for, or a "belief" about a world separate and autonomous from that world is dissolved. The constructs such as "beliefs" and "values," and even our academically cherished concepts of "culture" and "history," all entail psychological and philosophical states in which an individual holds a cluster of propositional or declarative ideas/ thoughts about the truth, nature, or existence of something else, be it material objects or other ideas/thoughts. In this state, the cluster and the something else are each understood as having distinctive albeit exclusive constituents. Such psychological and philosophical states necessarily presuppose Cartesian dualism—of thought and material contradistinctive.

Within the Tin Shed you don't have "beliefs" about the Animal First Peoples, rather you have direct experiences with them. "Belief" and "history" neither mediate nor veil your engagement with the world. As a graduate student at the University of Colorado in 1979 I had the opportunity of listening to Vine Deloria Jr. as he was being interviewed for a faculty position, which he was offered and he subsequently accepted. During the interview Davíd Carrasco asked Deloria something to the effect, "what are some of the key religious beliefs of the American Indian?" Deloria wonderfully articulated a response, including the statement I still clearly remember, "We don't have beliefs about our religion, we experience it."

A good student of mine, well versed in philosophy, having just read an earlier version of this essay, likely the preceding paragraph, objected, "Is it not the case that every culture throughout the world has 'beliefs,' that the concept of 'believing' is universal?" As we visited, I conveyed that I am using the term "belief" not in the sense of a deep conviction in the truth of something, as "faith" or "trust" in something. And I know there are indigenous terms that have been translated at "belief" or "to believe," though as Rodney Needham argues in his tour de force *Belief, Language and Experience*, these terms themselves are historical products of "Indo-European culture" and core topics of European philosophers (1972:41; 51–63). I am using the term to refer to a cogent body of thought understood as tenets held by a group, as doctrines of a people's beliefs. While this body of thought can have reference to the experiential world, it necessarily has ideational existence separate from it, a condition predicated on literacy dualism.

And as a graduate student, I was introduced to a certain other adage, this one relating to "history," that has also continued to resonate with me. Shared during one of the many lectures I attended, the phrase was insightful in the construction of the concept of "history," as well as implications of this construct. Whether correctly attributed to the Lakota leader Sitting Bull or not, he is purported to have said, "History means disrespect for the ancestors." He had certainly witnessed horrendous disrespect, with the physical assault on his forefathers, at the hands of the United State military and its missionary allies. But even more perceptively, the saying suggests the very nature of lineal time, of a past rendered dead and buried, no longer accessible, is disrespectful itself, erecting a barrier to the once viable interactions with one's animated ancestors.

The Shift. As we houseclean, throwing out such constructs as "beliefs," I'm not suggesting that there isn't a great body of knowledge, of *miyp*, "teachings from all things," of *tamálwit*, "the law," that is brought to bear in each and every experiential moment of interaction between Animal and Plant, Human and Spirit Peoples. The *miyp* inform the unit of references in each symbolic act of confluence of those participating. The *miyp* are embodied in the morphemes associated with each phoneme of meaningful sound, in each and every spoken word. They are embedded in the beaded design on a cradleboard or powwow dancer's regalia, and in the actions of the mother of the child and swirl of the dancer. The *miyp* are disseminated among the peoples through a particular learning style. And the *miyp* can be accessed and taught by elders and even by ethnographers, and can now be held in hand by you, the reader. The acts of re-telling of the narrative oral traditions of Coyote and Salmon, of the *'me'y'mi'y'm q 'esp schint*, embedded with layers of *miyp*, render the world meaningful, and indeed, perpetuated. The *miyp* are intrinsically infused in, a part of each experiential moment.

The shift is from viewing reality as composed of objects of some perceived permanency and an investment in autonomous "beliefs" about those objects, as mediated by the glass pane of dualism, to experiencing reality directly, as an interconnected event, as the transitory intersection of those participating. The shift is from viewing the Pythagorean theorem as a precise mathematical extrapolation of a naturally occurring right angle to applying a symbolic formula, $A^2 + B^2 = C^2$, that brings such expressions into being, creating them in nature and in the Parthenon. The shift is from viewing Aristotelian forms as observable in material objects to experiencing ultimate reality as transcendent Platonic Forms or "ideas," as the perennial "bones," upon which all of nature is a manifestation and reflection. The shift is in moving from literacy to orality.

It is a shift from viewing reality devoid of spirit, to experiencing reality as infused with spiritual animation and vitality, with *snqhepiwes* "where the spirit lives, from horizon to horizon," as *hewléexhewlex,* "spirit." The words and songs are not only informed by the *miyp,* but can be inundated with spiritual power, with *suumesh* or *wéeyekin.* Words that, when woven into the blanket of a story can *dasshússua* "breaking with the mouth", can "make the world." *Hnkhwelkhwlnet* is animated *'me'y'mi'y'm.*

The shift is moving from Cartesian Dualism and Aristotelian Materialism to a Monism and Spiritual Platonism.

And critically, the shift is from viewing the Native *'me'y'mi'y'm* as explanations about the world, as attempts at "suspension of disbe- lief" about reality, to experiencing the *'me'y'mi'y'm* as the world, as intensifying reality itself (Frey, Aripa, and Yellowtail 1995:175–77). If science is the "what" and literacy-based equations are the "how," in sync, the act of experimentation can bring forth a prediction about reality. If *hnkhwelkhwlnet* is the "what" and orality-based *'me'y'mi'y'm* the "how," in alignment, the act of re-telling can bring forth that which is told, bring forth reality. The *hnkhwelkhwlnet* transitory intersection is made possible by the *'me'y'mi'y'm* transitory intersection. In storytelling the world is perpetuated.

Head and Heart Knowledge are indeed contrasting ways of *viewing,* on one hand, and of *experiencing,* on the other hand, the world around us—very distinct mega-stories! Can it be more than just contrasting ways of *viewing* or *experiencing* the world, but con- trasting worlds made, indeed contrasting realities? Are we willing to acknowledge the possibility of multiple realities, of world based on a material reality and of a world based on a transcendent reality?

On one hand a reality made up of distinct, "split, dissected," quantifiable objects, of material reductionism, in dynamic inter-actions with each other, devoid of spirit, viewed from a position of hierarchy and dualism, viewed independently, as if behind a plate-glass window.

On the other hand, a reality of unfolding transitory experiential intersections of interrelated participants—human, plant, animal, spiritual beings, of equal kinsmen—imbued with spirit, an event in the making, ever unfolding, in the process of becoming. An *Ashkísshe* of ephemeral movement in replication of a swirling Heart mega-story. No plate glass here.

Held in your hand right now: a text understood as an object that seeks to mirror a reality of objects out there; *or* a text as an unfolding event made up of participants in relationship with each other, predominated by the voices of our hosts and the many "fam-ilies" of "peoples," as well as by an ethnographer, and by you, that is reality itself?

Rock formations along the Clearwater as stories of the Animal First Peoples. *Nez Perce National Historic Park, NEPE-HI-0959*

We can glimpse these contrasting ways of *viewing* or *experiencing* reality in the particular rock formations and plants along the slopes and flats of the Clearwater River in Idaho. They can be understood through a scientific understanding of geological and botanical processes occurring during a particular geochronological period in lineal time—a landscape full of "natural resources," such as basalt boulders and *Camassia quamash*, to be viewed, studied, and acquired. And those same rock formations and plants can be experienced as created through the actions of the Animal First Peoples, such as Coyote and Snake, occurring in time immemorial—a landscape endowed with gifts from the Creator, as embodiments of the Animal First Peoples, having existence, perpetuated and renewed during the re-telling of their stories, and as *qémes*, having existence during their re-digging from the earth and during their sharing with those in need. Multiple realities, co-existing, side by side, or perhaps one upon the other, or one inside the other?

Not so fast, perhaps it's not all black and white? In the evolution of Western science there have been detours offered, suggesting that Heart Knowledge and aspects of the Western intellectual narratives have some affinity, are not so divergent. While the foundations of the scientific method are anchored to the philosophical discourse of Pythagoras, Aristotle, René Descartes, and John Locke, along with others, there are challenges to an understanding of a reality based upon dualism and reducible to material objects. These challenges have come from theories such as monism, "idealism," and "process philosophy," and argued by such theorists as Alfred North Whitehead, Charles Hartshorne, and David Ray Griffin, among others. Process philosophy advocates an understanding of reality as process, change, and "becoming," built upon interrelationships... perhaps more akin to *hnkhwelkhwlnet*? And reflect on the rainbow and its transitory intersections of those participating, and how that instance resembles the assertions of quantum physics, particularly its Copenhagen interpretation and Heisenberg principle—the observer is incontrovertibly part of the observed. Did not the renowned physicist John Wheeler (1911–2008) also say that the "vital act is the act of participation"? And consider the influential philosopher Baruch Spinoza (1632–1677), who advocated what can be called a sort of spiritual monism. He challenged Descartes' mind/body dualism, contending that all of Nature was inherently unified, its substance ultimately indivisible, and that Nature was derivative of a non-monotheistic "God," much more similar to the Hindu Infinite and impersonal Brahman than the Christian anthropomorphic God. Nevertheless, these scientific and philosophical postulations have found little expression in standard applications of the scientific method, and "the shift" still has relevance.

◆ ◆ ◆

With his college degree, upon enlisting in the army, the young man was given an officer's rank. He would lead others into combat, and he took that responsibility to heart. Before departing he stopped in to have a good visit with the "Old Folks," the grandparents. A good reassuring visit it was. And just as he was leaving, Grandma gave him a small pouch to wear around his neck, at all times, for protection.

The fight with the Viet Cong was a battle unlike anything he'd anticipated. And after several months, among those he commanded, those he cared for, too many were being killed. His frustration grew until finally he asked his superior if he could leave the compound, not going far, so he could take a smoke and offer a prayer. To help get right.

It was a hot, muggy day, and the trail into the jungle ran along a stream of fresh water. Thirsty, he set his M-16 rifle against a tree, bent over and began drinking a little water. Just then a Viet Cong soldier dropped from a nearby tree, not more than ten feet away, with rifle pointed. He reached for his M-16, but as he did the impact of the bullet hit him squarely in the chest, and launched him back into the stream. And he remembered what he'd learned in boot camp, "you won't feel it at first, but then it will hit." He waited, as the cool water ran over his body. He waited. Waited. Then he looked down at his chest, and saw his khaki shirt ripped apart, the pieces of his tee-shirt exposed…and a small pouch, intact. But that was it! He sat up, then stood. The bullet had not entered his body. And one amazed Viet Cong dropped his rifle and ran. He lit his cigarette and offered a prayer like none other he'd given.

Upon returning home, the first thing he did was show the grandparents the khaki shirt, retell the story, and offer thanks from his heart. (Re-told from an interview with Tom Yellowtail circa 1976; also in Frey 1987:131.)

◆ ◆ ◆

Traveling in Agnes' stories? In the act of *re-telling* a lake is *made* blue? If retold, great stories will come? A burnt face *made* as a newborn child's? *Swirling* with Coyote? The sky *falling*? *Dasshússua*? From a knot on the Center Pole a few drops *emerged*? A *healing* Brew, dancers *becoming* Blue Jays, and the two bullets *lying* beside a young man? One *amazed* Viet Cong? And *hnkhwelkhwlnet*, that transitory intersection of the many participating, in orality, at a place…Rainbows all. The internal landscape of the Heart mega-story. I accepted these assertions on face value, patient, trusting my teachers, all along seeking to interpret their meanings. Now with a little better appreciation of the mystery, had I connected the dots in ways unimagined before? Had I explained *dasshússua*? Were there still dots yet to connect, something missing?

But I'm reminded of the ethnographic mission, to seek effective ways to present the connected dots, not so much an analysis or explanation, but a description of the stories. Perhaps my explorations into efficacy are less explanation and more description—Eliade's hierophany but another way to describe Cliff's swirling? And could that which had eluded being conveyed in print, in so many previous attempts, now be conveyed more authentically, another way? Aligning the "how" with the "what" of a mega-story? A better way to describe the elusive? Perhaps going so far as abandoning the time-honored "graphein" in ethnography? Leaving behind the written? And from that resulting depiction, could the collective stories of the indigenous be better appreciated as a cogent, coherent, and compelling body of knowledge and practice onto itself? Could those stories be of such value that they provide benefit to others?

Yet I also sensed deep down, I'd never ultimately connect the dots, never fully understand the efficacy of *dasshússua*. *Hnkhwelkhwlnet* and indigenous spirituality is beyond knowing, at its heart a *Great Mystery*, only to be felt. As mightily as I might try, there can be no explanation for, no mere description of the water flowing from that knot on the rootless Tree with a flick of an Eagle-feather fan, or the bullets received in the heat of a bar fight removed with a prayer and a root, or a Viet Cong's bullet failing to penetrate the flesh of a grateful one who wore around his neck a small pouch, or…of the blue of Coyote's lake. There can only be acceptance and appreciation, as you engage with others in these unfolding stories. While not giving up attempts to better replicate the words of the story, connecting the dots as a storyteller and retaining the bones of the story, I seek to transcend the description of the story. May the words of the story be lifted off the page, resuscitated and alive, revealing its *Mystery*.

And I awoke.

Sqigwts
"water potato"

Aligning the "How" with the "What"—
Bringing Forth the Stories of Others

With the shovels in the back of the pickup, we drive to the shores of the lake. Each year in October, on the fourth Friday of the month, two men, an elder and another man, often joined by other adults and children, dig into the mud and gather the water potato tubers. They gather the water potatoes for their own families and for all the Schitsu'umsh families, that they "may be nourished a little." Over the next several days, other Schitsu'umsh will also go to the lake's shore and gather the water potato.

After we arrive and share a warm greeting on a day that is often rainy and cold, the elder sings one of his *suumesh* (spiritual) songs and offers words. The prayer asked *Amotqn*, the Creator, for a good gathering of the *sqigwts*, "water potato,"

Flowering water potato. *Frey 1997*

199

that all those gathered here would be safe as they dug, that the many who could not make it down here today would be blessed by these "gifts," and he gave *lim lemt.sh*, "thanks."

There, do you see him? A muskrat is swimming close by, toward a thick stand of cattails emerging from the mud just along the shoreline of the lake. The elder watches closely the movement of muskrat and then says aloud, *"lim lemt.sh."* And so, we'd been instructed where to begin to dig. But we're also told that we're not to take from the muskrat. Nothing on the surface of the mud marked what we were seeking. Earlier that summer, the cattails intermingled with a "broad-leafed" water potato plant, with delicate white flowers. Today there is no visible sign of the plant.

Almost right away, about six to eight inches down, our shovels found the first water potato. It is a tuber about two inches long and three-quarters-of-an-inch around, with a brown skin covering; its botanical binomial name—*Sagittaria latifolia.* As it is partially cleaned, the others stop their digging and briefly glance at it in silence. With a second and third shovel, more water potatoes are revealed. Some are smaller, an inch or so, but most are larger, up to three and a half inches in length. Within an hour, all the water potatoes needed this year are gathered. Some years, more would be gathered. One of the men remembered how they used to gather "gunny-sacks-full" of the water potatoes, which would last through the winter.

The water potatoes are washed in the lake's water and placed in plastic and paper sacks to be taken to those who could not be here today. We're told that we can "prepare it just like a potato." As we're about ready to leave, the elder reiterates what he had mentioned as we dug, "take at least one of these and give it to an elder, or someone who could not make it down here today, someone in need of these water potatoes." (Re-told from experiences circa late 1990s along the shores of Lake Coeur d'Alene.)

◆ ◆ ◆

In my association with Lawrence Aripa, beginning in 1990, we loved to spend time along the eastern shore of Lake Coeur d'Alene, talking, with Lawrence reminiscing about the "old times." On some of those

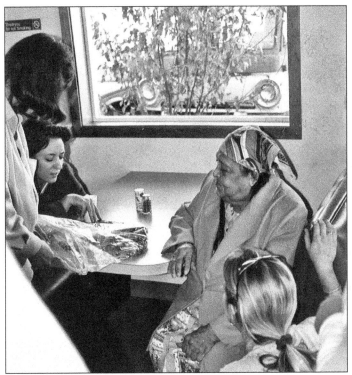

University of Idaho students presenting a bag of the *sqigwts,* "water potatoes," to Lucy Finley and other elders at the Senior Center, Plummer, Idaho. *Frey 1998*

occasions we'd gather *sqigwts*. He loved his *sqigwts*. In October of 1998 Lawrence passed away. I'd been told of the practice of providing a favored food for the departed. So just prior to attending the funeral and wake, I stopped at the area where we had spent so much time together, offered a prayer, and dug a few *sqigwts* from the lake's mud and then cleaned them. That evening I stood in silence and prayer before his open coffin, and placed the handful of *sqigwts* beside Lawrence. They'd accompany and refresh him on his next journey, with a taste he loved.

❖ ❖ ❖

The Coeur d'Alene call themselves the Schitsu'umsh, the "ones that were found here," in reference to *Chatcolet*, "Lake Coeur d'Alene," and to their creation story that places them as having originated at this lake. And it is from the waters and soils of this lake that one of their traditional root foods has flourished and has nourished: *sqigwts,* "water potato" *Sagittaria latifolia.* It is a root that is celebrated each August with "Water Potato Day," when area students, from on and off the reservation, arrive to gather them, under the guidance of elders. When asked in 2014 which plant or animal species should be the focus of a newly initiated research project, the immediate and unanimous response by the members of the Coeur d'Alene Cultural Committee, elders and traditionalists, was *sqigwts,* it so closely associated with their tribal identity.

◆ ◆ ◆

Sqigwts.org was a proof-in-concept project, developed during 2014–15, that sought to demonstrate the relevance of indigenous knowledge and practice that, in concert with scientific knowledge, could offer unique insights in addressing issues associated with climate change. For me this was an exciting next ethnographic step, bringing to bear literally decades of research, seeking to bring the indigenous to the forefront of conversation in a real-world application.

To accomplish the project's objective, the body of Schitsu'umsh knowledge and practice associated with the test case, *sqigwts,* first needed to be identified and described. As the funding for the project came through the Department of the Interior Northwest Climate Science Center and the USGS National Climate Change and Wildlife Science Center, Schitsu'umsh knowledge and practice needed to be rendered accessible and meaningful to USGS climate scientists. But as part of the "give back" to the tribe, it also needed to be accessible to high school students on the Coeur d'Alene Reservation and anywhere, along with the general public. And all rendered in such a manner as to retain Schitsu'umsh meaning associated with *sqigwts.* And finally, could Schitsu'umsh knowledge and practice address issues associated with climate change? No small task.

Sqigwts.org was developed through an interdisciplinary collaboration between members of the Coeur d'Alene Tribe, including elders, cultural and language experts, and members of the University of Idaho, including faculty in ethnography, natural resources, data management, and virtual world design. Leanne Campbell, manager of the tribe's Historic Preservation Program, Jeremy Kenyon, research and metadata librarian with the university, and I were co-principal investigators. Primary to the team were CarylDene Swan, with the Coeur d'Alene Tribe Historic Preservation Program; Michelle Clark, Coeur d'Alene Tribe Language Program; Audra Vincent, Coeur d'Alene Tribe Language Program manager; and Steven Daley-Laursen, professor of natural resources, who provided administrative oversight for this project. Brought on at the height of the research frenzy was Brian Cleveley, senior instructor, Virtual Technology & Design Program, University of Idaho, who was our virtual world wizard.

This project was initiated and completed using a best-practices research protocol, including a legal agreement that protects the intellectual property and traditional knowledge of the tribe, while providing an avenue for collaborative research. Acknowledging the tribal sovereignty of the Coeur d'Alene, and as the project involved "culturally sensitive" information, only after a thorough review by the tribe could the project's cultural content be publically disseminated. It was approved for public dissemination on September 9, 2015, by the Coeur d'Alene Tribal Council.

The Challenge. As the research unfolded, it became evident to the team that what the Schi̱tsu'umsh defined as their indigenous knowledge and practice, termed *hnkhwelkhwlnet*, "our ways of life in the world," embedded with *mi̱yp*, "teachings from all things," had unique structural and dynamic attributes. This was no surprise to the Schi̱tsu'umsh team members, and I too had some familiarity with *hnkhwelkhwlnet*. As articulated in the project, while *hnkhwelkhwlnet* has fundamental overlapping qualities with what is typically defined as Traditional Knowledge, "TK," and Traditional Ecological Knowledge, "TEK," there are distinctions. Even more challenging, *hnkhwelkhwlnet* is based upon fundamental ontological (what is real) and epistemological (ways of knowing) principles distinct from that of typical Western worldview and science. And in its traditional setting, *hnkhwelkhwlnet* is passed from generation to generation through the spoken word (orality) and storytelling, what is termed, *'me'y'mi'y'm*, "telling stories," and of course not via the written word (literacy).

How were we to describe *hnkhwelkhwlnet* that did not conform to established definitions of indigenous knowledge/practice? How is phenomena to be described that was itself not predicated on Cartesian Dualism—the unequivocal separation of thought/mind and material/body, but based on a participatory monism? How is phenomena to be described that was itself not subject to Aristotelian Material Reductionism—the causal primacy of what is empirically physical, on objects, but as an unfolding transitory event in which the spiritual is primary? How is phenomena to be described that was itself not predicated on literacy-based communications—predicated not on writing, but on orality?

Given these unique structural and dynamic attributes, how is *hnkhwelkhwlnet* to be rendered accessible, authentic, and applicable to climate scientists, as well as high school students, and even the general public? And given one of our primary target audiences, i.e., USGS climate scientists and the standard means by which these scientist access data, how is *hnkhwelkhwlnet* to be linked to and placed within an International Standards Organization (ISO) metadata repository predicated on scientific geo-spatial scheme, which can result in "scientizing the indigenous"? And overarching it all, given the ontological and epistemological schism between *hnkhwelkhwlnet* and the scientific, how are these two seemingly "mutually exclusive" epistemologies to be mediated? A lot of challenging questions framed this "proof-in-concept" project.

In all the research collaborations I've been involved with, this attempt to define what is so elusive comes closer to precisely putting into action and words the essence of indigenous knowledge and practice. While overlapping, this articulation goes deeper than, with critical distinctions separating it from other standard definitions of the indigenous, and significantly adds to the "TK" and "TEK" discussions. The team identified and described the unique structural and dynamic attributes of *hnkhwelkhwlnet* as: "Phenomena precipitated into existence as a transitory intersection of those participating—human, animal, plant, water, rock, spirit—all of which is anchored in place-based perennial, the *miyp*, 'teachings from all things,' that are conveyed through orality-based communications. It is an event made real by those participating, their relationships with each other guided and rendered meaningful by the oral traditions of a specific landscape."

The key dynamic and structural *hnkhwelkhwlnet* attributes are:

- transitory event, unfolding process (a reality not focused on and reducible to its discrete, physical objects),
- participatory (human not detached, not as an observer of the world), and actively engaged, attentiveness (human not as passive),
- collective and relational with other participants, including spiritual participants (the individual not in isolation, not autonomous from others),
- place-based to a specific landscape (not abstracted),
- orality-based (not literacy-based), and
- perennial teachings, intergenerationally disseminated, derived from the Creator and Animal First Peoples (not human invented meaning).

In attempting to convey *hnkhwelkhwlnet,* the research project not only sought to identify its unique content attributes, but also sought to present it in a format and means consistent with that content. As there is an unequivocal relationship between "what" is conveyed and "how" it is conveyed, drawing upon how the Schi̲tsu'umsh pass on these teachings we explored the dynamics and structures of traditional storytelling techniques. And as you would expect, there is a most intriguing alignment of *'me'y'mi'y'm* attributes with those of *hnkhwelkhwlnet,* the "what" with the "how." The key dynamic and structural *'me'y'mi'y'm* attributes are:

- unfolding storyline event,
- traveling a landscape,

- convergence of those attentively participating,
- experience unique to each participant,
- collectively relational, and
- orality-based, revealing of embedded perennial teachings

The Resolution. Taking my cue from the potentialities of the L3 modules and one of my graduate student's DVD thesis, and one morning in a chance conversation with Brian Cleveley at Starbucks, the application of another form of emerging technology would help realize the Sqigwts.org project and address the challenge. In searching for the elusive format that aligned the "how" and "what," an alternative means of conveying indigenous knowledge and practice through an interactive, 3-D Landscape was developed using virtual world technology. We would be giving up the pen for keyboard coding—this was ethnography conveyed through virtual reality (VR). Built upon a platform using virtual world technology and design (VTD), the structures and dynamics of the 3-D Landscape entail users taking the form of "representatives," i.e., avatars visible to others. With auditory and visual sensations, the representatives, each with their own profiles, interact in a computer-simulated world of perceptual stimuli, who in turn, can manipulate elements of the modeled world and thus "*experience* a degree of presence." Consider this intriguing alignment. The key dynamic and structural interactive 3-D Landscape attributes are:

- unfolding event,
- convergence of those attentively participating,
- avatar has a distinctive "profile," which influences the experience,
- collective,
- can be orality-based,
- traveling a territory, and
- discovery of embedded lessons.

We have sought to incorporate the critical structural and dynamic attributes in a *'me'y'mi'y'm* event into an interactive 3-D Landscape as the means for users to better gain insights into the meaning of the Schitsu'umsh *hnkhwelkhwlnet* associated with *sqigwts*. As with the storyteller's techniques of retelling a story, this format is but another

This virtual campfire scene is an example of the Sqigwts.org 3-D landscape.

means, the "how," of putting "flesh and muscle" on the "bones," the "what," the *miyp* embedded in the *hnkhwelkhwlnet*. Each is in alignment with the other. This dynamic means provided access to what is steadfast, allowing the user, as a participant, to experience a story coming alive, revealing its *miyp*. The 3-D pedagogy allows users the opportunity to "discover" perennial indigenous teachings, to make "interpretations" of their Schitsu'umsh experiences, and to apply that which is learned to one's life, to attain what the elder called "wisdom." Given the collaborative nature of the project, as "authenticity" was a critical criteria sought in this project, the 3-D Landscape was inclusive of the multiplicity of Schitsu'umsh voices, reflective of their "original expression" and "genuine representation." Story and orality, discovery, reflection and interpretation,

    Discover Sqigwts.org

To experience for yourself the meaning of *sqigwts,* and perhaps have your own *miyp* revealed, a huckleberry or two, go to www.sqigwts.org.

and wisdom go to the core of both indigenous *hnkhwelkhwlnet* and the digital format—an alignment that had eluded me when using a literacy-based "how."

In my forty-plus years of collaborative ethnographic researching and writing I have never felt as if we've developed a means of conveying indigenous knowledge and practice with this level of authenticity and depth of meaning than as with the Sqigwts.org project. The interactive 3-D Landscape begins to address those pestering challenges associated with literacy, materialism, and duality.

While the 3-D Landscape can never substitute for the actual encounter with an elder as he or she verbally re-tells a story, with it you can experience a little of the "heartbeat" of a story. It is intriguing how this interactive format derived from computer technology, which is itself an extension of literacy-based communications, can align with *'me'y'mi'y'm* and *hnkhwelkhwlnet*, which are only precipitated through orality-based communications! The project sought to "indigenize the digital, rather than digitize the indigenous."

Even the ISO metadata repository schema, the access points used by climate scientists to flag, identify, and thus frame internationally and scientifically standardized, geo-spatial-temporal data, were modified to help avoid compromising the meaning of Schitsu'umsh *hnkhwelkhwlnet*. Jeremy Kenyon successfully developed appropriate adjustments in the language codes and ISO schema that helped "indigenize" the organization's metadata repository.

Be it a scientist from Washington, DC, or a high school student from the reservation, the user selects a representative that reflects something of him or herself. He or she then proceeds into the 3-D Landscape's muddy shoreline, embedded with *sqigwts,* meeting an elder and muskrat. As the dialogue unfolds, the user needs to listen closely and make appropriate decisions on what to do next, for example, to pick up a shovel, dig there, or share a basket of *sqigwts* with one in need. What is expected is not made explicit. If the user responds by moving the avatar appropriately, revealed in the action are *miyp*-informed teachings, a little *hnkhwelkhwlnet*. But if the user doesn't respond as he or she should, the avatar is returned to the beginning of the experience and must start over. If the listener is not paying attention and acknowledging his or her participation in the story, the story telling would cease for the evening. Even the muskrat offers guidance. And as the experience might be a little different for each story user, as a Schi̱tsu'umsh avatar, the muskrat literally speaks to the user. But the USGS scientist avatar can only pay attention to the muskrat's actions. When we were demonstrating an early prototype of this scene with our tribal team members, upon encountering a muskrat without "voice," their first response was, "why isn't the muskrat speaking? He always speaks to us." Following the digging of the *sqigwts*, the user joins the elder and a scientist, and is able to ask questions of the digging experience, questions relating to both the indigenous and scientific significance in the context of climate change projections.

With the structures and dynamics of an interactive 3-D Landscape the user can begin to appreciate *hnkhwelkhwlnet* as an unfolding event brought forth by those participating. The user can begin to appreciate a reality not reduced to its material properties, not estranged from participation, not seen as if from behind a "plate-glass window." This interactive 3-D Landscape can provide access to the meaning and significance of *hnkhwelkhwlnet* that begins to acknowledge and address the challenges brought by Aristotelian materialism and Cartesian dualism. The user can begin to appreciate how, if this orality-based, storytelling dynamic is missing, so too can much of the meaning of the story. The interactive 3-D Landscape can provide access to the meaning and significance of *hnkhwelkhwlnet* in a manner a literacy-based format cannot. It can provide access to the experience of what a "transitory intersection of those participating" *feels* like, helping reveal *miyp*-informed teachings, a little *hnkhwelkhwlnet*.

◆ ◆ ◆

It's so exhilarating to still be able to have one of those "aha moments." As the research was in intense mode, with deadlines approaching and yet so much to do, I was reviewing some of the key qualities and attributes we sought to build into the 3-D Landscape experience, especially in the context of the dynamics of *'me'y'mi'y'm*. The word "empathy" kept jumping out to me, so essential to *'me'y'mi'y'm*, allowing the story to remain anchored to its steadfast *miyp* bones, while at the same time bringing teller and listener into the story, bringing the story alive with dynamics and flexibility—stable yet supple. While juggling *'me'y'mi'y'm*, I considered the tribe's history, particularly their successful farming days, circa late 1890s. The Schitsu'umsh pursued successful Euro-American farming practices, having a deep appreciation and understanding, an empathy for those distinct skills, while maintaining their traditional seasonal round—stable yet supple. "Connecting the dots," and it hit me—the dynamics of Coyote's story parallels that of the dynamics of Schitsu'umsh farming and huckleberrying—each is story, in fact, the same story. I discussed it with Leanne Campbell and she agreed. We consulted Audra Vincent, and with her language skills, the "aha" was termed, *snukwnkhwtskhwts'mi'ls ł stsee'nidmsh*, "empathetic adaptability."

◆ ◆ ◆

Traveling in Agnes Vandenberg's stories? *Swirling* with Coyote? The transitory intersection of those *participating*, in *orality*? And now *traveling* to the shore of Coyote's blue lake and *digging sqigwts*, and *experiencing hnkhwelkhwlnet* for yourself?…Rainbows all. What had eluded being conveyed in print, the dots were now connected in previously unimagined ways, conveyed more authentically, more compellingly. The "how" better aligned with the "what" of the powerful Heart mega-story.

Could these dots be extended, flushed out a bit further? Could the story of a water potato be extended and applied to the dynamics of a living people? And there is…*snukwnkhwtskhwts'mi'ls ł stsee'nidmsh*?

Such a desire.

Stsee'nidmsh
"adaptability"

A Spinning Wheel—
Bringing Forth the Stories of Others

It was a pretty big camp. Some twenty canvas wall tents, numerous "tourist tents," a few recreational trailers, and the tipis surrounded the Sundance Lodge to the south, west, and north. Spear Siding was known for its strong winds, so many took extra care in staking down their tents and associated shades and canopies. Late into the night the inevitable arrived. Before long everyone had stumbled out of their lodgings and each was attempting to anchor a tent, hold down a canopy pole, or add an extra stake. It blew hard for some twenty minutes, but seemed much longer. As the winds subsided so too did the camp, everyone returned to their sleep as best they could. Only with the morning light could the damage be seen. Tables and chairs, kitchen gear and food supplies, garbage cans and contents were strewn here and everywhere. Latrines had to be uprighted. Some canopies were blown over, a few with canvas tops were ripped, and only the pole frames remained of shades that had been covered with brush. Even some of the wall tents needed re-staking. Then there were the tourist tents, some seemed secure, but many faced new directions after their occupants had to re-stake them in the dark, and a few were completely flattened. But in all the chaos, the twelve or so Crow lodges (tipis) stood beautifully silhouetted against the Big Sky horizon. As the wind blew with ever greater fury, these

Students and teacher putting up the tipi in Moscow, Idaho. *Author collection, 1999*

conical lodges grew only more stable, hugging the earth tighter, accommodating the dismantling gusts. (Re-told from experiences during the late 1970s on the Crow Reservation.)

◆ ◆ ◆

D'Lisa Penny Pinkham reminded me that Tom's Medicine Wheel has remarkable parallels with the tipi. She is Niimíipuu, an experienced teacher in the Lapwai school district on the Nez Perce Reservation and principal of the high school, with a doctorate in education. In a presentation during my Turning of the Wheel humanities colloquium, D'Lisa talked about an indigenous pedagogy she had developed for her students. Using the image of the tipi as a visual and conceptual design for a larger understanding of a culturally relevant curriculum, she pointed out the metaphoric relationship between the Wagon Wheel and the tipi as understood by her family. The tipi poles were like the spokes of the Wheel, representing her individual students. Each distinct, each with his or her own unique stories, and yet together they come to make up a whole classroom, as D'Lisa said, a "family, a home welcoming to others." Critically, the tipi was the place where the individual poles came together and were placed in proper order on a four-pole foundation, upon which the entire lodge was now secured. This place of coming together is called *tiwe*. It is the foundation, the center, the hub, where no one pole could stand alone without the support of these others. Once erected, the poles were then wrapped with the canvas cover and firmly staked to the ground. As D'Lisa said, "If my students have a strong, sturdy tipi, they surely can tell some good stories in there!" And they can withstand any "colonizing winds." When viewed from within looking up, or from the vantage point of an Eagle gazing down, it's the unmistaken image of the hub and spokes of the Wheel.

◆ ◆ ◆

Each fall, for the last eighteen or so years, as part of our university's "celebration" of Columbus Day—now reclaimed as Indigenous Peoples' Day—it has been important to help remind students on campus that there continue to be rich, vibrant, and sovereign Indigenous populations on this land. And that it was they, the Native peoples, who had already "discovered" what immigrants would call, through their colonizing eyes and actions, "America." I have my students, without much coaching from me, erect a twelve-foot Crow lodge right in the middle of the campus, on ceded lands once the landscape of the Niimíipuu. Among the tasks is aligning the lodge with the east, offering those who would emerge each morning from its door an opportunity to give thanks to the Sun. In so orienting the smoke flaps, the smoke would also easily ascend out of the lodge without the prevailing westerly winds blowing the smoke back within. In erecting this "four-pole lodge" there is also a judging of the placement of the two rear and two front foundational poles; the poles to the west slightly shorter, creating a steeper angle on the back side, the side facing the prevailing winds. Then there is the particular order of placing the poles onto the four-pole base. The placement will create a distinct and differing configuration at this juncture of the poles. A next critical step is in deciding where on the "lift pole" the canvas lodge cover will be secured, a point on the pole that approximates where the crutch is formed by the intersection of

Crow Tipi, outside Helena, Montana.
Frey 1996

all the poles, a decision essential if there is to be an even, narrow spacing between the ground and the edge of the lower cover. With the cover tied to the lift pole and pole lifted from the rear of the lodge, the poles are wrapped by the lodge cover and with wooden pins, secured down the front of the lodge. The ends of the poles are adjusted outward, as wooden pegs are pounded into the ground, tightening the cover to the poles and to the ground, top to bottom no wrinkles, tight enough to create the "sound of a drum" when the lodge is hit, taut enough to grab hold of the earth, especially when the strong winds blow. All in all, no small set of tasks. All the while, "the grandmothers are watching," as the owners of the lodge are responsible for erecting it to withstand the strong winds. Were my students up to the task?

The silhouette of this Crow lodge on the horizon, with its particular pole alignment and cut of the cover smoke flaps, help distinguish it from a three-pole Cheyenne or Sioux lodge; not bad information to know for a Native person traveling buffalo county in the 1840s. A Cheyenne elder once told me that their lodges were really four-pole lodges as well, though the fourth pole was not often seen, as it was the spirit of the people. "That is why when the United States Calvary attacked our villages and killed our people, they could never truly succeed because they never could find the fourth pole." Following a little prayer, the lodge in the midst of a college campus is ready to welcome its "family." Once, after we had completed the tipi, as the students sat huddled tight beneath the smoke flap, a small feather gently floated down from the sky. A blessing. My students while erecting the tipi, experienced yet another expression of the dynamic Wheel.

◆ ◆ ◆

Snukwnkhwtskhwts'mi'ls ɬ stsee'nidmsh was a critical *miyp* revealed through the research associated with *sqigwts* in the 3-D Landscape project. The expression *snukwnkhwtskhwts'mi'ls*, "empathy," combined with *stsee'nidmsh*, "adaptability," offers insights into how the Schitsu'umsh have engaged their ever-changing landscape.

Empathetic adaptability can be defined as the competency to facilitate a level of understanding and feeling of the perspectives and positions of others, which in turn, allows one the ability to more effectively communicate and participate from the position of others, thus engaging in multiple ways of thinking and doing. Consider the definition of the phrase, *hnkhwelkhwlnet*, referring to "our *ways* of life in the world," emphasis on the plural *ways*.

Empathetic adaptability entails the capacity to think integratively. Integrative thinking is defined as the competency to attain, use, and develop knowledge from a variety of perspectives and epistemologies. It entails on one hand the competency to *think divergently*, distinguishing different perspectives and ways of knowing and doing. Integrative thinking is also the competency to incorporate information across perspectives and epistemologies. It is the competency to *think convergently*, re-connecting diverse perspectives in novel ways. It is a cumulative learning competency developed as a result of a keen awareness of others.

Snukwnkhwtskhwts'mi'ls is the necessary competency that brings storyteller and story listener into the story, anchored to steadfast bones yet supple re-tellings, swirling with Coyote and bringing forth the landscape; it is the competency for integrative thinking that continues an adaptive bringing forth of Schitsu'umsh landscapes when new participants seek to join the storytelling and travel their lands. Such new participants include Christian missionaries and agricultural techniques and technologies, capitalistic economics and Euro-American-based education. Each can be incorporated into the stories, the bones retained, while new ones are also added. Each is part of a re-telling of dynamic landscapes by Schitsu'umsh storytellers who have retained their voice, their sovereignty. Not only is a tension between contrasting ways of knowing dissipated, but so too are the possible hegemonic forces of assimilation calmed. *Snukwnkhwtskhwts'mi'ls ł stsee'nidmsh* characterizes how the Schitsu'umsh have successfully engaged a history of Euro-American social, ecological, and religious contact, and how they will continue to do so in the face of another new participant: rapid climate change.

From a Schitsu'umsh perspective, consider the metaphor of a tree and its branches. Empathetic adaptability is the capacity of not only the branches of the tree bending with the changing winds, but even of the capacity of new branches, from altogether different trees, being grafted onto that the tree, while the roots of the tree remain firmly anchored to the earth—as if a cedar branch was successfully grafted to a cottonwood trunk. The branches remain supple and dynamic, adapting, accommodating, and even embracing changing circumstances, while the trunk remains steadfast and stable. This competency to be able to embrace multiple perspectives is based in *snukwnkhwtskhwts'mi'ls*, "empathy." It is based on a person's ability to feel, understand, and appreciate the perspective of another person. But the "roots of the tree remain firmly anchored." While having the ability to embrace other perspectives, empathetic adaptability also facilitates the anchoring of one's own perspective, allowing a person to maintain his or her core perspective or way of knowing.

Snukwnkhwtskhwts'mi'ls ł stsee'nidmsh finds kinship with other articulations and applications. It is expressed in the 1999 ground-breaking and seminal work by Fikret Berkes, *Sacred Ecology*, and his definition of "traditional ecological knowledge" (TEK). For Berkes it is "a cumulative body of knowledge, practice, and beliefs, evolving by adaptive processes and handed down through generations by cultural transmission, about the relationship of living beings (including humans) with one another and with their environment" (2012:7). Berkes notes that among the Australian Aborigines, TEK is more than a body of knowledge, it is a "way of life," the verb-based act of living and doing, thus very similar to Schitsu'umsh *hnkhwelkhwlnet*—the ideational conceptualizing and knowing, the *miyp*, are not separated from the "living," from the "doing" *'itsk'u'lm*, from the physical world, from the experiential relational connections of the many participants. Nevertheless the typical application of TEK by Berkes and many scholars is on the "ways of knowing (knowing, the process), as well as to information (knowledge as the thing known)" (2012:8–9), thus diverging from an articulation within which ways of knowing and doing are indistinguishably interwoven.

In another application, empathetic adaptability is akin to what is termed a Multiple Evidence Base Approach (MEB), as authored by a workgroup including such scholars as Karletta Chief, Kathy Lynn, Kyle Powys White, and Daniel Wildcat, in their "Guidelines for Considering Traditional Knowledge In Climate Change Initiatives" (Chief 2014:20–21, 39). MEB advocates for compatibility of multiple knowledge systems, including indigenous and scientific, when addressing climate change.

Empathic adaptability is not unlike being a powwow dancer. While wearing his or her "traditional-style" regalia, the dancer moves with reserved dignity grounded with the earth. But while dressed in his "fancy dance" regalia or her "fancy shawl" that same dancer spins and leaps with vigor as if soaring above the earth. The dancer is free to dance either style, but in doing so he or she must be keenly aware of the differing skills and moves needed for and etiquette associated with each dance style—aware that a fancy dancer wears two Eagle-feather bustles, a male traditional dancer wears one or none at all, keenly aware that the fringed shawl is worn by a fancy female dancer but not by a jingle-dress dancer. Yet another distinct regalia may be worn at a college graduation, indicating yet another set of skills and moves the dancer may have acquired. Each regalia is distinct from the others, each appropriate for a different path, but each can be donned by the same dancer, with the competency to know the difference. The dancer would never attempt to spin and leap while in his traditional regalia, though he might in his graduation gown! From the many regalia a powwow is made whole and one, each of the many in its proper order and place following the Eagle-feather staff of the Grand Entry. From the many individual spokes, spinning together into a unified hub, "as driftwood lodges."

And we are reminded of Tom's Rock Medicine Wheel, with its shared hub connected with multiple spokes. As with a diversity of branches, so too with the many spokes of the wheel, each embraced and, if with competency, traveled; the spokes/branches offering supple dynamics to the onslaught of changing winds. Yet the adaptive spokes/branches are anchored to a steadfast hub/trunk, to the perennial *miyp*. Change without change.

Withstanding the onslaught of various pressures of assimilation and genocide, from boarding schools to land allotment, from military defeat to smallpox, from poverty to discrimination, is what elders call "tradition" or the "old ways"—or traditionalism, another term for *snukwnkhwtskhwts'mi'ls ł stsee'nidmsh*. It is the bending with the winds of a tornado without breaking. It is transforming the rigid dogbane fibers into strong and flexible twine, into a "living bag." It is a traditionalism that is found in the anchoring to the bones of the Animal First Peoples, to their perennial *miyp*, while expressing and manifesting itself, its integrity and meaning, through ever-changing regalia and dance styles, through ever-adapting subsistence techniques, through ever-altering storytelling styles and techniques of the differing as with any re-telling of a Coyote story. Stable yet supple.

When I first witnessed a great forked cottonwood about to be cut down to be used as the Center Pole in the Big Lodge, I anticipated seeing something "traditional." After driving some distance, over forty of us got out of our pickups and gathered around. In prayer and with an Eagle-feather fan in hand, the tree was first smudged with a burning braid of sweetgrass and then offered kinnikinnick and tobacco burnt in the stone bowl of a Pipe. As the smoke, sweet to the senses, ascended from that Pipe, through its wooden stem directed toward the sky, so too did the words of the Sundance Chief ascend with the smoke, asking permission of the Tree for its use in the Lodge. I shouldn't have been surprised, but all the same, I was taken aback when a gas-powered chainsaw was brought out and started up, its sharp steel teeth easily cutting the Tree from its roots. No "stone axe" here. With steel axes and chainsaws, the downed Tree was cleaned up, limbs and branches removed to reveal its two great forks, though their tips were left green with foliage. The forty of us lifted and pulled with coordinated effort the huge Center Pole onto the trailer designed for telephone poles. Then back in our pickups, we were off down the highway, the Tree in tow to its destination.

I ask in reflection, had any of the bones really been lost, had any of the *miyp* teachings really been discarded? Despite the high-pitched roar of the chainsaws and the pungent odor of burnt gas and oil that enveloped the Tree, it remained the conduit for the prayers of the dancers to the Creator. The Tree continued to be the avenue through which a healing might come to an infirm grandmother or wayward nephew, the *axis mundi* for a special gift from the Buffalo, the Eagle, or some other Animal Person bestowed on a dancer. And from a knot on the Tree water was drawn and flowed so others could be refreshed.

The ritual expressions and styles of the Sundance over time offer an illustration of an ever dynamic yet tethered edifice. Today, many of the overt ritual procedures of Sundance are rather distinct from the Crow Sundance as held during the 1800s, even though the same term is used to identify both (Lowie 1935:297). The structural alignment of the Sundance poles was reflected in another version of the Big Horn Medicine Wheel, modeled after a tipi, though large enough to accommodate numerous participants. A primary motivation for sponsoring a Sundance was to gain spiritual power to avenge the death of a relative. With intertribal warfare the Sundance flourished. When the United States military triumphed and the conflicts resulting in death ceased so too did Apsáalooke Sundancing, all in conjunction with an imposed federal governmental edict prohibiting such "uncivilized, un-Christian" behavior. With the federal restrictions lifted, Sundancing resumed on the Crow Reservation in the early 1940s. The Apsáalooke borrowed the form of the Dance practiced by their neighbors to the south, the Wind River Shoshone, under the leadership and tutelage of their medicine man, Old Man John Trehero (Frey 1987:35-36). It was during World War II, when relatives at home sought to offer prayers to those far away in harm's way. Added to this motivation for the 1941 Crow Sundance was the health of the sponsor's ill child. It is this Shoshone-derived expression of the Sundance that is witnessed today (Frey 1987:98–125). As dynamic as the last two hundred years have been, speculating on the Sundance of five hundred years ago, or since time immemorial, their expressions would likely be only vaguely familiar to us today. Or would they?

On this grand temporal scale, had any of the bones of the *Ashkísshe*, in whatever form and style through which they were expressed, really been lost, had any of the *miyp* teachings really been discarded? In the timeless *in illo tempore*, the Apsáalooke go without food and water, and dance hard, offer themselves in sacrifice for a loved one; they pray through an *axis mundi* and receive special communications and gifts of spiritual power and healing through that "center." The tipi of old is re-told, modified, its converging poles now aligned with a Center Pole. Hierophanies shine through, while history is trumped. Coyote's voice continues, accounting for and bringing forth the varied and changing styles and expressions.

American Indian religion scholar Joseph Epes Brown once relayed to me a wonderful story of "adaptive traditionalism." Joseph had spent time with Black Elk at his home in South Dakota during the winter of 1947, recording in depth the ritual processes and symbolism of key Lakota rituals. Black Elk wished to have the rites associated with the Pipe recorded, "for as long as it is known, and for as long as the pipe is used, their people will live; but as soon as the pipe is forgotten, the people will be without a center and they will perish" (Brown 1953:xiii). While traveling far from home, Black Elk was staying at the elegant Brown Palace Hotel in downtown Denver. He had a desire to hold an *Inipi* ceremony, which centered on the use of the Sweat Lodge. Normally, access to a Sweat Lodge would be no problem, but in downtown Denver? Resourceful and adaptive, Black Elk held his ceremony, right there in the middle of his hotel room with a window to an asphalt street of noise below. The Lodge was constructed by rearranging the chairs, covering them with blankets from his bed, and leaving an opening to the east. A few loose bricks from the fireplace wall were heated red-hot in that fireplace, placed in an ash bucket, and the bucket placed in the middle of the little Lodge. With a pitcher of water and a cup to ladle the water over the bricks, steam and prayers rose from that Sweat Lodge, in the middle of downtown Denver. And a soul was cleansed "from the inside out," a body reborn, words were shared from the heart with *Wakan-Tanka*, the Great Spirit, words to nurture and protect the "two-leggeds, the four-leggeds, the winged ones," "all my relations." Even in this altered form and style of presentation, the sacredness and efficacy of the *Inipi*, this rite of purification, was in no way compromised, its hallowed center found amongst the concrete and steel of the Brown Palace. In the context of our discussion of the Wheel, it is worth noting that, like Tom Yellowtail, Black Elk too traveled many seemingly disparate paths, without conflict. While having received a powerful vision as a youth and throughout his life traveling "the good red road," and as the "keeper of the sacred pipe" for his people, Black Elk was also a practicing Catholic and could perform the rite of catechism.

We can witness another example of empathetic adaptive traditionalism in how the Schitsu'umsh have engaged their intimate kinship-based relationship with plants and their landscape in an ever-changing context (Frey 2001:6, 10, 155–64, 172–76). In the instance of *sqha'wlutqhwe'*—camas, *Camassia quamash*—there remains is a strong reciprocal relation between "kinsmen" into the twenty-first century. For the human, there is still a responsibility for acquiring a vast level of *miyp* knowledge, including a keen awareness of the seasonal cycles and unique weather patterns that effect location and timing of the digging, as well as the obligation for acts of prayer and respect during and after the digging. Before the steel-blade of the *pitse'* digging stick, replacing its wooden predecessor, pierces and loosens the earth around the camas tuber, a prayer to *Amotqn*, "the Creator" and to the *sqha'wlutqhwe'* is given, asking permission to gather the tubers. A small gift of tobacco might also be offered, tobacco from a store-bought cigarette. Only that amount of camas needed by the family would be dug, never more. For its part, the *sqha'wlutqhwe'* responds with its own gift of nutrition, feeding the body and the spirit of humans. As noted previously, camas, when annually dug in this manner, responds by producing larger tubers when compared to camas left in the "wild," void of human interaction. Once dug and prepared, the human also has the responsibility of sharing the camas with those in need, and not hoarding it for self-gain.

Hudson's Bay Company fur traders and trappers first settled at Spokane House in 1810, down river from Spokane Falls, and by the mid-1820s were being observed by the Schitsu'umsh successively planting and digging white potatoes. By 1843, the Schitsu'umsh had applied their camas knowledge and techniques to this newly introduced plant and were annually digging white potatoes (Frey and the Schitsu'umsh 2001:59–61, 73–75).

The Schitsu'umsh continued to be adaptive innovators, applying traditional *miyp* knowledge to new opportunities, and by the late 1890s they were among the most successful, self-sufficient farmers on the Palouse. Schitsu'umsh agricultural success was most noticeable for families along the Hangman Creek region and particularly after 1892. That year the tribe received a half-million dollars from the United States in compensation for ceding their northern territory as part of the Indian Commission's 1889 agreement. The money was divided equally among the families, each member receiving an approximate $1,000 per capita payment. Most funds were, in turn, invested in state-of-the-art farm implements, wire fencing, and work horses. According to the reports of the Indian agents, wheat production alone rose from 8,000 bushels in 1892 to 27,600 in 1893, to 45,000 in 1894, and in 1896 to 100,000 bushels. Besides wheat and potatoes, Schitsu'umsh families were successfully raising oats, peas, and hay for cash income. This level of production suggests going beyond the subsistence needs of individual nuclear families to provide for extended families and those in need.

Some families had fenced farms and ranches ranging in size from several hundred to two thousand acres. This was the era when many families had two homes, one on their farm land and another at DeSmet. On the weekends, the families would congregate at and around the mission for religious services and social gatherings. As one elder remembered, this was a time when "we even hired Whites to help in the farming." He referred to this period as "a time of good feeling."

While their farming endeavors—noted in reports of the Commissioner of Indian Affairs—established them as among the most "successful" of all the tribes in the northwest region of the United States, their agricultural pursuits did not prevent Schitsu'umsh families from continuing their seasonal round of digging roots, gathering berries, catching fish, and hunting deer. For instance, the Vincent family, who had taken up subsistence farming, continued to hunt water fowl, dig water potato, and fish the trout of the lake. They hunted along the Little North Fork of the Clearwater River, and turned the "meat from over 30 deer shot on a hunt" into jerky. By the 1910s, the Schitsu'umsh were likely splitting their endeavors equally, half toward hunting, fishing, gathering, and digging, and half to agricultural farming. Stable yet supple.

While their success in farming came to an abrupt but temporary halt when the federal government imposed the Allotment Act of 1887 on Coeur d'Alene lands during the years 1906–09, the Schitsu'umsh have continued to apply their traditional knowledge and praxis to camas, water potato, huckleberries, and lake trout. The Schitsu'umsh are the oldest, continuous farmers of the Palouse, knowing how to successfully adapt, with changing technologies, to a dynamic climate. With their *pitse'* and plow in hand, with their adaptive traditionalism and *snukwnkhwtskhwts'mi'ls ɫ stsee'nidmsh,* the Schitsu'umsh can offer insights into our ever-changing landscapes.

◆ ◆ ◆

An outreach campus at DeSmet. In a partnership between Lewis-Clark State College and the Coeur d'Alene Tribe, I helped initiate, and coordinated two baccalaureate "learning communities," one in business management and the other in elementary education. An agreement was established between the tribe and LCSC during the 1992–93 school year. To better serve a place-bound student population, all classes were offered at DeSmet, on the Coeur d'Alene Reservation (with the exception of the senior year of the elementary education program). The business learning community began in the fall of 1993, with the education learning community initiated the following year.

What was particularly unique and exciting about the program was the possibility of completing a bachelor's degree in four years, while taking no more than two courses at a time. Because of the two-course load, students were able to maintain family and employment commitments while still going to school. Students would take two evening courses over a six-week period, with two six-week sessions during the fall semester and three six-week sessions in the spring, thus completing over the academic year the necessary thirty credits to stay on a four-year plan. In order not to compromise academic integrity, I offered some of the courses as linked. For example, the skills-oriented assignments of an English composition course were integrated with the content-oriented projects required in a marketing course.

The ultimate success of the program must be attributed to the students themselves. They were highly motivated and, as they progressed through the program taking the same courses together, they developed a strong support system for one another, "family learning cadres." When one couldn't make it to class, another took detailed notes. When a test was scheduled, the family gathered to study together. Knowing each other well, they sought to augment their family traditions, their *hnkhwelkhwlnet*, with new skill sets, with new competencies from another tradition. They embraced differing ways of knowing and doing, they embraced empathetic adaptability. As anticipated, four years after beginning the coursework we had our first graduates in May of 1997. It was gratifying to be able to provide stories of another kind to my Schitsu'umsh students who had over the years been so generous with stories they held close to their hearts. (Re-told from experiences in the mid-1990s on the Coeur d'Alene Reservation.)

◆ ◆ ◆

Traditionalism is thus not to be equated with a static or even stagnant community, but one that is alive and dynamic, as with a re-telling of a Coyote story from generation to generation, its style and techniques of expression accommodating the creativity and discovery of its varied raconteurs, as well as adjusting to external and internal pressures that would seek to knock the Wheel off balance, seek to bury the bones. While there is an unequivocal relationship between the "what" and the "how" of something, between the bones of an oral tradition and the style of re-telling that tradition, there can be multiple ways of re-saying the same thing. Take our experience of a transitory intersection of water mist in the air, in relation to sunlight, in relation to your perceptual and conceptual participation, as in the instance of what the Niimíipuu call *wacámyos* or in English "rainbow." Differing units of reference for the same referent. I can still vividly remember, at a Sundance encampment many years ago, listening to a wonderfully told story of a young boy hopelessly lost but eventually saved, "adopted" by the Little People. Almost immediately following this re-telling, another elder stepped in and said, "Oh no! It wasn't the Little People but the Buffalo People who took the boy in" and went on to re-tell some of the story her way (Frey 1987:156–57; Frey, Aripa, and Yellowtail 1995:71). I was never certain if the difference between the two accounts was in relation to *where* the story was being re-told, a sort of deictic technique anchoring the story to a particular place, as when we were just north of and viewing the Castle Rocks where the *Awakkuléeshe* are known to reside; or when we were camped at the edge of the prairie where the buffalo once roamed farther to the east and north of us. Or perhaps the difference was a *generational* distinction between the two raconteurs, a son and his mother, reflecting altogether differing communication styles, for differing audiences. Nevertheless, in both instances the same storyline was repeated and the bones of the story remained intact, the message, the "what" remained intact, differentiated only by subtleties in the styles of re-telling, in their use of units of reference, in their adjusted "hows."

I would have us consider that traditionalism is a timeless, re-occurring set of stories anchored to perennial bones. Coyote's story can be effectively re-told, be it orally in Apsáalooke, in Schitsu'umsh, in English, or in a dramatized school play or through a 3-D virtual reality landscape, by a son, by a mother, by an elder, or with permission, by an ethnographer, each differing in style, so long as each style leads the way to and is aligned with the indigenous perennial bones. The traditional ways of the Sundance and Jump Dance, of *snuk-wnkhwtskhwts'mi'ls ł stsee'nidmsh,* continue to reverberate, anchored to their bones, with renewing Indigenous meaning and identity for their dancers, in a historic world that has sought their demise. In traditionalism, the message remains intact yet styles differ; bones are stable yet flesh remains supple. The integrity and sovereignty of Allen and Cliff and Tom and Susie's Tin Shed/Sweat Lodge spoke is maintained; its path and territory continue to guide and are traveled, as are other paths of the many spokes in a spinning wheel.

◆ ◆ ◆

Traveling in Agnes Vandenberg's stories? *Dasshússua?* A *resuscitating* from the bones? *Swirling* with Coyote, his lake is *made* blue? Story *brought* to life? The transitory intersection of those *participating,* in *orality? Traveling* to a lake's shore *digging sqigwts,* and *experiencing hnkhwelkhwlnet* for yourself? Now *snukwnkhwtskhwts'mi'ls ł stsee'nidmsh* extended further, to a spinning Wheel, the swirling of the Heart mega-story. Tipis and traditionalism. Rainbows all.

But could the reverberation of anchored bones render a resuscitation closer to home, allowing me to connect the dots in the direst of moments any of us will ever have to face? Could the stories of others be applied to my own story? Could the macro be applied to the micro; could the stories that can heal humanity's relationship to the earth and color its lakes, also heal and color the self? Could something that is not, be awakened?

Snukwnkhwtskhwts'mi'ls
"fellow sufferer"

A Healing Story—
Bringing Forth One's Own Story

You never know when you might stumble and fall; get knocked off our path. You never know when you or someone close might face a seemingly insurmountable challenge—a dilemma relating to health, a relationship, a job, an overwhelmingly grave situation. How each of us responds is as diverse as there are spokes on a wheel. Each of us will seek out that certain path that best navigates the dark territory. The following is my particular story.

In December of 2005 I was diagnosed with third-stage Hodgkin's lymphoma. I was fit, or so I thought, age fifty-five, happily married, with a loving family, professionally successful, and was about to begin a most unanticipated journey that threatened it all. I blamed no one. In fact, felt no anger. But the cancer could not be ignored. Acknowledged as a huge bump on the path, to be jumped over, if I could.

Soon after being diagnosed I was having lunch with Cliff SiJohn, as we often did at the Coeur d'Alene Casino, but this time I was sharing a new development with him. His words helped initiate the critical path in my healing journey. Cliff emphasized the importance of appreciating the complementary, though distinct processes of "external healing" and "inner healing." He spoke of "Putting your full trust in your doctors, in the external healing" and in what he called, Head Knowledge. But he also stressed that, knowing of my own spiritual path with the Apsáalooke and the Sundance, I needed to pay attention to my "inner healing" and to what he referred to as Heart Knowledge. "To listen with your heart, be attentive. That's your responsibility, something you can take charge of; not your doctors." "Attend to both, equally," Cliff stressed. (Re-told from experiences; also in Frey, Yellowtail, and SiJohn 2008:188.)

◆ ◆ ◆

He stands there, in Eagle-feather headdress and beaded buckskin regalia, with an Eagle-feather fan in hand, sharing the podium with some of the world's foremost religious leaders, including the Dalai Lama. First speaking in his Apsáalooke language and then in English, Tom Yellowtail offers words of prayer for world peace and compassion for all. He is an *akbaalíak*, "one who doctors others," a medicine man, a Sundance Chief, and his words are readily received by the over 5,000 in attendance—Christian, Muslim and Jew, Hindu, Buddhist and Taoist alike—that 1993 October day in Chicago at the Council for a Parliament of the World's Religions. Like many others from his own community in Montana, he demonstrates an uncanny ability to speak and travel multiple and distinct paths simultaneously, for him the ways of both the Sundance and of Christianity. While in the Sundance Lodge, he dances with Eagle plumes, blows the Eagle-bone whistle and prays to *Akbaatatdía*, "the one who made everything." While in the Little Brown Baptist Church he reads from the Good Book and prays to Jesus Christ. Tom Yellowtail is able, with competence, to effectively communicate and participate with others, indeed nurture and support others, from diverse communities, so distinct and seemingly irreconcilable. He understood and spoke of the world as a great Rock Medicine Wheel, a Wagon Wheel, with its distinct but equal spokes and universal hub.

◆ ◆ ◆

How would I attempt to travel what I had come to appreciate as contrasting paths, so seemingly mutually exclusive, simultaneously, side by side? After all, the world of Head Knowledge is the world of Western biomedicine, of the physical action and reaction of scalpels, chemo drugs, and stem cell transplants, anchored in the objectivity of the scientific method, on discrete causal objects. The world of Heart Knowledge is the world of American Indian spiritual healing, of the pulsating force coming through an Eagle-feather fan, emanating out of an event, a transitory intersection of those participating.

Cliff said, "Attend to both, equally." But when we're confronted in our lives with such seemingly incompatible differences, when the "difference" seems so mutually exclusive, how are we to go about negotiating our way? How are we to effectively communicate and, in some manner, go about engaging, collaborating, with the many strangers amongst us, with those of our vast humanity? If we're to enter the Sweat Lodge of Heart Knowledge, would we have to give up our seat on the well-worn, wooden bench, would we have to give up Head Knowledge?

Where do we look for guidance; where was I to look for guidance? What huckleberries would I need to pull from my basket, to rely upon if I was to travel the mutually exclusive?

Wagon Wheels and Medicine Wheels? Sundance participants, Baptist parishioners, Indian Health Service practitioners? The interplay between the supple and grafted branches, the flesh, and a steadfast trunk, the bones? Between the diverse spokes and ubiquitous hub? The interplay between the unique and the universal, between our collective diversity and what we share in common? Are there lessons to be learned? Huckleberries to be placed in our basket? And how would I best heed Cliff's advice, attending to both the internal and external healing, both the Heart and Head Knowledge ways?

For Tom and Susie, the Wheel can facilitate the separate integrity of each of the many while embedding them within an interdependency of the greater whole. The Wheel can provide a map for traveling the many paths without dilemma, without having to make an either-or choice. It's a map that can chart a course, a map that can create a path when followed with competence. It's a map of the world, brought to life in deed and action, embedded with values of inclusion, of interconnection, of equality. Regardless of how seemingly irrevocably distinct from the other, the varied paths we encounter can be traveled without threat of their mutual exclusivity.

Competency of the Spokes. But it is a matter of knowing your map, of knowing its terrain. For Tom and Susie there was a critical competency in knowing which context and setting to be a devout Christian or a sincere Sundancer, a skilled nurse or a spiritual healer. Knowing the map goes beyond just acknowledging or even just respecting the distinctions of the spokes; it is hard work, it takes effort. Tom and Susie repeatedly demonstrated their capacities to effectively converse and communicate with Baptist parishioners, with Sundancer participants, and with Indian Health Service practitioners alike, of applying the subtle etiquette, nuances, and languages of each. While in such distinct communities, Tom and Susie worked with the members of each so easily, always in collaboration, helping sustain their respective Little Brown Church, Sundance Lodges, and IHS hospital communities, without mutual exclusivity. It was little wonder that Tom, like Allen Old Horn, was at ease incorporating overtly Euro-American images to convey essential and nuanced Indigenous meanings, like that of the "tin shed" or the "wagon wheel," with its association with white settlers and Manifest Destiny. It's a competency in knowing that only when the individual logs of driftwood are kept distinct and strong in relation to the others does the lodged driftwood survive. Tom and Susie, like powwow dancers, could effectively don the many regalia and dance the varied paths—"traditional" or "fancy" dance—distinguishing the unique and separate significance of each of the many spokes, when acknowledging the indispensable and interdependent relationship of the many within the greater whole—the Grand Entry.

◆ ◆ ◆

Around the same time I had visited with Cliff, one of Tom Yellowtail's granddaughters contacted me. She was desiring to "hear her grandpa's voice again." Tom had passed on "to the other side camp" over ten years earlier, in November of 1993. She knew I had an audio copy of Tom telling his Burnt Face story, recorded the summer before his passing. Her son was in trouble, going through a treatment program for his methamphetamine addiction, and the granddaughter felt this particular healing story would be of immense help for him. So I burned a compact disk copy of Tom's entire telling of the Burnt Face story, lasting over forty minutes, and sent it to her to give to her son's counselor. Though I had been sharing the Burnt Face with students for years, with this granddaughter's request came my own renewal with Tom's voice and his most cherished story. The timing could not have been better. Tom's voice would again be heard, giving life to Burnt Face.

◆ ◆ ◆

Re-telling of the Wheel and Burnt Face. In my own unfolding healing journey, I would attend to Tom's stories of the Wheel, with its spokes and hub, and now also to Burnt Face, the story of a rite of passage *par excellence*. These two stories would indeed offer a map, a means to meet the challenges, to chart paths through a dark territory—huckleberries to guide and nourish. A connecting of the dots.

The Wheel allowed me to simultaneously travel what seemed mutually exclusive. I gathered many of the "wagon wheel huckleberries" while on my personal life's journey with my adopted families. Parts of that journey are shared here, other segments are more fully re-told in the essay, "If All These Great Stories Were Told, Great Stories Will Come" (Frey, Yellowtail, and SiJohn 2008:185–205). I chose to travel the spoke of Indian Names, Eagle feathers, the Sundance way, and Heart Knowledge, while at the same time travel the spoke of chemotherapy, radiation treatment, an autologous stem cell transplant, and Head Knowledge—without discord, in balance, equally. I certainly brought to bear my own levels of competency in being able to dance the distinct and unique spokes of the Apsáalooke Sundance way and Western biomedical way, in my healing journey of 2006 and again following my relapse in 2009. I danced even while I reclined under an IV connected to chemo drugs and a small pouch of my own stem cells; just as I did with the spirit of the Buffalo.

As I sought to pay particular attention to my inner healing, as Cliff advised, it was Tom's most cherished narrative that further refined a path, that helped navigate through a most perilous and unfamiliar territory—a young Native boy would help chart the course of action for an adult Anglo man.

Without warning, we could stumble and fall, become ill. *It's evening…Over there, they're running through camp, chasing each other… and a boy falls, his face landing in the hot coals of the fire pit.* For a young Apsáalooke boy a face is hideously scarred after falling into a fire pit. And for me, a body infested with malignant cells.

Confusion and solitude resulted. *He comes out of his tipi. They gather around…they see the scar…Someone calls out, 'hey, Burnt Face!' Months follow, he feels bad, ashamed. At ten years old, the young boy keeps to himself, traveling* alone, *setting up his camp* far *from his family and village. Then it comes to him. He'll go to the mountains, to fast, to pray, seeking help.* For a young boy it is a life of ridicule and rejection, of living alone, as if without family, orphaned. For me it was the awkwardness of others not knowing just quite what to say, how to relate to someone with cancer, or perhaps it was going incognito, as my bushy eyebrows and graying head of hair vanished, along with my identity. But for both of us, the isolation was soon replaced with the loving support of family and friends. Prayers given, preparations made.

◆ ◆ ◆

Soon family and friends were making jerky and extra moccasins. When Rob Moran, my "elder bro," a Little Shell Chippewa, first heard the news, he immediately drove over, some 350 miles from his Warm Springs, Oregon, home. He offered prayers, salmon from the Deschutes River, and much needed laughter. I had a Sweat Lodge in my backyard, and the rocks were heated and we entered the Little Lodge. Rob brought strips of blue and white cloth and tied them to the overhead saplings supporting the Lodge's coverings, renewing its connection with the Sundance Lodge and to the two Flags of the Center Tree. With his medicine things laid out before us and the burning of cedar, Rob prayed to the Creator to watch over his "younger bro," and all those in need of help. Each week thereafter, Rob called and sent emails, offering a joke or a story, an update on the family, and a renewal of his concerns.

A short time later Josiah Pinkham, a close Nez Perce friend, had me down to his home, just south of Lapwai. He offered a Healing Sweat and meal of traditional foods. We were joined by two elders and his brother. It was a powerful Sweat of prayers, sharing, and heart talk. As Josiah said, "we wanted you to know that we would be there with you for your entire journey, we had your back." One of the elders, Leroy Seth, shared even more, "a little bonus," he said with a smile. As he sat next to me in the darkened Lodge, the steam thick in the air, Leroy began to swoon and became lethargic. Once outside and clear-headed, he told us that while in the Lodge he "heard a song, coming from near the fire pit, sung by the Little People or, maybe, Children!" He went on to relate how he had felt and shouldered some of my challenges, a "gift to you."

After the meal, Josiah presented me with a beautiful Pendleton blanket, while his wife, D'Lisa, gave me a candle in a dragonfly holder and a supply of *qawsqáaws*, a medicine root used in the Sweat Lodge. I had brought with me my Buffalo Skull, wrapped in a black blanket, a blanket Leroy had given me a couple of years prior as part of his giveaway, and presented it as a gift to Josiah. In the days leading up to the Sweat, it had come to me that the Skull should now belong to Josiah. I had received it many years before from Joseph Epes Brown, when I taught his courses for him during that sabbatical leave. (Re-told from experience; also in Frey, Yellowtail, and SiJohn 2008:191.)

◆ ◆ ◆

During the winter of 2006, Cliff asked if I would join him in his family's Jump Dance. His family welcomed all in the community, setting an early March date. Cliff knew of the seriousness of my health situation. Kris, my wife, and Jennifer Gatzke, one of my graduate students, also accompanied me, having done so in other

Jump Dances. Cliff often encouraged me to bring along some of my students. We planned to attend only the first night.

Upon our arrival that evening, as he had done each year, Cliff warmly greeted each of us with a warm handshake, saying "welcome home." Kris and I presented Cliff and his wife Lori with three small gifts—a Pendleton blanket in the style I had used while Sundancing, a smaller blanket for Lori's new grandchild, and a porcupine quilled Medicine Wheel medallion with an Eagle plume attached, which had been given to me many years ago by a Lakota artist. Soon the air was filled with "heart talk" and *suumesh* song. Someone would make their way onto the floor, offer heart talk of their family's joys and challenges, and then sing his *suumesh*, medicine song, as others would then join in, "jumping," dancing with him in support of his family's needs and hopes.

Well into the evening Lori asked if I'd join Cliff on the dance floor, as the two of us then walked counter-clockwise before the other participants, over one hundred men, women, and children. Knowing Cliff's eyesight was very poor, especially under the dimmed light, it was an honor to help guide Cliff around the dance floor as he sang his *suumesh* songs. And then we stopped and Cliff spoke. His words caught me off guard. Cliff spoke to everyone about me, my relationship with the Crow and the Sundance, what I meant to him and the Coeur d'Alenes, and asked, given my cancer, that all pray for my health. He then had me give my own heart talk. Alone, I circled the floor and spoke. I don't remember much of what I said, much too nervous I guess, but spoke from the heart.

When I completed my circle, standing again beside Cliff, he announced and bestowed a Coeur d'Alene Indian name on me, *Kw'lkwi'l Sqqi*, meaning Little Red Hawk. The name is in reference to the red-tailed hawk, explained Cliff to those assembled, "a patient and observant bird," who then "acts quickly and deliberately, swoops down, picks up what can feed and nourish, and shares it with his family, with others." And he spoke of me as a "patient observer," who then "acts deliberately," as he "thinks and writes about," and "helps our people." As we returned to our seats, Cliff took his red bandana from around his neck and had me place it around mine, and called me "brother." On such prayerful occasions the red bandana is worn with pride by all the members of the SiJohn family.

Having received this special name, I felt I needed to attend the second night and have my giveaway. But as we were going to our car after the Jump Dance, Cliff and Lori approached and insisted that I spend the next evening at home, resting, and said that they had already taken care of the giveaway for me. When we spoke next, Cliff said the giveaway had gone well, and the Sundance blanket had been given to a young Coeur d'Alene girl, now also blessed.

◆ ◆ ◆

For each of us, Burnt Face and myself, there awaited a long journey of humility and perseverance, of sacrifice and offerings made. *He travels alone to those high mountains of the Bighorns. He wears out each of four sets of moccasins his mother had made...There, high on the mountain, the sunrise and sunset clearly seen, he goes without food and water, offers daily prayer with Indian tobacco, with the carved stone pipe his father had given him. Under the watch of the Sun, he moves huge rocks, there, that one, and there, to form a great Wheel, an offering, twenty-eight spokes with a rock hub, like the Sundance Lodge. It takes him awhile. It's an offering, showing his sincerity, a gift to whoever might come, perhaps to the Awakkuléeshe, the Little People, who inhabit this area.*

My own journey involved travel to Lewiston and the St. Joseph Regional Cancer Center in 2006, and then to Seattle and the Fred Hutchinson Cancer Research Institute in 2009, undergoing days, weeks, and months of chemotherapy and irradiation, their chaotic side effects—fatigue, nausea, neuropathy—and an invasive stem cell transplant. Throughout it all, I assembled my own "rock offerings." Among the gifts I held tight to and laid out in daily prayer were my Indian Names—*Maakuuxshiichíilish*, Seeking to Help Others, the name Tom bestowed on me during a Medicine Bundle ceremony in 1977 when he brought me into his family, and *Kw'lk'il Sqqi*, Little Red Hawk, the name Cliff SiJohn conferred on a brother in 2006.

I also held tight to my gift of Medicine—*Bishée*, received during my fourth Sundance in 1978. This was a journey that called on me to be attentive to what I most cherished, and, with renewed vigor, to what I must do with these special gifts, these "rocks," now and throughout my life's journey. As I laid out my rocks I realized I had laid bare what was most cherished, attending deep to my bones and the spirit within. This segment of the journey was one of sacrifice and perseverance, in the hope that a healing would come, always holding tight to the special gifts, and my bones.

There are no guarantees. As Tom noted in his re-telling, Burnt Face could have perished high on that mountain. But the healing journey can also meet with success, with transformation. *And they do come, the Little People; they'd been watching him. They take him in, adopt him; he calls them his "Medicine Fathers," and his scar is removed. It's like a new born child's face.* On the Monday following the 2006 Jump Dance, I was scheduled for another Pet/CT scan, having had a baseline scan just a couple of months before, in December. Because of some intense night sweats, the oncologist wanted this early scan to make sure the chemo recipe was not missing the mark. On Wednesday, my doctor shared the results with Kris and me. There was no indication of any abnormality, no cancer! A little over two months into the six months of treatment, and there was no sign of my third-stage Hodgkin's, from my left-side abdomen up through my chest and into my neck. Incredible news. I am still amazed! I immediately called and shared the news with my Mom, son, sister, and uncle, then "bros," Cliff and Rob, then Josiah and Leroy.

This by no means suggested that the journey was over. The oncologist was very pleased to be sure, but the cancer, I was told, could still exist at a microscopic level, not detectable by the scan. So the chemo continued into June, completing the twelve treatments. And with the chemo new challenges arose, side effects such as neuropathy in my feet and later after radiation, diabetes and motor neuron disease. (Re-told from experiences; also in Frey, Yellowtail, and SiJohn 2008:197–200; the original impetus to share this 2006 healing story came at the suggestion of Suzanne

Crawford O'Brien, a revered colleague, who invited me to include it in her 2008 anthology of indigenous healing stories).

There were no guarantees that the healing journey was over. In 2009 the cancer returned, a relapse of my Hodgkin's lymphoma, calling for a more invasive and drastic approach—a stem cell transplant. My wife and I traveled west to Seattle and the Fred Hutchinson Cancer Research Center ("the Hutch"). As before, I sought to swirl with Burnt Face and a Wheel, charting the course that would again seek a new-born child's face, a scar removed. And this time my healing would also entail literally getting down to my bones, seeking a resuscitation from them.

I was most assuredly reborn as if a child, the malignant cells destroyed. Together with the chemotherapy and radiation, the Sundance prayers coming from family and friends, as with a pat of Tom's Eagle-feather fan, *baaxpée* entered deep within and pulled what had sought to knock me off the path. As with the waters of a lake, from my bones flesh was given color. I have no illusions as the journey continues, and am thankful for each day, living each to its fullest. Life so precious, that can stiffen so quickly.

Following the successful 2009 stem cell procedure I lost a lifetime of built-up immunity; the chemo and radiation had destroyed the malignant cells along with my resistance to the most common of afflictions. I had to re-take all my childhood immunization shots, as if a child, including my mumps and measles vaccination. I was indeed reborn as a child, reborn supple, able to now re-tell my story to you. As with Burnt Face, though an uncertain future, each day is truly a blessing.

A Language of the Hub. While at Fred Hutchinson and immediately following the stem cell transplant procedure, something else was lost, and something else realized. As part of my 2009 autologous stem cell transplant, I underwent two days of intensive chemotherapy and four days of Total Body Irradiation (TBI). The zapping went deep into my bones, seeking to purge my entire body of cancer. But in so doing, it rendered those bones lifeless, no longer able to produce the red and white blood cells and platelets I needed for life. Only

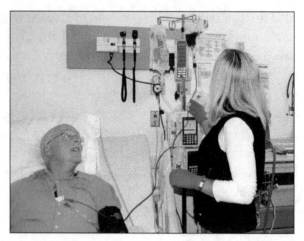

Receiving the stem cells and a few weeks later, a "pat on the back," Seattle, Washington. *Kris Roby 2009*

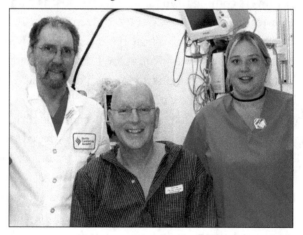

with the infusion of my own cleaned stem cells would my bones, days later, be re-awakened, my own resuscitation.

Those four days of irradiation in Seattle were the same days of the Sundance, held in Montana. My son Matt was now helping sponsor that Dance. During the past summer and fall of 2008, and at a Naming ceremony for a "granddaughter," I had been in conversation and planning with Janet and Rayburn Beck, longtime Sundance Shoshone family from Fort Washakie, Wyoming. They had become family, and we offered and prepared to sponsor the

Apsáalooke Sundance the following summer. Arrangements were made, people contacted, three Medicine Dances held, considerable funds raised and secured, with Leonard Bends, the Sundance Chief, agreeing to run the Dance. Then my relapse. And Matt would stand in my place, supported by Kelly, his significant other, and by family and friends. Matt would himself "go in and blow the Whistle" the following year and pray using his Name. As a young child during a Bundle ceremony, Tom bestowed on Matt the Indian Name, the *Awakúikiiaateesh* "little dwarf," saying "may he be as strong as the Little People."

As I stood before a medically induced ray, so too did my family and friends dance and absorb the rays of the sun. In a chamber of lead-lined walls, I too heard the prayer songs and stories of the Sundance and Burnt Face, re-sung and re-told in Tom Yellowtail's voice, played on a CD player. For an eight-day period, following the effects of this traumatic and radically chaotic rendering of my physical being from the TBI and chemo drugs, my bone marrow was totally compromised, shut down—I could no longer produce the life-giving fluids my body thirsted. I was no longer viable, but dependent on transfusions of the red blood cells and platelets provided through the generosity of others. The supple marrow that had flowed from and through my bones, that nourished muscle and flesh, did no longer. I was at the threshold none of us seek, but inevitably we must all confront and…cross over.

But out of this chaos emerged another sort of time and place. There emerged a liminality, a "betwixt and between," what Arnold van Gennep (1960) and Victor Turner (1967 and 1969) have perceptively identified and articulated for us in the anthropological literature. It's a "timeless-spaceless" domain, betwixt and between the temporally and spatially defined spokes. It's where and when you get one of those rare opportunities to truly and deeply listen, with few extraneous distractions, devoid of mundane sensibilities and concerns, as in the Big Lodge or atop a hill, or perhaps while on a healing journey. You get an opportunity to see what is right before you, but normally veiled by convention and establishment, to sort through to what is most vital and essential, a chance to take being attentive to an altogether new level. Something close to, if not absolute, clarity. I had visited with an *Awakkuléeshe*, then saw through the eyes of *Bishée*, and now...

Out of the chaos, during this liminal period following my stem cell transplant, it was not fear or anxiety or even apprehension I felt. Out of my lifeless bones emerged an overwhelming and crystalline sensation of what I can only identify as empathy and compassion. As I continued to walk the halls of my hospital ward, with life-giving IV fluids attached and my Medicine Bundle close at hand, I felt my heart palpitating, reaching out to those around me—some patients on the road to health, others moving in another direction. I had never before experienced such an innate connectedness, and deep attentiveness to someone else's situation, such an outpouring of unselfish caring for them—at a place transcending my physical viability, at a place eclipsing either Sundance or biomedical ways, yet inclusive of both.

While difficult to put into precise words, during my betwixt and between I felt the very essence and meaning of empathy, intermixed with a generous dose of compassion. In both expressions, the categories of "self" and "other," if not eliminated, are at least blurred, each to some extent an extension of the other. At the time I was not familiar with the Schitsu'umsh term *snukwnkhwtskhwts'mi'ls*, "empathy," and the aptness of its literal meaning—"fellow sufferer." And consider the derivation of the English word "empathy," from the Greek word ἐμπάθεια or *empatheia*, meaning "physical affection or passion," having its roots in ἐν (*en*, "in, at") and πάθος (*pathos*, "suffering" with "passion")—"in suffering." Resuscitated from my bones, through my veins and palpitating heart, was a new life and a *keen awareness*. The most powerful of awakenings.

Throughout my healing journeys, I was able to transverse not only certain differentiated spokes, with a degree of competency, but there was also this hub and rim of our "shared humanity" that I crossed. While engaging with oncologists, surgeons, and nurses, emanating out of Head Knowledge dualism, or while engaging with Sundance *akbaalíak* and family members, emanating out of Heart Knowledge holism, distinct from one another in so many remarkable ways, they all so clearly shared and extended to me a universal human face of empathy, care, and compassion, transcending their fundamental differences. That "pat on the back" can penetrate oh so deeply, be it extended from the hand of a doctor in a white coat or from an *akbaalíak*'s hand holding an Eagle-feather fan.

In reflection, it was a language I first experienced many years ago, with such sincere expression in Tom Yellowtail's face. I can still vividly remember, in so many instances, when a family member and often a perfect stranger, perhaps a non-Indian, would be seated nearby and convey to Tom his or her particular illness or distress, just prior to being "doctored" during a Medicine Bundle ceremony. You would see in Tom's face, his eyes, indeed his entire being, a complete absorption, a degree of listening that it was as if Tom had himself entered into and was experiencing the pain and suffering of his patient. And then a few moments later, with the Medicine Bundle opened and Eagle-feather fan in his hand, Tom would begin to "doctor" his patient as they faced east. The Eagle-feather fan pulsated over the patient's body, penetrating deeply, and then pulled away, and with it the affliction, pointing the fan to the East, "letting it go with the westerly winds." It's little wonder that Tom could connect so easily with so many diverse people as he stood at that Chicago podium in 1993. And do not all the great spiritual traditions of the world—Hindu and Buddhist, and Taoist, Jewish, Christian and Muslim—all affirm the face and hand of Divinity, of the Infinite, to be ultimately that of empathy and compassion? It is little wonder that Tom and Susie could connect and travel so easily with the many distinct spokes in their lives. A "pat on the back" now has such renewed and invigorated meaning. Empathy, a necessary competency to travel the diverse spokes. Upon reaching the hub, empathy interwoven with compassion, an omnipresent language.

Another Language of the Hub. There was yet another huckleberry offered that summer of 1974, a huckleberry that, like empathy, could provide a language that transcended the idiosyncratic spokes that can divide, that can bridge the seemingly "mutually exclusive" among us. Another huckleberry to navigate a dark landscape. Another huckleberry of the hub, of our shared humanity.

I can still see with such clarity that first meeting I had with Tom Yellowtail. I had phoned and asked if we could visit on a tribally sponsored project I was involved with that summer of 1974. Upon arriving at his rural homestead I found Tom tending to his pigs, fixing the fence that seemed susceptible to their burrowing ways. There was a calm to his demeanor, as he gently spoke to these large beasts in the tone I soon learned was akin to that spoken to his own grandkids. And we struck up a conversation. I was always amazed at the almost immediate rapport we had with one another, as if we had known each other for years. Yet we came from such radically different backgrounds, seemingly had little in common. I was the younger by forty-five years, very urban-oriented, from a middle-class family, shrouded in white male privilege, raised far from Tom's way of life. Yet we could relate and converse with such ease. We soon shared a complete trust in and with one another that would only intensify over the next nineteen years. But in reflection, how was it that two people, so different from one another in so many ways, could come to share so much in common, so effortlessly, so readily?

For Tom and me, an additional language of our hub, as you might have already surmised, was the power of story. It was story conveyed in narrative, in song and dance, even in a pictorial representation on a beaded bag, a vest, or a cradleboard. Through the sharing of the many oral traditions, through *baaéechichiwaau,* "re-telling one's own," and of our own life's stories, *basbaaaliíchiwé,* "re-telling my story"—of heroes and tricksters, of quests and transformations, of sorrows and joys and humor—we easily conversed and trusted, we easily transversed our differing spokes. Through our stories, Tom and I felt, we cried, we laughed, with remarkable affinity. Stories, the languages of our diverse spokes. Story, the language of our shared humanity.

Successfully speaking the language of story has meant having a competence to listen and engage deeply, with the heart, with honesty and humility, as Tom did often for perfect strangers, so akin to empathy itself. During the act of re-telling a narrative, done with all the skills and techniques of an elder raconteur, with all the power of the spoken word, the intention is to welcome the listeners and then transform them into participants, fully engaged within the unfolding story, traveling and speaking with Coyote. And on those special re-tellings, the Animal First Peoples "come *alive*...they *swirl around* you as the Turtle is saying his thing or as the Chipmunk is saying something...they *swirl around* you...this is Chipmunk talking to you...this is Coyote talking to you...all these things *suddenly come alive*." It is of little wonder that the languages of story and of empathy are fundamentally complementary and interrelated modes and styles of sharing and feeling between and among people. After all, if the storyteller and story participant are to be successful, each must have some degree of competency in *snukwnkhwtskhwts'mi'ls*, as a "fellow suffer," with empathy.

And we are reminded, as Cliff and Allen first asked, "When it is your turn to pray, what are you *going to do*, are you *going to say*?... What are you *going to do* with what you've been given?" To re-tell and bring forth the stories in action and deed is to also assume responsibility for them, for the acts of re-telling and *their consequences*. Story, in and of itself, is capable for great beauty...as well as horrific darkness. As expressed in the lives of Tom and Susie, it is the responsibility that seeks to tell stories that nurture, to heal, to create. And not to injure, harm, destroy. Not to take, but to give back. A responsibility to share with those in need. To be honest, respectful, and humble. To tell stories that have empathy and compassion at their bones. With empathy, we are able to tell and project stories of beauty, as well as able to appreciate the stories of others, be they stories of beauty or darkness. To have empathy for another's story, to appreciate it, does not mean acceptance of it. Our stories of beauty need to reject those of darkness. As with Burnt Face and Salmon, our stories should be animated by empathy, and filled with lessons of empathy and compassion.

It was through narratives—of Tom's Wheel and his Burnt Face— that a path was charted through a dark territory and maps offered to transverse the seemingly mutually exclusive ways of the Sundance and biomedicine. As a hub for a healing journey, what better way than with Burnt Face showing the way, his the universal archetypal "rite of passage" (Eliade 1954, 1958; Turner 1967, 1969; Van Gennep 1960). It was in seeing science itself as narrative, a mega-story, that allowed me to better converse in it—science with its own storyline, a chronology of historical heroes, with their quests and discovered knowledge, seeking to improve the human condition. Science at once a distinct spoke, while also story, allowing me to access and travel it and the many diverse spokes. And it is through narrative that the format and style, indeed the very content of this essay is defined and conveyed to you. These are stories that have created my world and redefined me in relation to my indigenous hosts, my colleagues, my students, and my family, now defining me in relation to you—they are "stories that make the world." And in their re-telling, they are stories offered to you, for you, the reader. Hopefully I've been able to re-tell these stories in a manner welcoming you within, as a traveler with me and my hosts, with Coyote and Burnt Face, and the Little People. And if so, perhaps there's been a huckleberry or two that was added to your own basket? Tom would remind us, that whatever irrevocably divides our spokes is not so great that it cannot be bridged by some expression or capacity of our shared humanity, through some form of common language, some form of hub, *snukwnkhwtskhwts'mi'ls*—empathy, *'me'y'mi'y'm*—story. And as one ultimate expression of our shared humanity, "are we not the stories we tell," imbuing and renewing at once, our origins, our destinies, our worlds, ourselves, for "in the stories we are" (Frey 1994:5).

◆ ◆ ◆

I had a giveaway during the 2007 Jump Dance, a year following the healing gifts just received. Blankets had been purchased and a short narrative was written and printed, chronicling my healing journey. With Cliff's guidance, on the dance floor I spoke of my tremendous gratitude in having received the prayers of so many, both from within the Big Lodge and Longhouse, and of the healing gifts received. In spoken and print words I "re-told my story," *basbaaaliíchiwé*. Gifts were passed out to all assembled. Following my stem cell transplant I again had a giveaway, this time at the conclusion of the 2012 Sundance. Again, blankets were distributed and a heart-felt thanks extended to all present, as I shared my name and my story. *He travels back home…returns to his people. They don't recognize him at first… They ask him to tell them his* name, *to tell* his story, *to his family, his friends, to everyone. Burnt Face re-tells his story…There, the trail ends.*

I am Rodney Frey, of German and English ancestry. I am Professor of Ethnography and Humanities. I am *Maakuuxshiichíilish*, "Seeking To Help Others," of the Apsáalooke Whistling Water clan. I am *Kw'lk'il Sqqi*, "Little Red Hawk." I've traveled multiple spokes, following the Sundance way and the teachings of Jesus, the Buddha, and Lao Tzu, sitting on the warmed wooden bench with Head Knowledge and oncology, while also traveling within the damp of the Tin Shed with Heart Knowledge and *baaxpée*. Each separate spoke brought me to the same destination, to the Wheel's hub of story and empathy. As I had swirled with the *Awakkuléeshe* and *Bishée*, so too did I swirl with Burnt Face, aligning with their perennial bones, if only momentarily. And from my bones a life was resuscitated, fluids again flowing from and through them. My bones are stable, my flesh supple. I am an unfolding story, perpetuated as I give voice to its words. I am an unfolding story, the transitory intersection of the many participants, anchored to my *miyp* bones. "Heart outpouring" palpitates from my chest, flowing forth with *snukwnkhwtskhwts'mi'ls* to the many. And I am thankful, thankful to the many who made this re-telling possible. I am, we are, a part of a *Great Mystery!*

In your hands you now hold my healing *basbaaaliíchiwé*. May its words and what lies beneath be lifted off the page, they too resuscitated, and a huckleberry or two placed in your cedar basket.

And I awoke with *such a desire.*

Ahkúxpatchiahche
"inner ear protruding"

When We Walk the Halls, Into the Rooms
of Strangers[1]

I suspect most of us, if not all, have experienced *walking the halls* of a hospital, hopefully as a visitor to bring support or a little joy to a loved one or a friend. As you've walked past doors, many wide open, have you wondered about those individuals inside—who are they, why are they there—each a perfect stranger? As a young ethnographer in 1974, working with the Apsáalooke to improve their healthcare delivery, I *walked the halls* of an Indian Health Service hospital, seeking to understand those behind the doors. I had certainly *walked the halls* in 1976 when as a desperate father I took my unconscious year-old son into a hospital for tests, then totally oblivious to the strangers behind the doors. But I was particularly attentive to those behind the doors when I *walked the halls* during my own healing journeys with cancer, in 2005 and again in 2009.

Beginning in 2018, a year after my retirement from the university, I started doing some deliberate *hall walking,* as a lay chaplain for Gritman Medical Center in Moscow, Idaho. I was one of eight volunteers, each of us doing daily rounds and serving on-call for a week, in the halls of the Medical-Surgical Unit, the Critical Care Unit, the Emergency Department, the Family Birthing Center, and occasionally the Infusion Center. The walking led me through the doors and into the rooms of perfect strangers. In each instance, it became clear that the patient was traveling along some stage of a journey, inevitably involving a crisis, either getting better or not. I asked myself how I, as a novice chaplain, could create a relationship in a moment's notice that best serves them, that offers an ear, makes a connection, that speaks the right words, in a poem, in a prayer? How can I jumpstart a caring relationship with a perfect stranger?

Upon entering a room, I introduce myself, with my identifying badge worn upfront, "I'm Rodney, a lay chaplain, a good listener," followed by "I've come to see how you are doing today." Often taking a knee, leveling our eyes, I listen deeply. I try my best at being attentive, picking up a cue or a reference. The patient's first words often lead to follow-up inquires, while all along, still listening. Revealed are a range of crises, each stranger's healing journey different from the next, each expressed uniquely. Feeling *joy* or simply *relief* upon being notified that they are about to be discharged after a surgery or long illness. Or *apprehension, uncertainty* in words spoken or written on a face, in the eyes. Or in one's final hours, *resignation* or *fear*, and then the *grief* expressed by the patient's loved ones. From *calm* to *heightened anxiety*—a multitude of possible human expressions. And, as the listening continues, each stranger carries a range of possible worldviews, of possible stories with them. From atheist to no affiliation or agnostic, to Catholic, Episcopal, Jewish, Protestants of various persuasions, Orthodox, a "born-again" evangelical, to someone practicing a Native American tradition, to a spiritualist, a Buddhist, a fundamentalist "end-days are upon us," to even a "warlock." Each different from the last, each unique from myself. So much revealed from under the covers of a patient's bed. And I ask, when I enter the rooms of perfect strangers, what is the quality, the capacity, the stuff that I need to bring with me to help create a relationship meaningful to each unique individual?

My Gritman chaplain ID badge.
Frey 2002

Stories. Doesn't it all begin with a story? At the nexus of our inter-actions with one another, is it not the stories we tell that connect us? Are we, as human beings, not the weavers of narratives—*Homo narrans*, or rephrased, *basbaaaliíchiwé*, "telling my story"? The Apsáalooke term speaks to the importance of re-telling those spe-cial events that have transformed and defined us—sharing them with friends and family, even with strangers, such as yourself, the reader of this book. I listen for and to the stories of others as I also dig deep and bring forth my own story, in ways appropriate to the circumstance. If I'm to assist another, I must seek to link my words and actions to their story, their words and actions. Offer that which resonates with each patient.

In my instance, my story speaks of the "huckleberries" I've received from mentors and those special life-changing events stored away in my cedar basket. Huckleberries pulled out to light a path, to guide, to assist, to help one's self or, now, in this situation, pulled out to help another in trouble. And I ask, can my huckleberries, now held in hand, be applied as easily as they seemed to have been applied to my journeys as an academic ethnographer? Had I listened well enough to my mentors and to my own life-changing events? Had I gathered the best huckleberries, the best parts of my story to now enable me, as a chaplain, to navigate the halls of a hospital, into the rooms of perfect strangers? Patients themselves on various life-changing, life-threatening journeys, with their own stories? The following vignettes offer brief glimpses behind the doors in a hospital, inspired by actual events, though modified, out of respect for patient privacy and their confidentiality. All patient and fami-ly-member identifiers have been changed.

◆ ◆ ◆

As I was completing my rounds for the day, the case manager asked if I could return later that evening, as family members were flying in to see their parent who was dying. The case manager mentioned that they were strong in their faith. I arrived before the family to spend a few moments alone with the patient, orienting myself to the patient's circumstances (hooked up to IVs, a ventilator, and monitors) and, although the patient was non-responsive, I introduced myself and shared words of comfort and a short prayer. Shortly thereafter, the family arrived, having traveled to Moscow from all over the country. There were five family members in all. Of them, the eldest was a "take charge person," and I think we worked well together. This family member was constantly asking relevant questions of the doctors and nurses and kept the family informed. Another relative called for prayer.

I don't recall the specific order of events, but over the next few hours, we orchestrated family group prayers, along with making sure there was one-on-one time for each family member with their loved one. Time alone, to hold a hand, to say what had been unsaid or just what was in the heart. A time to shed tears in private. At this ultimate transition into the mysterious, it is so essential to accompany the dying as best we can, if only briefly, with gentle words whispered in the ear, a soft grip on a hand, the tender rubbing of the brow, with a human touch by a family member, a nurse, a chaplain. At some fundamental level, the patient just might feel that love therein conveyed.

I knew I was not equipped to provide the form of prayers typically offered in their church at these stages of dying, but I did my best to provide comforting words and prayer. My prayers are generally ad hoc, not scripted, focusing on issues at hand and emphasizing the love of God. In these particular prayers, I referenced the Trinity and Jesus Christ and included the names of the patient and family members, as best I could. On a couple of occasions, I led the family in the Lord's Prayer. One family member specifically asked to have the 23rd Psalm read aloud, which was also shared on a couple of occasions. (I had a copy on my iPhone along with various parables and phrases from the Gospels I've shared with patients.) Throughout, I listened to the conversations and asked a few relevant questions here and there, getting to know a little of the background of some family members. I remember that one family member was particularly distraught, as in recent years they had lived with the patient while going to school. I don't think I connected well with this family member, but others seemed to provide solace. As we continued to gather around the bed, various stories were shared from the patient's life, eliciting a smile, a laugh, and a few tears from family members. Stories that bond with a life; stories that could bond with lives yet to come. In other passings, if not initiated by a family member, I'll ask if anyone wishes to share a special story. And a life could be continued after death.

I don't remember the specific time, other than it was in the early morning hours and the family members were exhausted. Getting some degree of assurance from the nurses that their loved one was not close to passing, we agreed to get some rest and return later that morning. That time came all too soon. I arrived just before the family members and noticed some of the physiological signs of impending death. As family members assembled, we continued in group prayer and encouraged each member to again have some one-on-one time if desired.

At some point that morning, one of the family asked my religious affiliation (knowing from the language of my prayers I was not likely of their church). In reluctance (as I don't prefer to overtly talk about my own story), and without elaborating, I said I was "ecumenical, inter-faith, having been baptized and confirmed in the Methodist Church, partook of the Episcopal Eucharist with my mother-in-law, and had recently become a member of the Unitarian Universalist Church." (At that time, it took a special relationship with a patient or their family for me to identify a little of my Sundancing story). It turned out that one of the family members was a practicing Buddhist, and familiar with UU. In this situation, my sharing likely assisted in our growing relationships. Fortunately, my religious affiliations seldom come up, but when I do identify myself as a UU, I'm very cognizant of the "baggage" Unitarian Universalism can bring to some devout Christians.[2]

During those morning hours, when it seemed appropriate, I did leave for short periods so I could complete my rounds with the other patients on the Medical-Surgical floor. But as the patient moved closer to passing, I stayed with the loved one and the family. When the patient finally passed, I provided a group prayer, referencing family members and the journey now being undertaken by their loved one. "The last breath here was the first in Eternity." I was honored to spend some eight hours with this family during their most intimate of transitions, this quintessential rite of passage for both the dying and the living, and to come to know and feel a family's love for a very special person.

As observed, any empathy and compassion I sought to bring was well expressed by each of the nurses, staff, and doctors that attended the patient and the family. They were calm and professional and did the little things that made all the difference—rubbing lip balm on a patient's dry lips, adjusting pillows, ensuring the patient was as comfortable as possible, bringing in extra chairs as family members arrived, keeping a family well informed, and offering warm and reassuring comments and gestures throughout. And given the many months of day-in and day-out stress and exhaustion, the care these amazing folks brought to a loved one and family was fresh and focused. As I start my rounds, I would always extend a "how are you doing?" to these special people.

Soon after serving this family, my beloved ninety-nine-year-old mother-in-law passed on. During her transition, surrounded by family, friends, and her priest, I heard for the first time the prayer for the dying from the Episcopal Book of Common Prayer. I was struck by the beauty and poetry of its words, so comforting, a prayer so appropriate for a Christian. Adjusting some of the words to better resonate with a particular gathered family, I'd use this prayer in future situations. One of those situations occurred all too soon.

◆ ◆ ◆

I was on-call and it came in early in the morning. The nurse relayed that they had the loss of a fetus, and the young parents, being strong in their faith, would like prayers and, if possible, a baptism. I told the nurse that I didn't feel comfortable performing a Christian baptism, but could offer a "water blessing." Conveying an urgency and unable to locate a priest or minister, she said they'd appreciate it. Upon arriving at the hospital, the nurse escorted me to the room where I met the parents and their loved one. Having carried the child for so long close to its mother's heartbeat, imbuing it with hopes and dreams and love, they were understandably very distraught. Sensing overwhelming grief, I offered my sincere condolences, and immediately asked, in lieu of a baptism, if they would like a "water blessing" for their child and for themselves. They agreed, and we proceeded in prayer as the nurse brought forth a dish of water. I focused my words and actions deliberately, purposefully, with as much compassion as possible. I spoke of blessings, preparing, cleansing, transition, and eternal love. The parents had dressed their child in the special clothing they had intended for the trip home from the hospital. Addressing the Trinity and Jesus Christ, my ad hoc words flowed, seeking to connect and comfort, culminating with words and water dripped from my fingers onto the head of their loved one, and the two who so grieved. Pulling out my cell phone, I then read aloud, as prayer, a modified version of the prayer for the dying from the Book of Common Prayer. Just before I departed, the parents asked if I'd pose for a photo, holding their child cradled in my arms. That was a tough moment to be sure, the child looking so innocent, as if simply sleeping, but at the same time I was holding, feeling such a motionless, cold little body.

◆ ◆ ◆

In the five-plus years I had served as a chaplain, I had not as yet served an identified Schitsu'umsh patient, although their tribal lands were just 45 miles north. And then one day the opportunity arose. As my listening and our visits unfolded, he identified that he followed the Native way, although he also followed the Christian way, as he said, "both prayed to the same Creator, who we call, 'the Old Man' or 'Amotqn'"—"the One who Presides at the Head Mountain." We had some good visits, as I attempted to soothe his anxieties and concerns, while offering ad hoc prayers addressed to the Old Man. Later he shared with me that he followed the Jump Dance tradition.

He also shared that his daughter had visited the day before and after both went outside, she had smudged and cleansed him with the burning of a sweet grass braid and prayer. "It really helped," he said. After I mentioned that I'd soon be traveling to Montana to attend the Crow Sundance and would have prayers sent his way, he said he too had attended a Sundance, years earlier. This was the first time as a chaplain that I felt comfortable enough in my relationship with the patient to offer the sort of prayers more overtly reflective of that which I speak in my full-moon, Medicine Bundle ceremonies, as we addressed the Old Man in our prayers. As with other patients, after each visit, as I'm leaving the room, I'd let him know that I can come back at any time, even two in the morning, just to listen, just to sit with him. And directly facing him, I would say, "you are Loved."

◆ ◆ ◆

In a hospital, I'm reminded that the entire length of a human lifespan is represented, from the Family Birthing Center to the Critical Care Unit to the Emergency Room. One day I had the opportunity to feel the joy of holding a baby, just days old. She was so pure, so beautiful, a precious bundle of Love! It had been far too long since this old man had held a newborn, though the striking contrast with the stillborn child hit home, nevertheless both were so loved, so precious. As I reflected on this new baby I now held, I thought to myself that I must remember, as a chaplain, each and every time I hold the hand of someone at the other end of life's journey, that they too began so beautifully. Their long, unique journey, full of life's joys and sorrows, of hopes and dreams and disappointments, is now worn on their face and in their soul. And this little baby teaches me, that each and every one of us, in whatever stage of our life's journey, after removing all the baggage we've collected along the way, unique to each one of us, we are ultimately, at our core, still what we began as—a precious bundle of unconditional Love.

◆ ◆ ◆

And as a chaplain *walking the halls* of the hospital, I ask myself, what in my own story, which huckleberries should I seek to bring to the rooms of patients, to add to their journeys, to their stories? How do I best jumpstart a meaningful relationship with a perfect stranger?

Empathy. I remember with clarity my first visit with Tom Yellowtail in 1974. I had seen Tom running the Sundance a few days before, a Sundance Chief, a Medicine Man, an *Akbaalíak*. Following the Dance, I phoned and asked Tom if we could visit on a project I was doing for the Tribe. Upon arriving at his home outside of Wyola, Montana, I found Tom behind some old outbuildings and a corral, feeding some six pigs. He spoke softly, with care, slowly and deliberately, and he paused periodically, as if listening. I would often see this demeanor when Tom was approached by a relative, or someone who had driven a great distance, or a perfect stranger, asking Tom for help, requesting a blessing, a prayer, some "brew," or to be "doctored." As the words of the request filled the air, Tom stood in perfect stillness, deeply attentive, nodding his head, responding with a "hum" as he gently yet deliberately grasped the hand of the requester with his right hand, while placing his left lightly over the clasped hands, acknowledging the distress. It was as if he took in the suffering, and I saw it reflected on Tom's face, on his brow, in his eye and voice.

Regardless of whether it was a close relative or a perfect stranger, Tom always seemed to connect with the individual. He built that necessary bridge of empathy that could usher forth care and compassion. The Apsáalooke term for "attentive" is *ahkúxpatchiahche*, "to have perked ears," from the root words "inner ear" and "protruding." While the years of ethnographic research I've conducted—using its participant observation and interviewing techniques and teaching the same to my students—contributed to my own skills in attentiveness and listening, my steadfast role model has always been Tom Yellowtail. As I enter through the doors into the hospital rooms of perfect strangers, I so often recall the imagery of Tom with his pigs and perfect strangers. And I remember feeling that warm grasp of Tom's hands enveloping my hand, that human touch, when I softly grip the hand or tenderly rub a brow at that time of transition into the mysterious.

◆ ◆ ◆

When I was first diagnosed with cancer, as you recall, I shared the news over lunch with a close friend, my Schitsu'umsh "brother," Cliff SiJohn. His words drew me back to Tom's Medicine Wheel and his demeanor. Cliff said, "You've got to trust your doctors and what they'll do. Put it in their hands. But you must do your part. There's work to do; do it with your heart. They'll be responsible for the Head Knowledge stuff and you'll be responsible for the Heart Knowledge stuff." Cliff knew I was engaged spiritually in the Sundance. And he said, "Be attentive." *Stmi'sm*, listen deeply. As Cliff had told me in the past of the importance of being attentive, "listen as the wind, brushing through the leaves of the trees, tells you something." And I was immediately reminded of Grandpa's demeanor with pigs and perfect strangers. I suspect Cliff's words could apply to any of us, regardless of our backgrounds, when confronted with a serious crisis of any sort. Each of us can and should take responsibility for our own Heart stuff, from whatever story it arises, from whatever tradition it comes. Each should be attentive, listen deeply. It is what each of us can do.

During both my healing journeys, I never really feared the lymphoma, never got angry at it, never felt depressed, never saw it as somehow "an enemy," to be fought, battled and defeated, though it certainly represented the antithesis of my existence. I knew that a dominant metaphor in our society for cancer was, "fight it as an enemy." But I recalled Cliff's comments, "You must do your part," reaffirming to me that I had a voice and a choice in the matter; I had some responsibility for my own health. As I came to this impediment, this "huge yet vague, shadowy boulder" in my path, as I saw it, was I to attempt to crush it with equal or greater force, with my own "rocks,"—something hard, dense, inert? At this most critical moment, at this crisis, with everything at stake, was this how I would define myself, something akin, reducible to that of my enemy? Or would I choose to engage it with something else, my own most precious gifts—the love of family, my Indian Names, the gift of the Buffalo from the Creator? Familiar with the *Tao Te Ching* from a course I had taught, I was reminded of passages inspired from it. There's no greater misfortune than feeling, "I have an enemy," for when you and your enemy are alike, there is no room left for your own treasures. When two opponents meet, the one without an enemy will triumph (verse 69). The softest things dissolve the hardest things, as water runs over, around, and through a mountain, rendering it but sand (verse 78). For me, this Taoist approach to my cancer helped bring clarity, conviction, and inner strength. I'd rely on another sort of "rock," and in the process, discover the source and place of my own bundle of unconditional Love, own resilience. My treasures had nothing to do with lymphoma, and everything to do with my life's story.

The lymphoma was as different as different could be. I accepted it as something potentially destructive that would accompany me in the months and even years ahead, indeed, for the rest of my life, as there is only "remission;" the door to this strangest of strangers, even if once closed, could at any time reopen. "You have to do your part,…Be attentive" Cliff said. So, I sought to live each day as a gift, thankful, and with the resolve that it would be a journey shared with my cancer. It remained a bit of but less a stranger, holding it at arm's length. In a sense, we shared this alike, my lymphoma accompanying me in each stage of this unfolding journey, an unwelcomed, fellow journeyer. Ironically, and I know how odd this might sound, but I would owe to this difference my gratitude for a special gift that was about to be bestowed. With my attentiveness, out of the *difference* would come….

Following those four days of full-body radiation in Seattle, there would be days and nights that for me seemed without end. I was no longer viable; my red and white blood cells and my platelets were no longer being produced deep within my bones. At this juncture in my rite of passage, I entered what is called a "liminal state," of "betwixt and between." Where all the superficial and superfluous in my life seemed lifted away, left behind, revealing a state not of anxiety or fear, but of complete calm and heightened attentiveness. As if entering a great hall, like none other, full of stillness and void, with walls lined with doors opening to what?

Each day, as I got out of my bed, I found myself *walking the halls* of the University of Washington Hospital, hooked up to life-sustaining IVs. As I passed by open doors, I was anything but oblivious, gazing into the rooms of perfect strangers. Each was on their own journey of crisis, some getting better, others not. I'd later credit my own hall walking as a patient as a great precursor for better understanding those halls I'd walk as a chaplain.

On one of those walks, while in that liminal stillness, which I can still vividly remember, out from the rooms flowed a totally unanticipated experience. With crystalline clarity, I had a sensation I'd never experienced before. An experience that would forever change me. Difficult to put into words; it was an understanding, a feeling of some intimate connection to another's condition, which minimized if not removed any separation with a perfect stranger. It was as if removing the distinction between "self" and "other," or even of dissolving the "self" into the "other." An openness and keen awareness of another's situation, almost as if two hearts beat as one. The words that best describe the sensation are a profound empathy.

Out of the stillness of that great hall, through a door opened, if only momentarily, flowed an intimate awareness, a deep connection with and empathy for the journeys of others, *ahkúxpatchiahche,* "inner ear" "protruding," and what the Schi̱tsu'umsh call, *snuk-wnkhwtskhwts'mi'ls,* "fellow sufferer." A connection whose possibility, even if only a shadow of the former, I hoped would await future encounters with perfect strangers. With the superfluous and superficial removed, at the core of our shared humanity, I felt an essential essence was revealed. Initiated by an unwelcomed *difference,* came a moment of *no difference,* that made all *the difference.*

◆ ◆ ◆

I've found that one way to help affirm to a patient that I am truly listening is to briefly paraphrase in my words the words they had just spoken. Even applying an appropriate simile or metaphor to encapsulate the patient's unexpected journey. Aligning my response words with the patient's, helps demonstrate attentiveness, a level of empathy on my part, in essence saying, "I got it, I understand." In conveying my concern and care in this manner, it can help build a level of trust and sharing. I've also found that in rephrasing the words of a patient, the patient gets an opportunity to also listen—to correct any misrepresentations on my part, and just perhaps, to see themselves in slightly new ways, discovering aspects of their own story that have been blurred or have never before been revealed. But of course, if my paraphrasing misses the mark, my words not aligning with the patient's, there might be an awkward moment between us or even an early exit from their room.

◆ ◆ ◆

The Wheel. As Tom opened the doors to perfect strangers, along with his tremendous capacity for deep attentiveness and his unwavering desire to assist others, I realize that there was something else Tom brought to his exchanges. He brought his "Wagon Wheel," with its many possible Spokes, yet shared Hub. It's an imagery replicated in the Bighorn Rock Medicine Wheel, assembled by Burnt Face as an offering while on his fast. An imagery seen by an Eagle flying above, in the structure of the Sundance Lodge, the *Ashkísshe,* "representation [of the world] lodge," and an image reflected in the actions of the dancers within. The Sundance Lodge is also referred to as the *Ashé isée,* or in English, "The Big Lodge." Linked with the term for the Medicine Wheel, *Annashisée,* "place of the big lodge" or simply *Ashé isée,* "big lodge." And then there's the imagery of Tom, standing in full regalia with Eagle-feathers in hand, before some 5,000 on a 1993 Chicago stage, praying to *Akbaatatdía,* "Creator." Beside him were priests, rabbis, imams, and the Dalai Lama, each praying with the words of their tradition. A chorus of many Spokes. And together, their distinct spoken words harmonized, interwoven into and from the shared Hub.

◆ ◆ ◆

He offered to take me in, a stranger, providing a tent to sleep in and a few meals, while I witnessed the three days of my first Sundance in 1974. Within the Lodge was the Sundance Chief, Tom Yellowtail, as he prayed for others at the Center Pole, and to whom I'd visit with in a few short days. It didn't take long to learn that this non-Indian Good Samaritan was well respected by the Apsáalooke. In the months and years ahead, I'd periodically seek out his advice and guidance. He chose his words carefully, as our conversations were augmented by long and, for me, uneasy pauses of silence. He was unusual in many ways. While practicing and advocating his Catholic faith, he also actively partook of the Sweat Lodge and Sundance ceremonies. Unusual in that he was a Franciscan priest. As he conveyed to me, the Catholic and Sundance practices were mere reflections of the same ultimate Divinity. And like Tom and Susie Yellowtail, Father Randolph didn't blend or mix and match the distinct traditions, but kept the Mass fundamentally separate from the Sundance, though he did burn cedar at the beginning of Mass, read the Gospel for the day in Apsáalooke, and had an elder pray in Apsáalooke at the end of Mass. It's intriguing that at the same time, in the same place, coming at the Divine from completely different traditions, these critical mentors affirmed the same conclusion.

◆ ◆ ◆

The pivotal teachings of Tom and Susie Yellowtail, in conjunction with Father Randolph, have been foundational to my worldview and my practice. They too had *walked the halls* of a hospital numerous times, entering rooms of strangers, attentive, offered prayers with Eagle feathers or rosary beads in hand. They could just as easily pray to *Akbaatatdía* in the Sundance Lodge, as to Jesus in the Little Brown Baptist Church or during a Catholic Mass. Susie, who had *walked the halls* of a Boston hospital as one of the first Native woman to earn a nursing degree, could just as easily listen, engaging with sweet grass or with a stethoscope.

As a result of their role modeling, of living the world as a great Wheel, I seek to align with and acknowledge the core of each patient, shared by all, while also appreciating and respecting the distinctiveness, worn uniquely by each patient. As with a macrocosm, so a microcosm, the exterior mirroring the interior. As the outer world is a great Wheel, so too is it within each of us. And I am reminded of the newborn within each of us. As each of us travels a unique, distinct path, seen clearly in our garments worn, the Spokes, at our core resides the Ubiquitous, the Hub. At the heart is that "precious bundle of unconditional Love," another expression of our shared Divinity. Consequently, I found I could just as easily offer prayer in reference to the Trinity and Jesus Christ (a non-starter for most Unitarians Universalists!), as I could provide words referencing the Old Man. And there are words in my lexicon, from a Mary Oliver poem or a Buddhist meditation, that can align and connect with and bring comfort to an agnostic or atheist or even a warlock. I view each of the revered words I use as "thought-coverings," for a deeper shared Ultimate Hub, in whatever way it is overtly defined.

◆ ◆ ◆

Prayer Words. At this point, let me offer a short reflection on the power of spoken prayer words. As so many of us do, I take the revered words of prayer very seriously. I seek to speak deliberately, purposefully, as my words have effect. The same word spoken can have many subtle but differing meanings. While also true, the same meaning can be referred to by multiple words. And in both instances, the words spoken in prayer can have even further implications. Here's my take on prayer words, summarizing some of my previous thoughts shared already. While a word is a "thought-covering" (a Buddhist notion), i.e., a morpheme cluster representing something, which thus accommodates the possibility of differing words referring to the same phenomena, e.g., the "Hub," that does not dismiss or undermine the animating power of the spoken word. As you may recall, I was first made aware of the power of the word while working with the Apsáalooke in the mid-1970s, at a time when a majority of the population were fluent native speakers (though certainly bilingual English). They have a phrase, *dasshússua*, literally meaning, "breaking with the mouth." When a word, spoken from the heart, is voiced, it has the potential power to animate and alter reality. This is why the Apsáalooke don't say "goodbye," it's too final, but say instead, *diawákaawik*, "I'll see you later." Hence the power of an Indian Name to affect the disposition of a person's life journey. When Tom and Susie adopted me into their family, during a Medicine Bundle Ceremony in 1977, Tom bestowed on me the Name, *Maakuuxshiichíilish,* and translated it to mean, "Seeking to Help Others." I've been humbled by the Name ever since, knowing its animating force, while seeking to fulfill its expectation. At the moment when a spoken word and those interconnected with it are inexorably linked to the Divine, the Divine can materialize into reality. This notion is extended further by the great scholar of world religions, Mircea Eliade, calling the process an "hierophany," a shining through of the Sacred. When symbols brought into action (the act of speaking words aloud, the making of a sand mandala, a pilgrimage to a sacred site, the fanning of a person with Eagle feathers, even the viewing of the white of a Church wall, if only transitory) replicate and align with the archetypal *axis mundi* or *in illo tempore* of the Sacred, the meaning and power of the sacred shines through into the world. The symbolism of the ritual acts and prayer words of the Christian Eucharist or the Muslim Hajj, both have efficacy. Whether it is the Trinity and Jesus or the Old Man I speak in prayer as a chaplain, or if it is *Akbaatatdía* "Creator" and *Bishée* "Buffalo Spirit," I speak in prayer during a Medicine Bundle Ceremony, all connect to the same source. From that transcendent singular Divine source flows the Sacred into our multiple material realities, infusing into our diverse lives. Spokes to the Hub, and the Hub to the Spokes, the power of words spoken in prayer, from the Heart.

◆ ◆ ◆

Helping me put this inclusive and rich Divinity into words, I've also been fortunate to have taught a seminar on world religions for some twenty years at the University. My vocabulary and thoughts have been greatly influenced by the *Bhagavat Gita*, the *Tao Te Ching*, the *Torah*, the *Quran* and the *Dhammapada*. The words of the Gospels have held an immediate relevance, linked to my upbringing and to many I serve. Several years ago, I had the opportunity to learn from the "Jesus Seminar," which involved over 200 world Biblical scholars who have studied in-depth the five books of the Gospels (adding Thomas), to better discern what are most likely the actual words of the historic Jesus. Their research opened for me new and insightful meanings into the Parables and key passages attributed to Jesus. And from the University seminar also came an appreciation of the transcending Infinite Divine equally expressed and represented in, for example, Krishna, the Tao, and Christ. The words of the many religions may differ, but the Divinity remains steadfast.

While only scratching the surface of their depths and complexities, let me offer some observations on the Spokes and Hub as reflected in a few of the world's major religions. While these are rather academically-toned comments, they relate to the humanity behind the doors of a hospital room, helping bring a little context to a patient's words or better framing any questions posed to a stranger. Most assuredly, each of these traditions have, from subtle to overt ways, left imprints on my life and soul. This is Grandpa Tom's Rock Medicine Wheel mirrored in the Great Religions.

Spokes. As we are reminded by Tom, the Wheel is made up of many different Spokes. The Spokes are the different traditions of the world, each with their own language, own rituals, own way of life. Each built upon and expressive of integrity. While each is distinct and unique, each is equal in importance and worth, none greater than another, none dominating. Each Spoke to be respected, of value. The Spokes can be heard spoken in such diverse languages as in the "Gospel According to John," Krishna's edicts to Arjuna in the *Bhagavat Gita*, Pythagoras's "Theorem," Emily Dickinson's "A Light Exits in Spring," William Burke's "Salmon Always Goes

Up River," Charles Darwin's *On the Origin of Species*, or even Niels Bohr's "wave-particle duality and the complementarity principle." The door to a stranger's Spoke is opened with empathy, seeking an appreciation of and respect for that which is distinct and different in the patient, their unique story, so I can align my words accordingly. Let's briefly explore the diversity of the Spokes as reflected in a range of world religions.

In the instance of Judaism, Christianity and Islam, they share in the stories of Genesis and the Prophets, such as Abraham/Ibrahim, who is acknowledged as the father of all three religions. The story of "Abram," meaning "exalted father," is centrally important to each tradition, dealing with the covenant with God. Yet digging deeper, key differences emerge. For Jews it is a story emphasizing migration, of a "journey" with God to the Promised Land and what it means to be the Chosen People. For Christians it is a story focusing on "faith," having faith in God while departing on an uncertain journey, and faith in the willingness to sacrifice your son, Isaac. For the Apostle Paul, as articulated in the "doctrine of salvation by grace through faith in Christ," "faith" is an abiding conviction and key to becoming a Christian (thus opening the door to Jews and Gentiles in the fledgling Christian community of the 1st century AD, as opposed to the Jewish notion of "birthright" as a key to membership). For Muslims it is a story of "submission," i.e., "muslim" means "one who submits to God," and it is a story of submitting to the Allah's call to leave a homeland and to sacrifice your son, Ishmael (who, with Hagar, goes on to establish the *Kaaba* at Mecca and the first *Hajj*). Submission builds upon the notion of conviction to emphasize action. Note: Jesus is considered one of the great Prophets in Islam.

As a chaplain, my spoken words can reveal so much. I often include the Lord's Prayer as part of any Christian prayer. But, as I learned early on, I must also be aware of the particular religious community to which the patient belongs. In saying the Lord's Prayer, it is meaningful when my spoken words are joined in unison by the patient's and family's voice. But I must also recognize the distinction between how this universal Christian prayer ends if my prayers are to resonate with the patient, as Catholic and Protestant endings each differ. To confuse them can cause dissonance and a disconnect.

There seems to be a worldwide sharing in the notion of "sin." From the Latin, *sons* "guilty." Of all the variables that we might encounter, some form of "sin" could be deep under the covers of a patient's bed. Likely not coming up in conversation, the concept could predicate, be subsumed within a conversation. I'll define "sin" generically as a transgression against the ethical and moral teachings of a tradition. While many world religions share this or a comparable concept, once we dig deeper, there too are nuanced and even fundamental differing meanings, with big implications. For example, how sin is conceptualized can relate to how the afterlife is understood, which itself could also be deep under the covers of a patient's bed, in the back of their thoughts and feelings. A casual misuse of the term "sin" on my part, even if assumptive embedded in our dialogue, can lead to misunderstandings and a shortened visit with a patient. The following discussion highlights some of the diversity and subtle differences in how "sin" is understood by the world's religions.

In Judaism, "sin" in Hebrew is *hata*, "to go astray." Given an all-powerful God, Yahweh (there is little room for a counteragent of similar power, e.g., the Devil), the focus is on acts of human behavior and on the "here and now" aligned with God. Sin is less focused on the implications for the soul. There is no "original sin" and no baptism (though having a ritual of water purification). Sin is understood more as a "misstep" away from God, akin to a *mistake*. As humans are endowed with the ability to learn, to learn from one's mistakes, we get repeated attempts at getting it right. As you are the source of bad choices, of evil, you are the one who can learn from them. If cited, Satan is used more as a metaphor for someone's evil inclination. In seeking not to go astray, the focus in Judaism is on God as Creator, Revealer, and Redeemer; the *Torah*—God's "instruc-tions," moral and ethical code in the first five books of Bible; and on "Israel" as a living people of a place and land since biblical times. In Judaism, one seeks orthopraxy (correct behavior in social justice and freedom; to spare others from suffering) as a means to overcome sin, but it is an orthopraxy manifested in the "here and now" with other mortal human beings that is important. The ultimate focus is not on an everlasting life in a Heaven per se, though eventually all will reside there. (This concept is debated and rather agnostic.)

In Christianity, "sin" in Aramaic is termed *hōb*, which means "debt owed to another," and in Greek is *hamartia,* "missing the mark." Given the "Duality of Divinity," i.e., a loving God, the Father, and Jesus Christ, the incarnate Son, in Heaven, in contrast to an evil Satan in Hell, each in battle for the human soul, sin is an essential part of the cosmology, as reflected in doctrine of "original sin." Acknowledging subtle definitional distinctions between Catholics (e.g., affirms state of guilt and distinguishes degrees of sins—venial vs mortal, "seven deadly sins"), Protestants (e.g., affirms state of guilt with all humanity having sinned, a universal moral corruption) and Eastern Orthodox Christians (e.g., not so much a state of guilt as a "terminal spiritual sickness" that debases the image of and relationship with God), sin is fundamentally *disobedience* to God, i.e., "a word, deed or desire in opposition to the eternal law of God" (St. Augustine of Hippo). Sin is an evil act, and for many is understood as an alignment with Satan. For some adherents, sin is a loss of love for God, elevating self-love in its place. Redemption is pursued through sacramental acts of faith in Jesus Christ of the *Gospels,* such as baptism, confession, communion, credal affirmation, acceptance of Christ as one's personal savior, and in living by the example of Jesus. In Christianity one seeks salvation through "faith" in and "relationship" with Jesus Christ who died for your sins—uniquely combining orthodoxy (correct belief, conviction, doctrine) with orthopraxy (correct behavior) as a means to overcome sin, and attain deliverance of the soul and everlasting life in the Kingdom of God, in Heaven.

In Islam, "sin" in Arabic is *khatiya,* meaning a "transgression, iniquity." Given an all-powerful God—Allah, sin is an act of not following Allah and his teachings, but more specifically, it is an act of *forgetting* to follow His will. As with Judaism, there is no all-powerful counterforce, though there are Devils. For some, Devils can be attributed to leading one astray. As humans are not born of sin, there is no "original sin" and no baptism. As an act of forgetting, it is through deliberate acts of atonement and repentance that sin is overcome. Atonement comes in acts of submission to the Five Pillars of Islam: 1. Witnessing to the one true God; 2. Acts of ritual prayer five times daily; 3. Charity—sharing one's wealth; attending to orphans, the destitute, and disinherited; performing good deeds; 4. Fasting during the month of Ramadan; 5. Partaking of the *Hajj*—pilgrimage to Mecca. All are anchored in Allah's revelations via the angel Gabriel/Jibril to the prophet Mohammad, "peace be upon him," as recorded in the *Quran*. For Muslims one overcomes sin by seeking orthopraxy (correct behavior) as a means for one's soul to have everlasting life in Paradise.

In Hinduism, "sin" in Sanskrit is *pāpa* and means "vice." As there are multiple routes to Divinity (the many *Yoga* paths) and given the all-encompassing nature of the Divine (the one Divinity—Brahman, inclusive of the 330 million Gods and Goddesses), the term *papa* in the strictest sense refers to actions antithetical to the moral and ethical codes of one's *Dharma,* actions which bring about negative *karma*, adverse consequences, i.e., re-born into a lesser state of being. Such actions are not directly related to and enshrined in a specific Divine doctrine, nor a violation of God's will, per se. To avoid sin, the focus is on following one's *Yoga* path, such as *Bhakti*, *Raja* or *Jnana*, and in adhering to one's *Dharma*, one's true self and its social, ethical and moral responsibilities at each stage of one's *samsara* or cycle of re-births. We see this played out in the unfolding drama between Krishna (the eighth avatar of Vishnu, the preserver God) and Arjuna (a warrior prince) in the *Bhagavad Gita*, and the quintessential command, "act, renouncing the fruit of your actions." The ultimate destination of one's *Yoga* path is *Moksha*, when you are liberated from the continuous cycles of *samsara*, and the burdens and sorrows, the fears and pains associated with the desires of the mortal life. You are liberated into the oneness of the Infinite, into bliss and ultimate joy. You are united with Brahman/Atman (i.e., the ultimate Divinity in the cosmos and within the soul). In Hinduism, one overcomes sin by seeking orthopraxy (correct behavior) as a means to *Moksha*, but it is not for personal salvation of one's soul and everlasting life in Paradise.

In Buddhism (as in Hinduism) "sin" in Sanskrit is *pāpa* and defined as "vice." As a religion not adhering to a personal God or Supreme Being per se, sin stands for the pursuit of thoughts and actions that cloud and undermine clarity of mind, leaving a person suspectable to "attachments," e.g., love of self, love of possessions, love of a profession, etc. As with the Hindu doctrine of *samsara*, one seeks to move from the continual cycles of suffering at each reincarnation, to a state of *Nirvana* and *Sunyata* (similar to but not exactly like *Moksha*). In *Nirvana,* desires are "extinguished" (the fuel is taken away), and one is liberated and released from suffering. In *Sunyata,* one attains "emptiness," all is extinguished (the fire itself is taken away), and one enters a transcendent state of "boundlessness," like "a drop of water in the great endless ocean." Though it does not mean "nothingness," as the "self" is dissolved and reconstituted into the Infinite, the Eternal. To avoid sin and gain *Sunyata,* one seeks to follow the "Four Noble Truths": 1. *Dukkha*—acknowledging suffering as the condition of human life; 2. *Tanha*—greed, hatred, ignorance, attachment—is the cause of *Dukkha*; 3. *Dukkha* can be abated by following the Eightfold Path, which focuses on the clarity of mind being attentive and awake to all, on acts of compassion and non-violence for all living beings, and through the mind, on truth and overcoming ignorance; 4. When *Dukkha* is abated, *Nirvana* and *Sunyata* are actualized. For some adherents, Buddhism is more a philosophical or even psychological approach to life than a spiritual path. While the Buddha and the Eightfold Path can get you to *Nirvana* and *Sunyata,* upon arrival, for some branches of Buddhism, there is the realization that there is no Buddha, no Eightfold Path, no personal God. As reflected in the Eightfold Path (e.g., right speech, right conduct, right livelihood), aspects of Buddhism are reflective of orthopraxy (correct behavior). Other aspects of the Eightfold Path (e.g., right mindfulness, right concentration) involve realizing a mental state of *emptiness of action and thought*, as through forms of meditation, a means to *Nirvana* and *Sunyata* that is neither orthopraxy nor orthodoxy (correct thought). Like Hinduism, in Buddhism there is no personal salvation; no everlasting life in a Paradise.

"Sin" in Native American traditions is difficult to equate, and some elders argue the concept does not exist. Perhaps examples coming closest are the Niimíipuu term, *qepsi'iswit* "to be mean toward another," and the Schitsu'umsh term, *hnch'esn* "wrongdoing toward another." In these instances, they entail acts violating the moral and ethical code embedded in the kinship system, expressed as harming another person and acting selfishly, with greed. It is an act that will inevitably come back to harm the doer or their family, similar to the Hindu notion of negative *karma*, but occurring in the more immediate, not in a next life. There is no "original sin," no battle between God and Satan for the soul; bad behavior is not understood as a violation of and disobedience to God's will. Rather, sin as bad behavior originates out of and is operationalized within the structure of ethical and moral social relationships. In this regard, it is akin to Hinduism. Along with "coming back to you," there are social responses to and social consequences for committed acts of harmful behavior. To avoid sinful behavior, one must act aligned with the *miyp* "teachings" of the Animal-First Peoples, such as Coyote, Salmon, Sedna, Changing Woman, and Raven, who were themselves brought forth by and are extensions of the Creator— *Akbaatatdía* (Apsáalooke; the one and the many Divine conceptualization comparable to Hinduism). The teachings are conveyed in the oral narratives, retold periodically and enshrined in the geological typography of the landscape. For Native Americans, these cherished stories are the equivalent in stature and importance to the *Bhagavad Gita, Torah, Gospels,* or *Quran.* One seeks orthopraxy (correct behavior) as a means to overcome bad behavior, and, as with Judaism, what is significant is the orthopraxy's manifestation in the "here and now" with other mortal human beings. There is no Heaven, nor Hell. Upon death, everyone's spiritual being journeys on and resides in "the lands across the river," re-joining with all the departed ancestors, comparable to Judaism.

The world's religions reflect so many distinct and differing Spokes, an endless rainbow of rich, vibrant colors. Even a pivotal concept such as "sin" has many diverse meanings. While there will seldom if ever be a Buddhist, Hindu, or Muslim under the covers of a Gritman hospital bed, an appreciation of the rich diversity of the world's religions better prepares me for the subtle nuanced differences I do encounter with perfect strangers.

◆ ◆ ◆

After I was first diagnosed with lymphoma in 2005, Cliff SiJohn said, "You got to trust your doctors.... and their Head Knowledge.... But ...you'll be responsible for the Heart Knowledge....And listen." His words immediately drew me back to Tom's attentiveness and the Rock Medicine Wheel, with its many Spokes and singular Hub. Could I walk both paths, the Head and the Heart, doing so simultaneously, and doing so even upon my relapse in 2009? As you recall, Janet and Rayburn Beck, my Shoshone family, and I were sponsoring the 2009 Crow Sundance. Just weeks before the Dance, the cancer knocked me off course, and I had an appointment in Seattle at the Fred Hutchinson Cancer Research Center. It was the health of my son that in 1976 initiated my Sundance journey; now Matt along with Kelly reciprocated, stepping in for me at the Sundance. As Burnt Face had assembled the rocks of the Medicine Wheel, I too assembled my own "rocks," "my treasures"—a family's love, my Indian Names *Maakuuxshiichíilish* and *Kw'lk'įl Sqqi̱*, and the gift of a Medicine Father—*Bishée*—holding them in daily prayers to *Akbaatatdía*. And then there were the prayers of the many coming from the Sundance Lodge, as Eagle-bone whistles blew to the beat of the Drum. On the same exact days of the Dance I took in intensive chemotherapy and Total Body Irradiation, part of undergoing an autologous stem cell transplant. Who could have scheduled it any better! As the Sun's rays blessed those in an open-air, log and tree Lodge, I, in a small, lead-lined room, was bombarded with radiation rays, while listening on a CD player to Sundance songs and Grandpa Tom telling of Burnt Face. And the distinct paths I attempted to navigate, seemingly so mutually exclusive, coalesced, leading me into that liminal state of betwixt and between. As I *walked the halls*, hooked to IVs, deeply attentive, with all my superficial baggage left behind, with one step in Head Knowledge and the other in Heart Knowledge, out from the rooms of once perfect strangers, out from deep within, came that overwhelming and crystalline sensation—best described as profound empathy.

◆ ◆ ◆

Ontological Diversity. On reflecting deeply on Tom's Wheel, on Sundance spirituality, and on the power of the spoken word, all are premised on holding a certain corresponding ontology, that of Heart Ways of Knowing, in contrast with Head Ways of Knowing. These are two rather distinct views of reality. I certainly adhere to the scientific paradigm, with its foundation in Cartesian Dualism and Aristotelian Materialism, in its objects and objectification, in its rationalism and empiricism. But I also adhere of the Indigenous/mystical reality, with its foundation in Monism and Spiritual Platonism, in an interconnected, participatory world of unfolding events brought forth from the transcendent Forms. The world of *hnkhwelkhwlnet* "our ways of life in the world." This is the world of Sundance healings and the miracles of Jesus. My two journeys with cancer were successful because of the science of chemotherapy and a stem cell transplant, along with prayers of Sundancers and a Medicine Bundle. As Susie Yellowtail held, I too hold that there is more than one ontological Spoke in the universe. There need not be mutual exclusivity.

On a practical note, having multiple ontologies helps me to understand and align with patients oriented one way or another, or anything in between. If a patient is caught between the seeming exclusivity of one worldview over another and a decision needs to be made, help that patient discover for themselves, their own path. In the room of the critical care unit, inundated with all the scientific-based medical technology and procedures and the staff well-trained in its applications, there was more than ample room for the spirituality of prayer. As the patient passed, the nurses monitored what was necessary, but respected and accommodated the prayers of the family. As a chaplain, I too needed to effectively navigate multiple worlds, the world of my patients and their families, and that of the nurses and doctors, from the medical-scientific to the spiritual-religious, so many Spokes to travel.

◆ ◆ ◆

Several years ago, a colleague from the University and I drove to DeSmet, on the Coeur d'Alene Reservation, to visit a friend at the Education Building, next the church. Along the way, we talked academic politics and laughed at trivia. As we pulled up beside the Catholic Church to park, we both looked up at what had always been a plain white wall and were amazed to see what someone had beautifully painted on the side of the Church. It was vivid, in vibrant pastels; it was the image of the Madonna! We turned to each other and both commented how splendid a painting of the Virgin Mary it was, covering the entire side of the Church. Then, when we looked back up again at the wall, there was nothing but white! This Sundancer-Unitarian had a most unexpected visitor—the ultimate symbol of nurturing Motherhood, of unconditional Love!

◆ ◆ ◆

Hub. We should not let the Spoke's "different as different could be," its glare, blind us and get in the way of discovering what is right in front of us. As Tom continued, all the different Spokes radiate from and are anchored to a singular source, the Hub. While the Spokes are each specific, idiosyncratic, exclusive and defined, the Hub is necessarily non-specific, is inclusive, all-encompassing. That which connects all, that is in all, that extends out deep through each Spoke to the outer Hub—the Rim. The Infinite, the Divine. And we are reminded of *chnis-teem-ilqws* "I am your relative, I am part of all peoples—human, plant, animal, fish, spirit." Ubiquitous and universal, yet ultimately undefinable.

Out from the Hub emanates the spark, the spirit, the energy, the light, the power (and I search for the right words), infused in an interconnected, interactive dynamic web, each vital relationship influencing another, making all possible—animating, renewing, life-giving, transforming. And we are reminded of *snqhepiwes* "where the spirit lives, from horizon to horizon," and *snukwnkhwtskhwts'mi'ls ł stsee'nidmsh* "empathetic adaptability," and the Buddhist doctrine, *paticcasamuppada* "interdependent co-arising." From the Hub, the Spokes are rendered flexible, ever-adapting, ever-changing. Yet deep within that dynamic of the supple Spokes, at the heart of the Ubiquitous Hub, are also the steadfast *miyp* bones, the universal Forms, the Sacred archetypes (and the possibility of hierophany). The Eternal, the Divine. A turning Wheel that is malleable yet immutable. Ultimately, truly undefinable.

Nevertheless, with all its mystery, the Hub is that which can be felt palpitating from deep within one's Heart and glimpsed reflected in metaphor. There is Krishna's attempt at conveying to Arjuna something of the Infinite, "a thousand suns blazing in the sky is but a faint reflection of its radiance," *Bhagavat Gita 11:12.* And then there is Elijah being told to stand on the mountain as the Lord would soon pass by. A great wind came that shattered the rocks, but no Lord. A great earthquake came, but no Lord. A great fire came, but no Lord. In the stillness, "the gentle whisper" of the Lord came to Elijah, (1 Kings 19:11–13). In my own transformative gifts from Sundance spirituality, with the Little People and *Bishée*, came a much deeper appreciation of and openness to the spirituality in other religious traditions, all emanating from the same Hub. Came a transitory, vibrant image of the Madonna on a Church wall! How kindred the Spirit is. The door to a stranger's Hub, yet another metaphor for the nameless, is opened with attentiveness, to seek an appreciation of that which interconnects, which is shared-in-common with the patient, that "precious bundle of unconditional Love," in whatever way it is overtly defined, in whatever metaphor used. I listen deeply to better align my words with those of the patient's Hub.

◆ ◆ ◆

I danced hard, with focus, during that fourth Sundance, letting go of the superficial, the superfluous, emerging into liminality. Charging the Center Pole, dancing back, charging, dancing, as my Eagle-bone whistle blew to the sound of the Drum and Song. Each step a prayer. Then I was hit, knocked down, and I watched as my body laid there on the ground covered with cattails, mint, and sage, as I traveled on. A deep, dark rocky canyon, looking up, seeing nothing; traveling to a deep, dim pine forest, looking up, seeing…; then a shadowy, cottonwood grove, seeing nothing as I looked up; and I was up in the white, fluffy clouds, and then looking out…

I *walked the halls*, hooked to IV fluids, in that Seattle hospital, with the superficial, the superfluous left behind, emerging into liminality. With doors opened, looking into the rooms of strangers. Hall after hall after hall, room after room after room. Each step a prayer. And then out from the rooms…

With crystalline clarity, I knew I was looking out through the eyes of *Bishée*, Buffalo. With crystalline clarity, out from the rooms flowed a deep empathy with perfect strangers no longer. Such an innate interconnectedness. No separations, no distinctions. Such a spirit-infused web of transitory participant relations. As also revealed by an *Awakkuléeshe* on a hillside and by the Virgin Mary on a Church wall. A shared-in-common with *all* of ever-emerging creation, flowing out the transcendent, deep within myself, deep outside myself, from the Hub. While remote from most our experiences—Sundancing, a stem cell transplant, a fast on a hill—the unfolding relationships can reveal themselves in our daily lives, if we're attentive. Even revealed while traveling along the mundane of our Spokes. Reflect on what it takes to bring forth a Rainbow or a flowering Camas? And in those transitory intersections of participant relationships, when the moment of intersection coalesces with the *axis mundi* or *in illo tempore* archetype, comes the viewing through the eyes of another, comes a feeling of the sufferings of others, comes the crystalline clarity of empathy. Comes an hierophany of the Divine that transforms my life.

◆ ◆ ◆

Besides variations on the shared ontology of Monism and Spiritual Platonism, another shared-in-common among the world's religions is the "ethic of reciprocity, of sharing" found in the *Golden Rule*. As stated by Barbara Brown Taylor (2019:77), "It can be argued that all great religions have [the Golden Rule] as a benchmark on what makes them great. They ask the members of their tribe to use humanity as the benchmark for how to treat those outside the tribe." The "Golden Rule" is itself expressive of what can be considered at the heart of the teachings of all great religions—empathy and compassion—love. Like "sin," the "Golden Rule" too could be deep under the covers of a patient's bed, though not specifically coming up in a conversation, but predicated in it. It is intriguing to note that these two pivotal religious components, "sin" and the "Golden Rule," are fundamentally antithetical. Let's briefly explore examples of this shared-in-common.

In Judaism, it is expressed as, hurt not others in ways that you yourself would find hurtful. "You shall not take vengeance or bear a grudge against your kinsfolk. Love your neighbor as yourself: I am the LORD," *Leviticus* 19:18. In Christianity, "All things, therefore, that you want men to do to you, you also must likewise do to them," i.e., do unto others as you would have them do unto you, *Matthew* 7:12. And "Thou shalt love the Lord thy God with all thy heart, and with all thy soul, and with all thy mind. This is the first and great commandment. And the second is like unto it, Thou shalt love thy neighbour as thyself," *Matthew* 22:37–39. In Islam, "None of you [truly] believes until he wishes for his brother what he wishes for himself," i.e., love your brother as you love yourself, *An-Nawawi's Forty Hadith* 13.

In Hinduism, "this is the sum of duty, your *Dharma*: do not do to others what would cause pain if done to you; treat others as you treat yourself," *Mahābhārata Shānti-Parva* 167:9. In Buddhism,

"One who, while himself seeking happiness, oppresses with violence other beings who also desire happiness, will not attain happiness hereafter," *Dhammapada* 10. *Violence.* And "Hurt not others in ways that you yourself would find hurtful," *Udanavarga* 5:18. In Native America, as expressed in the Apsáalooke term *bacháxpak iilío* "to share something with someone" and the Niimíipuu term *téeke* "to give and share [food] with others," there is the ethical responsibility to help all others who are in need, as they would help you when you're in need. It is nicely illustrated in the Schitsu'umsh narrative of Rabbit and Jack Rabbit (Frey and Schitsu'umsh 2001:112).

◆ ◆ ◆

Dreams have always been meaningful for the Apsáalooke, potentially as an important communication from the spirit world. While visiting at his home in Wyola in the late 1970s, Grandpa Tom and I were talking about this and that, but I don't recall exactly what. Grandpa then paused, turned to look me in the eye, and said, "Rod, Jesus paid me a visit! I was with a group of others, laying on my back. I saw him approach us. Looked just like you see him in the pictures. I asked the others if they saw him? No. He came right up to me and shook my hand. It was so warm to the touch. He was as close as you and me." Nothing else was conveyed about the dream, and I didn't ask. But I fully realized the Grandpa could visit with *Akbaatatdía* and his Medicine Fathers as easily as with Jesus Christ, all emanating from the same Hub.

◆ ◆ ◆

Compassion. As I enter the rooms, I wear a Gritman ID badge with my picture, first name and "Chaplain" stenciled on it, helping identify me. I cannot engage a patient without also acknowledging to myself the names that fully identify me, that anchor my story, each indeed a "treasure." Rodney Paul Frey, my birth name, imbued with all the hopes, dreams, and love of my parents, and all my worldly and spiritual experiences etched in the landscape contours of my life's journey. And from Grandpa Tom, *Maakuuxshiichíilish*, "Seeking to Help Others," along with Cliff's *Kw'lk'il Sqqi* "Little Red

Hawk," "a patient observer,"..."who helps" others, each Indian Name deliberately bestowed, with their own animacy to bring forth and to inspire, sparking something deep within, at the core, in my heart. Each name intermingling, each in essence seeking to help others in need. Seeking to bring what the Apsáalooke call *baalaásdee,* "compassion," the root word of which is *daasé,* "heart." After a visit, as I'm leaving the room of each and every patient, I'll turn to face them directly. They will hear from me the words, "I will continue to hold you in my heart, and offer prayer." And clearly hear, "Know that you are Loved."

◆ ◆ ◆

Sincerity. And finally, when I engage that perfect stranger, I ask myself, can I offer my huckleberries with my heart, with my utmost *díakaashe,* "doing it with determination"—sincerity, honesty, integrity, authenticity? While there can be many essential, overarching meanings to this term, I first recall seeing it on the faces of the Sundancers and in their actions in 1975. They revealed and exhibited to me something altogether self-effacing, so authentic, so sincere, on faces and in actions entirely focused and intentionally engaged. The Apsáalooke so appropriately call it *díakaashe,* literally meaning "doing it with determination." In front of that Sundance door, as I witnessed within, I fell to my knees and tears filled my eyes. And I found *díakaashe* virtually each and every time I engaged Grandpa Tom, on his face and in his actions, and as I viewed him engage so many others. Could I do the same as a chaplain, as I too engage perfect strangers?

◆ ◆ ◆

The most immediate and important way I can show my *baalaásdee* "compassion" and *díakaashe* "sincerity" to a patient is expressing it in my undivided presence and through the right balance of silence and sound. With attentiveness taking priority, I seek to open my inner ears to whatever words may come from the patient. A silence not of my mind chattering away, flooded with "what do I say next," with this thought and that thought, but of a stillness, receptive to the emotional and spiritual stirrings and rhythms of another's heart. A silence more of a void, waiting to be filled with the patient's troubles and concerns. Waiting to be filled with the patient's *basbaaaliíchiwé* "telling my story." Filled, along with words, with the little things— body language, tone of the words, even patient belongings. A story has many expressions. A silent presence available 24/7; "just have your nurse give me a call, even if two in the morning." Offering a presence in silence can mean just sitting quietly beside the patient for a half hour or more. A stillness of presence that does take discipline and practice; my babbling mind can be so distracting. Going hand-in-hand with presence is patience. The work of the heart should never be rushed.

Given the Spokes and Hub embedded in their shared story, my silence is broken with spoken words in alignment with the patient. Be it in the words selected in a conversation, in a poem, in a parable or in a prayer, or in words written on my face and in my body language, I seek to speak deeply from my heart to their heart. My ad hoc words are chosen with care—deliberately, purposefully—aligning as best I can with the patient and the gathered family. In addition to *the what* I seek to convey, critical is *the how* it is conveyed. I pace my words so they can be clearly heard, slow and loud enough, but not too, as I face the patient, often eye-to-eye, if eyes are not closed. As in the example of the Lord's Prayer, I'll recite it aloud not as if memorized—rote, mechanical and flat—but as re-membered, renewing the words of the prayer each time with life, bringing emphasis, intonation, pauses, bringing facial and bodily expression, bringing heart to each voiced expression. Before offering a prayer, I'll occasionally preface any words with a silent pause, to center ourselves in the moment, and to better open myself up to and select my words for the patient, for all those present, and for that which interconnects us. It is a presence and a balance I seek to apply equally, to a newborn or to one dying or deceased, or to anyone else at whatever stage along life's journey they might be, as we and our storytelling intertwine. Throughout, my sound always in deference to my silence.

◆ ◆ ◆

What I Seek to Bring into the Rooms. As I enter the room of that stranger under the covers of a hospital bed, it is as if I'm entering a place that for many is dark, cold, and foreboding, and certainly unfamiliar and of concern. As a lay chaplain, with empathy in hand and now standing or seated beside the bed, I begin with my name and by listening with deep attentiveness, augmented by a few exploratory inquires. My hope is that the patient might feel welcomed and safe to share something—if only bits and pieces—of their own unique story, as well as our shared humanity. To do a little of their own *basbaaaliíchiwé*. To allow me to enter their particular place, now in turmoil.

We continue with my attentiveness, augmented with spoken and occasionally in unspoken dialogue; so much can be said in silence, as through the eyes. The continuing may take numerous visits over a few days. And throughout I seek to bring to bear my inner ear and a helping hand, to provide encouragement, solace, hope, perhaps a laugh, some compassion. "You're not alone!" I seek to be an "attentive companion," to hold a hand, if only for a short duration, while along their journey. And might even place in that hand a soft cloth stuffed frog, a beautiful quilted throw or requested rosary beads, all kind donations to the hospital from others. An extended presence in silence can itself offer comfort. Doing it all with authenticity, honesty, and sincerity. I certainly do *not* seek to bring into the rooms any proselytizing, judging, giving advice, counseling, or fixing a problem.

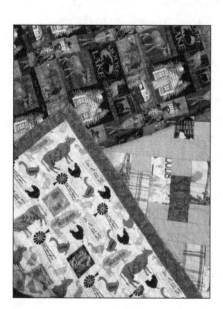

Kindly donated quilted throws.
Photo: Shelley McGregor

With empathy guiding my way, eventually I'll offer the words of a poem, or of a parable, or of a prayer, as best I can, words that attempt to align with and are appropriate to the patient's Spoke, while cognizant of our shared Hub. With my words and presence, hopefully I have stitched a quilt, with just the right patches of fabric, design, and color, held together with threads of sincerity and padded with batting of compassion, that renders that which is under the covers less dark and cold, and more a place of refuge. I seek to eventually leave a patient's room as if I had been honored to have entered something akin to their particular church, or special mountain view, or inspired poetry, or beloved music, or......a place that has brought comfort and grace, peace and beauty. The place that enshrines one's "most precious gifts," their "treasures." Perhaps even a place where the patient can discover and travel with their own equivalent Burnt Face, along the Spokes of their own Wheel, helping map a territory so unfamiliar, arriving at their own Hub. A place where the patient can discover, for themselves, their bundle of unconditional Love. And from that Love, the possibility of resilience, renewal, restoration, wholeness of Heart. Even the possibility of an hierophany—a shining through of the Divine. Leaving a sterile hospital bed transformed into place a little more like a candlelit sanctuary, wrapped in a warmed patchwork quilt, with the possibility of......?

A place temporary to be sure, certainly only partial, never a substitute, always in the process of becoming, and ultimately *aspirational*. In the relatively short time I have with a patient, I may only begin to align my words and presences with the patient's Spokes and Hub, only begin to stitch together the fabric and design of their particular quilt, but that should not prevent me from attempting to do so. If any sort of alignment can get closer, a few foundational bricks of the candlelit sanctuary laid, all the better for the patient.

Of course, all my efforts can fall short of rendering a patient other than a stranger. There is no formulaic guarantee that a connection will be made. Occasionally, there will be obstacles—physical, psychological, something else—beyond our control. The patient just might not want to visit at the time, or feels they are not ready to share with a stranger, albeit even a chaplain. Time itself can constrain the degree of rapport. Given the particular overlapping sequence of a patient's admittance and a chaplain's seven-day assignment, more time might have been needed to open our hearts. If the patient is continuing beyond the seven days of a chaplain's scheduled week, hopefully any level of relationship developed by one chaplain will only expand with the next assigned chaplain.

Then there are the obstacles I bring into a patient's room. I have limits in my ability to align. I'll always be a student, with much yet to learn of the world's Spokes and Hub. And my personal integrity can also be an obstacle. If I'm to speak from the heart, my words must be spoken with honesty. While I can more easily align the universality of our shared Hub, e.g., speaking the equivalence of Jesus and the Old Man, the diversity represented in the Spokes can bring challenge. I can provide a "water blessing," accompanied with prayer words such as "cleansing" and "blessings," but while I have respect for it, I cannot bring myself to voice it and provide a Christian Baptism, which washes away "sin." You'll not find words in my prayers referencing such notions as "hell," "personal savior," or "original sin." For the benefit of the patient, when moments of any elements of my personal integrity are askew or even clash with those of the patient, I'll seek to temporarily silence any overt hint of my convictions. Nevertheless, when deep aspects of our Spokes and/or Hub remain unaligned, my presence insufficient to connect, a stranger may persist.

I do acknowledge, that while there is so much each of my fellow chaplains share with one another, we each also bring into the rooms of perfect strangers our unique stories, endowed with distinct huckleberries and gifts, encapsulated in differing personalities. It just might be that another chaplain could better connect with and serve a patient than I.

While I'll always respect the right of a patient to share or not share their story, and acknowledge the many possible obstacles, I'll nevertheless always seek, with all my heart, to be attentive and to be in some level of alignment. As in the Indian Name Grandpa Tom bestowed on me, "*Seeking* to Help Others."

If those gently spoken words do get close to aligning—the beginnings of the right patches of the quilt stitched, the foundational bricks of the properly lit sanctuary laid—heard could be my words prefaced with, for example, "In the name of our Lord Father, who created you; in the name of His son, Jesus Christ, who redeems you; in the name of the Holy Spirit, who sanctifies you….." Words coming from my heart touching another's that just might bring a calming, a reassurance, a hope, just might bring a resilience. And with that someone now less a stranger might come a sparkle in an eye, a glimmer in the corner of a lip, a tranquility in the voice, or an eyelid closing in restful peace.

And now at home, in a full-moon Medicine Bundle Ceremony and every day in my backyard "prayer circle," my prayers are continued for all those seen in the hospital—the sick, the recovering, the newborn, the dying, their families, and their hospital caregivers. This time the spoken words coming from my heart are substituted and prefaced with *Akbaatatdía*—"Creator" and *Bishée*—"Buffalo Spirit," my Medicine Father, accompanied with *báape ítchimaa cháachk* "today is a very good day," followed by the specifics of all those in need. As I complete the words of the prayer, I'll express my sincere gratitude with *ahó, ahókaash* "thanks, thanks a lot."

"I'm Rodney, a Lay Chaplain, and I seek to be *with you*." And now, when asked "what church do you attend?" I briefly mention, "I'm *inter-faith*,…baptized and confirmed in the Methodist Church, have partaken of the Episcopal Eucharist with my mother-in-law, a member of the Unitarian Universalist community, and follow the Native teachings of my adopted grandparents, Tom and Susie Yellowtail." I seek to bring into the room of a perfect stranger: attentiveness and empathy,… acknowledgement and respect for their unique Spoke,…affirmation of our shared Hub, in whatever way it is defined,…compassion and service to others,…and doing so with sincerity. I seek to leave a patient with a candlelit sanctuary, wrapped with their own warmed stitched quilt, and enshrined with their own treasures, with the possibility that they can discover their own resilience. All aspirational for certain. Huckleberries pulled from my cedar-bark basket, consumed by chaplain and patient, and now given to you who holds this book. And I wonder if these "seekings," these attributes, these aspirations, these huckleberries, all "bones" derivative of and distilled from their *miyp* teaching stories, some seemingly so simple, cannot also be brought with all of us as we *walk the halls* and enter the many differing rooms of the perfect strangers encountered *outside* of the hospital?

◆ ◆ ◆

I carry my cell phone with me as I enter each patient's room, with the ringer turned off. In it are access to phrases, poems, and prayers, such as from Mary Oliver, Albert Camus or Romans 8:38–39 or Psalm 23. Parables such as the Mustard Seed, Sower of Seeds or Watchful Servant, and many other texts I've come to appreciate. If the moment warrants, I re-tell or read any one of them to a patient. The following is one such text, adapted and modified from a Buddhist meditation.

In the stillness, may you hear the
voice that whispers deep within ...

"you are Loved."

May you continue to be filled with loving-kindness,

May you be peaceful and at ease,

May you be well,

May you be whole,

May the Spirit abound within you and flow from you.

In the stillness, may you hear the voice that whispers deep within

...

"you are Loved."

From my heart to your heart,

"you are Loved."

◆ ◆ ◆

And I *woke* with *such* a desire.

Notes

[1] Some of the following materials resulted from a fellow chaplain who had heard from a family member about my assistance with their dying parent. I was then asked if I'd write up the experience and bring it as a case study to the other Gritman chaplains to discuss. It was subsequently published in *SpokaneFāVS: Faith and Values,* 29 January 2020 and in Gritman Medical Center's *Newsletter,* 30 July 2021. This chapter was reviewed by Gritman Medical Center's legal counsel, the HIPAA/Privacy Officer, and the Administrative Team, and complies with the HIPAA Privacy Rule, which protects individual's records and other individual identifiable health information, 11 September 2023.

[2] Though I had attended a Unitarian Church during graduate school, I became active in the Unitarian Universalist Church of the Palouse after the 2017 publication of *Carry Forth the Stories.* I've found in the UU community an alignment of our values, an opportunity for personal and philosophical growth, an acceptance of my Sundance spirituality and theology, and a community extending love to all. It is interesting to note that one of the principal organizers of the first World's Parliament of Religions (as it was called then) was Jenkins Lloyd Jones, a Unitarian minister. The 1893 Parliament is credited as the first international interfaith initiative. And one of the participants in the centennial celebration of the Parliament of the World's Religions in 1993, providing the opening prayer, was Tom Yellowtail.

Ilúuppe Tatáche
"to be flexible; to be solid"

Integrating the Spokes and the Hub for
the General Public[1]

The stories of the intersection of diversity and commonality, of empathy and intentional engagement, of compassion and sincerity traveled with me as an ethnographer, along the *hallways* of the academy and into university classrooms of perfect strangers, and into the Indigenous homes of perfect strangers. Could I connect, jump-start meaningful relations with these perfect strangers? Let me add some further extensions and implications, new applications of Tom's Wheel, with its Hub and Spokes, and his empathy, revealing some of their intellectual and affective nuances for ethnographers, for chaplains, and for us all.

As a faculty member, with occasional administrative roles, I first taught and researched at the University of Montana (1979–80, as a sabbatical replacement for the revered religious studies scholar Joseph Epes Brown), then at Carroll College in Montana (1980–86), Lewis-Clark State College in Idaho (1987–98), and lastly at the University of Idaho (1998–2017). The Wheel's sensitivities and capacities served me well in the classroom as I engaged my undergraduate and graduate students, planting seeds of Spokes and Hub, seeds to be nurtured with empathy. The Wheel's sensitivities and capacities served me well as I engaged perfect strangers, while conducting applied, collaborative, ethnographic research projects with such

Native peoples as the Coeur d'Alene, Crow, Flathead, Nez Perce, Spokane, and Warm Springs Tribes. These were projects that ranged from the cultural impacts determined as part a Natural Resource Damage Assessment of the mining activities in a traditional Indian homeland, to Native perspectives on Lewis and Clark's Corps of Discovery and the forces of assimilation they brought, to developing an Indian language arts curriculum for a non-Native school district, to identifying the nature of and applying Indigenous knowledge in helping address climate change. Each of these varied projects demonstrated the power of story, of the act of re-telling the sacred narratives, what the Apsáalooke call *baaéechichiwaau,* "re-telling one's own" and Schitsu'umsh, *'me'y'mi'y'm,* "telling stories." Stories such as those of Coyote or Salmon, of Chief Child of the Yellow-root or Burnt Face. Stories at the heart of each of these Indigenous communities, since time immemorial. Stories at the nexus of not only withstanding the hegemonic winds of the dominant society but of providing the adaptive, pliable fibers assuring cultural renewal and persistence into the future. In these differing research collaborations, the empathy of the Spokes and Hub allowed me to travel together with those who sought to apply their voices and re-tell their stories, stories that inevitably sought a healing in the earth and with humanity.

In my initial application of an academic pursuit, wasn't it fortuitous that my first ethnographic research project, during that summer of 1974, sought to aid in the delivery of health care? On the Crow Reservation, the government's Indian Health Service physicians, though well trained in the latest advances in medicine, often had difficulty in understanding and communicating with their patients, particularly the older, more "traditional" Apsáalooke. I worked with elders—key among them Tom and Susie Yellowtail—and we put together an introduction to Apsáalooke concepts and perspectives on illness and healing. With such knowledge in hand, it was hoped the physicians could better work with and deliver health care to their Crow patients, hoped that when they *walked the halls* of their hospital, they could better jump-start relationships with perfect strangers.

General Education. Following my cancer journeys, in the summer of 2010, I was asked to serve on the University of Idaho's General Education Steering Committee. We were to review and redesign the core curriculum required of all the university's undergraduates, representing about a third of their total course work, distinct from their courses in their major. Reflect the "best practices in a liberal education." With its noble intentions, general education typically entails broad learning in the liberal arts and sciences, building skills in communication, in analytical and creative thinking, and in problem-solving, for lifelong intellectual and aesthetic, civic and ethical, real-world engagement. And I pondered, is this not an *education* applicable beyond the academy, to the *general* public, its intentions important to all of us? How can we jump start meaningful relations with the perfect strangers of the general public?

While serving on the steering committee, I helped initiate a new course requirement in American diversity and assisted in refining the nature of the "integrative learning," which took the form of the Integrative Seminars—ISEM 101, ISEM 301 and the Senior Experience. Both diversity and integrative learning are pivotal components in the revised general education curriculum. In summer 2011, I chaired the subcommittee that developed the specifics for these Integrative Seminars. Among other objectives, these seminars were to apply the university's Learning Outcomes and use multiple disciplines and perspectives, such as the humanities and social sciences, to explore a single topic of contemporary relevance, as selected by the instructor.

It is interesting to note that in my initial diversity proposal, I had focused on coursework in Native American studies. As the University of Idaho, a land-grant institution, is located squarely on ancestral Niimíipuu lands; as the public lands adjacent to the university are acknowledged in the 1855 Nez Perce Treaty as "usual and accustomed" lands remaining to this day accessible to enrolled Nez Perce members for hunting, fishing, and gathering; and as so little is known about the Nez Perce Tribe, which continues to be a sovereign nation just a few miles away from the university's campus, (or about any other Idaho Tribe, in fact) by the dominant White society, I felt this coursework would be essential to any new diversity requirement. Unfortunately, my skills at committee member negotiations fell short. I could not get a consensus buy-in and had to settle for a more expansive diversity requirement, which in and of itself had great benefit. The new diversity General Education requirement meant many more of the diverse Spokes in our American society could be represented, explored, and appreciated by students. Below is the General Catalog description:

> **J-3-e. American Diversity (One course).** As we live in an increasingly diverse and multicultural world, the purpose of these courses is to prepare students to understand, communicate and collaborate with those from diverse communities within the United States and throughout the world. The American diversity courses seek to increase awareness of contemporary and historical issues surrounding the social and cultural diversity in the U.S. Students engage in critical thinking and inquiry into the issues, complexities, and implications of diversity, and how social, economic, and/or political forces have shaped American communities. Diversity includes such characteristics as ability, age, ethnicity, gender, race, religion, sexual orientation, and socioeconomic status. One course chosen from the approved American diversity courses listed below. (The diversity course was an additional requirement alongside an already existing international requirement. From the 2014–15 University of Idaho General Catalog.)

Integrative Studies: Spokes and Hub. Over the years, I had the opportunity repeatedly to teach each of the three types of Integrative Seminars. All were favorites, though the ISEM 101 holds a special place. The ISEM 101 seminar I particularly loved was entitled "the Sacred Journey," which, in its year-long version, provided an introduction to the world's religious traditions—Native American, Hindu, Buddhist, Taoist, Judaism, Christianity, and Islam—while attempting to address the Learning Outcomes within its designed pedagogical structures. I asked my students, at the core of each of these seven distinct religious configurations, were they not each in approximation with the others, and together archetypal of something grander? And I asked, how did they align, in Spokes and Hub, with their own tradition, their own unfolding story? In the questions I asked my students, there were no correct or incorrect answers sought. Rather, I expected serious reflective engagement from them.

From 2012–15, while continuing to teach, I also served as the University of Idaho's Director of General Education, responsible for implementing the work of the steering committees. It was during this time that I developed, wrote, and added a formal definition for a critical component of the General Education storyline. It was based upon the insights gained from the American Academy of Colleges and Universities (AAC&U), the lead national organization focused on general education (via its conference presentations and conversations with colleagues, and its publications), but also in conjunction with my own lived stories of Spokes and Hub. In the university's General Catalog, "integrative studies" is thus defined in the following manner:

> **J-3-f. Integrated Studies—ISem 101 Integrative Seminar (3 cr), ISem 301 Great Issues (1 cr), and Senior Experience.** The purpose of these courses is to provide students with the tools of integrative thinking, which are critical for problem solving, creativity and innovation, and communication and collaboration. Integrated learning is the competency to attain, use, and develop knowledge from a variety of disciplines and perspectives, such as the arts, humanities, sciences, and social sciences, with disciplinary specialization (to think divergently, distinguishing different perspectives), and to incorporate information across disciplines and perspectives (to think convergently, re-connecting diverse perspectives in novel ways). It is a cumulative learning competency, initiated as a first-year student and culminating as reflected in a graduating senior. (From the 2014–15 University of Idaho General Catalog.)

In a broad sweep, aligned were the traditions, the diverse, the unique Spokes, the *difference*, with divergent thinking, and the transformational, the shared, the ubiquitous Hub, the *no difference*, with convergent thinking. All essential complementary processes in a balanced Wheel, in a winning relay team, or in lifelong integrative engagement, making *all the difference*. And I was reminded of the imagery of Apsáalooke term for clan, *ashammalíaxxiia,* "driftwood lodges." In that river of life, full of eddies, fast currents, and sharp protruding boulders, it was in the tight interweaving of the distinct pieces of driftwood, each *different* from the next, that there was *no difference*, and it made *all the difference*. Distilled in this definition and learning outcome were elements from the Academy, the AAC&U, and from the Indigenous, the Spokes and Hub, into one specific application, a pedagogy for action, "integrated studies."

As General Education director, I understood that, if integrative thinking and behaving, as witnessed in the lives of Tom and Susie Yellowtail, and experienced in my own healing journeys, were to have any success in impacting students, the divergent Spokes and convergent Hub must be engaged with deliberation and purpose, through experiential learning. Tom and Susie practiced and lived that which they spoke. A relay race is run. I experienced first-hand the scientific and spiritual applied to a healing journey. Integrative thinking doesn't occur passively, by just viewing it or talking about it, or simply by juxtaposing this and that course randomly, as if in isolation from one another, over a four-year period. If it were to have some success in sticking, integrative learning should involve focused, deliberate, and purposeful learning activities, a pedagogy that spins, separates, reconstitutes, and reconnects the Spokes and Hub in a single experiential event. And in a sequence of events that extend and are reiterated over a number of years. Such is the intent of the ISEM 101 seminars, ISEM 301 seminars, and the Senior Experience. Thinking beyond the university, I ask, shouldn't all our lives be lived continually with intentional engagement?

The students' learning activities of deliberate spinning, separating, reconstituting, and reconnecting should involve not only an external journey but also an internal one, a microcosm of the macrocosm. To impact students, I was convinced that integrative thinking should consider not only how we behave in relationship to others, but should also be directed within, exploring the self. It is a self that embodies a multitude of memories, identities, and dreams, some more overt, others hidden deep behind veils of ego and ignorance, injury and prejudice. It is a self, parts of which are hard to crack open. But it is an exploration that can reveal to what extent one's actions are influenced, indeed governed, by one's own inner voice. An exploration acknowledging that if there is to be empathy for others, there should also be empathy of the self. A deep exploration that can help reveal aspects of one's uniqueness as well as qualities of one's shared humanity. At times of disappointment or even failure in one's actions, an exploration that can provide a self-critique, confirming or confronting. An exploration that seeks a sort of gestalt, with one's exterior behavior synchronized with one's interior landscape. Integrative thinking of the soul seeks an alignment of one's behavior with oneself to help one take ownership of and responsibility for one's actions, for one's telling of one's own story. An exploration of the exterior without connecting it with the interior, can render integrative learning simply an academic exercise, something compartmentalized and separate from the student's personal experiences and thus their lifelong unfolding story. Perhaps it is cliché, but does not action without an inner compass render only a lost soul? This form of intimate exploration does take deliberate and purposeful learning activities, a pedagogy in reflection and introspection, focused attentiveness to the self. Such is sought in the ISEM seminars. And I wonder, shouldn't all our lives be lived with intentional reflection?

Empathy Revisited. As part of my General Education responsibilities, I was to assist in helping assure that the General Education curriculum, as an aggregate of courses, met the University of Idaho's Learning Outcomes. Greatly influenced by the AAC&U's "Essential Learning Outcomes," the university's Learning Outcomes were designed to provide the "best possible contemporary liberal education." Upon graduation, each student would be equipped with these outcomes, along with the skills of their specific major field of study.

At least that was the hope, our aspiration. As I closely reviewed and contemplated their meanings and ways of implementation, I was struck by one particular competency—itself essential and foundational for the success in each of the five learning outcomes. That capacity was *empathy*. Consider each of them, with my added empathy-contingent skill in italics.

1. Learn and Integrate—Through independent learning and collaborative study, attain, use, and develop *knowledge in the arts, humanities, sciences, and social sciences,* with disciplinary specialization and the ability to *integrate information across disciplines.*

2. Think and Create—Use *multiple thinking strategies* to examine real-world issues, explore *creative* avenues of expression, *solve problems,* and make consequential decisions.

3. Communicate—Acquire, articulate, create, and convey intended meaning using verbal and nonverbal methods of communication that *demonstrate respect* and *understanding in a complex society.*

4. Clarify Purpose and Perceptive—Explore one's life purpose and meaning through transformational experiences that foster an *understanding of self, relationships,* and *diverse global perspectives.*

5. Practice Citizenship—Apply principles of ethical leadership, *collaborative engagement, socially responsible behavior, respect for diversity in an interdependent world,* and a service-oriented commitment to advance and sustain *local and global communities.*

Empathy, through and through these aspirational relationships. I ask, are not these empathy-infused aspirational principles applicable beyond the university; could they not also apply to chaplains and to us all?

Something Grown. I feel fortunate to have experienced a rich social and ethnic diversity at an early age, in my home community and in a public-school setting, and then as an ethnographer in Native communities. Be it in the classroom, in athletics, in a weekend social gathering, or at a ceremonial event, multiracial, multicultural interactions framed much of my life. So, I ask myself, was I able to effectively engage diversity, to the extent I did, because I had empathy—somehow I was already endowed with it? Or did my empathy grow as I continued to engage diversity, in high school, college, and professionally—is empathy somehow learned? If I had not had these pivotal multiracial relationships growing up, in what state-of-affairs would my empathy capacity be today? I've come to hold that empathy and the doorways of diverse relationships it opens are each mutually interwoven, co-created, a sort of positive feedback loop. While more nuanced and with other factors in play, empathy is greatly cultivated by experiencing a rich diversity in one's life, and diverse relationships are successfully engaged by one's heightened capacity for empathy. Rephrased, empathy, the animating fluid, is nurtured as relationships, the structural conduits, expand. In turn, those relationship expansions nurture the swell of empathy. And of course, the inverse is also the case.

For me, the General Education takeaway was in creating a pedagogical setting, such as the Integrative Seminars and American diversity courses, that was deliberate and rich with all forms of diversity, so even those students previously diversity-deprived had an opportunity to increase their own empathy capacity, as well as lifelong opportunities for relationship expansion. "All forms of diversity" include such variants as in gender, race, ethnicity, religion, epistemology, sex, age, gender identity, socioeconomic status and class, mental and physical ability, as well as local, national, and global cultural affiliation. It is necessarily a pedagogy of deliberate engagement with diversity, its meaning presented with some degree of depth, in historic and cultural context, with some degree of appreciation. Else it be a confrontation with a stranger that can misunderstand, unnerve, repel, or even elicit fear.

Spokes and Hub Revisited. Having spent only part of that summer of 1974 with Tom and Susie Yellowtail—albeit an intense several weeks—by the time I departed for Colorado, I was calling them, "grandpa" and "grandma," and they calling me, "grandson." We were once perfect strangers to each other, the overt differences so glaring, I wonder in hindsight if it was something shared-in-common that brought us together, "as if we'd known each other all along." Let's not forget that to jump-start a relationship with a perfect stranger, with empathy guiding our way, there is also the shared Hub. We want to engage the stranger certainly by exploring the diverse Spokes, but also by searching for what is shared-in-common. Intentional integrative engagement entails both divergent and convergent thinking. In its year-long version, the Sacred Journey seminar explored the Spokes of seven diverse religions and what they possibly shared at the Hub. We should not let the Spoke's different as different could be, its glare, blind us and get in the way of discovering what is right in front of us. A difference so different in one's own or another's politics, religious convictions, ethnicity, age, sex, nationality, status and privilege, gender identity, whatever "ism,"—and the list goes on—should not get in the way. If only for a moment, can we put the Spoke on pause? This can be the greatest challenge, but with the greatest reward. In the diversity pedagogical setting, having students juxtapose the varied Spokes alongside their reflective selves can facilitate the highlighting of the distinct as well as the shared contours of that stranger's and those students' landscapes. Finding common ground, if only a small parcel, is a start. With a pause and a juxtaposition, followed by reflection and action, comes the possibility of jump-starting a relationship with a perfect stranger. Perhaps this is an argument for the value of intentional diversity engagement for us all.

And I ask, with empathy guiding our way, perhaps empathy is to be revealed upon arriving at our destination, at the Hub? As conveyed in the words of the Indian Name Grandpa Tom would bestow on me, *Maakuuxshiichíilish*, a Name implicit with perhaps something he saw glimpses of in me and certainly a hope for what would become even more so, was that what two perfect strangers shared-in-common that summer of 1974? In sync, I know I felt and saw that same something, fully expressed, in Tom from the beginning. Empathy, a means to and the end itself? Empathy imbued throughout the Wheel, along its Spokes and at its Hub. Something at the core of our humanity, shared-in-common, revealed in its depth at the depths of my liminal state in 2009.

Value of a General Education. I am convinced that a General Education curriculum, with an integrative "backbone" and arteries flowing with empathy-infused "blood," would result in graduates with "nimble minds—solid core and limbs—flexible bodies." Would result in *ilúuppe,* yet *tatáche,* the Crow terms meaning "to be flexible," "to be solid." In their intellectual and artistic endeavors, empathy, diversity appreciation and integrative thinking would lead them to be more adaptable, innovative, a creative thinker, a critical thinker, with effective skills in communication and collaboration. As artists, not only be able to clearly and attentively feel, but also think. As scientists, not only be able to clearly and attentively think, but *also* feel. For both, to be able to clearly and attentively distinguish the pieces, the parts, while also reimagining and reconnecting those parts into new combinations, a new or a renewed whole. Empathy, diversity appreciation, and integrative thinking facilitate self-aware-ness, and, with it, clarity in and responsibility for choices we make. With empathy, respect for diversity, and integrative thinking, the graduates could better identify and address various forms of social schism, expressed in such behaviors as bigotry, scapegoating, trib-alism, or balkanization in a society. Integrative thinking, premised on empathy, promotes tolerance and respect for difference, the ability to feel and understand something of another's perspective, to listen and be attentive to the diverse Spokes. Integrative thinking also facilitates making connections and reconnections, and finding common ground, the possibility of a ubiquitous Hub, with once strangers, now opponents no longer. I wonder if what I had advo-cated as a director, another iteration of Grandpa's attentiveness and Wheel, had rubbed off and influenced me as a chaplain? Helping provide the flexibility and adaptability I'd need to engage each of the diverse prefect strangers I encountered as I *walked the halls* of the Medical-Surgical Unit? In living deliberately, respecting diversity, with empathy-infused integrative engagement, would not only ethnographers and chaplains, but each one of us be nimbler, more flexible, yet solid at our core, as we *walk the halls* of our contemporary world and engage the many perfect strangers? Huckleberries for us all, applied to the many?

◆ ◆ ◆

And I woke with such a desire!

Notes

[1]Some of the General Education materials in this chapter were previously published the *Journal of Northwest Anthropology*, 2021.

Tsi'łhnkhukhwatpalqs
"the trail ends"

To Carry Forth the Stories—
Great Stories Will Come

We started this essay with four "Awakening Stories"—the Tin Shed, the Wheel, a Prayer for My Son, and Burnt Face. Mysteries to be sure, yet *Mystery* to be revealed. They are reflective of the meanings of *baaéechichiwaau*, "re-telling one's own," re-telling the cherished oral traditions of a people, and *basbaaaliíchiwé*, "telling my story," re-telling the significant stories of a person's life. Stories that have jumped started my own story, an anchoring from which my journey unfolded. In turn, these stories have led us into other stories, into the Tin Sheds and Sweat Houses of perfect strangers, and through the Halls of Hospitals and the Academy into the rooms of perfect strangers, swirling with the stories of Tom and Susie Yellowtail, Cliff SiJohn and Allen Old Horn, and so many others, including those of myself, Rodney Frey. We swirled with such disparate stories as Burnt Face, Salmon and Coyote, Head and Heart Knowing, cancer abated and an inner ear protruding, Sundancing and *Bishée, Sqigwts* and 3-D virtual reality, visits from the *Awakkuléeshe* and the Madonna, *walking the halls* of a hospital and General Education. And may our various storytellers become less strangers to you. May there have been, embedded in our stories, now revealed to you special *miyp*, "teachings from all things," indeed *st'shąstq* "huckleberries." As they have certainly transformed me, brought the contours of my journey to you, in the act of re-telling them, these huckleberries are now gifted to you, to be placed into your cedar basket for safe keeping, huckleberries awaiting their own re-telling, awaiting the possibility of continued transformation.

In my *stmi'sm*, "listening," in being *ahkúxpatchiahche*, "attentive" to the stories swirling within the Tin Shed and Sweat House, and in the rooms of Hospitals, stories diverse, stories ubiquitous, revealed were two special *miyp* huckleberries—the power of *snukwnkhwtskhwts'mi'ls*, "empathy," and the guidance of the *Ashé isée* "the Medicine Wheel." Stories brought to life by empathy, conveying teachings of empathy— stories by and of empathy and compassion. Empathy, the "how" and the "what" of these stories. And is not *stmi'sm* and *ahkúxpatchiahche*, themselves, this deep listening, another form of empathy applied? As Cliff SiJohn asked us to do, "be attentive, listen as the wind, brushing through the leaves of the trees, tells you something." And I wonder, is not this a listening that leads to an expression something akin to the ultimate meaning of Divinity as revealed in the great spiritual traditions of the world? And Tom Yellowtail stood so connected with the many diverse people and spiritual leaders at that Chicago podium, stood Spokes *and* Hub. Tom's Wheel certainly offers an ambidextrous map, indeed "strategy stories" for traveling the many diverse Spokes, while at the same time conversing in our shared languages, without threat of divisiveness and schism. And interwoven throughout it all, yet another undeniable huckleberry, the value of "story" itself, *'me'y'mi'y'm*, in both its expressions, *baaéechichiwaau* and *basbaaaliíchiwé*.

◆ ◆ ◆

Now let me leave you with a few final thoughts—reiterating our huckleberries, shining a little more light on them, as I pose a question or two in the process. When we *walk* into the homes of our Indigenous neighbors, or we *walk the halls* of a hospital and enter the rooms, or upon graduation, *walk* from the commencement stage and enter the many doors awaiting, or as we simply *walk* the streets of any town or city, and enter the rooms of our diverse America, I wonder if empathy, attentive to our stories infused with diversity and commonality, doing so in sincerity is not the key in helping jumpstart relationships with perfect strangers? Even, with only deep attentiveness, can come the possibility of finding gratitude for the strangest of strangers. Even with only focused listening can come the possibility of having gratitude for the different as different could be.

Tom and Susie Yellowtail, Allen Old Horn, Cliff SiJohn and Father Randolph remind us that there are so many strangers amongst us, so many Sweat Lodges and Tin Sheds, so many *hallways to walk* in our world, distinguished by such divisions as class, ethnicity, economics, gender or religion, by cultural distances, distinguished by academic disciplines and theoretical paradigms, distinguished by political affiliations. Is there not great merit in seeking to enter the Sweat Lodges of others and be swaddled in the blankets of our hosts, woven with the fibers of ethical permission and collaboration, patterned in their particular perspectives, learning styles and epistemologies, blankets that can, in turn, be given away to provide comfort for others? If we're to effectively engage, communicate, and work together to build community in a world of so many strangers, are not the lessons from the Hub, of our shared humanity, just as critical as the lessons from the Spokes, the lessons of our human diversity? If we're to travel within and outside of the many Sweat Lodges, with the many strangers amongst us, can we with competence don the regalia of the many Spokes, while also speaking our shared languages, languages of empathy and of story? Can there even be a humanity without *snukwnkhwtskhwts'mi'ls* and *'me'y'mi'y'm*?

When there is the perception of an irreconcilable mutually exclusivity between two points of view or ways of knowing, and that exclusivity is left un-attended, the result can be a combination of distrust, misunderstanding, miscommunication, dysfunctional operations, and inability to achieve goals. The result can be entrenched partisan politics or religious intolerance, "my way or the highway." Surely intransigent exclusivity and separation, segregation by another term, should not prevail. We know where balkanization can lead. Do we have to wait to be galvanized by some external threat, some sort of catastrophe, to re-discover what we already know, what we already can do?

As exemplified in lives of the elders, such as Cliff, Tom, and Susie, one can remain grounded in a scientific paradigm, in a world of discrete objects and Head Knowledge dualism, while also experiencing a world as a transitory co-creation of those participating, a world of Heart Knowledge holism, monism. One can engage and communicate with the world via literacy, viewing it through Shakespearian sonnets and scientific treatises, while also via orality, experiencing an unfolding world while swirling in storytelling. In literacy, reality is described; in orality, you are in reality, it being perpetuated. One can keep the well-worn wooden bench of the natural and social sciences warmed, without need of reducing indigenous knowledge and practice to mere "fantasy" and "quaint beliefs and practices," to imaginary "myths and superstitions," or relegating it to some pre-scientific stage of human cultural development, of "primitive," misplaced observations and explanations about what otherwise cannot be understood. Geology and Coyote can each account for those rock formations. The Wheel can provide a map for traveling the many paths without dilemma, without having to make an either-or choice. Regardless of how seemingly irrevocably distinct from the other, the varied paths we encounter can be traveled without threat of their mutual exclusivity. The integrity of one's tree trunk can remain viable while grafting onto it branches from other trees.

◆ ◆ ◆

Doesn't it start with an empathy that is honest in its motivation and action to be deeply attentive to another, a self-effacing empathy? An empathy that, in its quintessential expression, removes separation and dissolves the "self" into the "other," as if two hearts beat as one. A non-discriminating empathy. And not an empathy that is in any way shrouded in ego, hubris or ulterior motive, a self-serving empathy. Not an empathy imbued with a rush to judgment. If ego over empathy is brought to the door of a stranger, surely that door would be closed. And isn't it only after gaining a sense of the stranger's perspective that we can begin to assess and critique the one now engaged, that we can bring the interests of the self to bear in the unfolding relationship, that we bring a helping hand, or simply walk hand-in-hand, or perhaps hold another at an arm's length, or even bring a stiff arm to the relationship, depending on the context? Of course, the first action the most likely option for a chaplain!

I wonder if it is not self-effacing empathy that is the lifeblood that flows through and animates the architectural bones of our stories? And when those veins are opened to others and with the blood coalescing, uniting into a whole, "self" and "other" become blurred if not dissolved, as the Wheel's Spokes and Hub spin in balance and harmony? I wonder if it is not self-effacing empathy that is at the core of the various relationships sought in our aspirational principles—empathy imperative for relationships of acceptance, respect, and understanding—empathy a prerequisite for justice and equality, and above all, empathy, brought to its conclusion, into action, compassion? Compassion, without the guiding hand of empathy, can miss its mark. I wonder, if empathy, attentive to our separate traditions and our shared humanity, and attentive to the possibilities of transformation, is not essential in helping create and sustain all our most meaningful relationships? Something at the core that helps define the essence of our humanity? As asked and affirmed by so many traditions, in so many ways, when we lose our capacity to feel the suffering of others, we lose our humanity. And I wonder if empathy, born of diversity, growing into compassion for one another, maturing at the heart of our shared humanity, has the possibility of rebirth into…?

◆ ◆ ◆

It was at a tribally sponsored meeting of local officials at the Benewah Resort, along the shores of Lake Coeur d'Alene, some fifteen years ago. Cliff was helping facilitate, with members of his family and the "family drum" present. Cliff had seen my involvement at numerous powwows over the years, as I mostly viewed from my seat, occasionally was on the dance floor during an Intertribal song, and once with a woman's shawl draped over my shoulders. He knew I must have had some familiarity with the drum. As the meeting was to commence, the SiJohn Drum was to offer a song. Cliff motioned to me to come forward, handed me a drumstick and a seat around the drum. I was honored, but...I attempted to keep in pace and rhythm, voicing sounds unfamiliar to my throat, worried I'd continue beating on the drum when the song ended. You know, Cliff never did invite me to sit again at this family's drum. It was a competency not yet mastered.

◆ ◆ ◆

The Wheel can be kept balanced, any schisms bridged, the mutually exclusive rendered irrelevant, when successfully donning the varied regalia of our collective diversity, while speaking the common languages of our shared humanity. But it does take a will, desire, and an effort to muster the competencies of the varied dance styles and of the shared languages. It takes more than a causal familiarity with the drum or the wish for a tasty huckleberry, but hours and hours of preparation and effort. Inclusivity over exclusivity takes hard work. Self-selecting into siloes is easy. Embracing a stranger takes effort.

As with Tom, there is a particular competency, above all others, that must be mastered and evoked, that allowed him to hold in one hand the Eagle-feather fan, and the other the Gospel of Mark, while standing alongside the Dalai Lama. It is the essential competency needed to successfully travel with kinsmen along the Spoke of familial relationships, and all the more needed when traveling with strangers along Spokes separate and diverse. And as if you haven't already connected the dots for yourself (and I suspect you have), what keeps the wheel greased and turning, facilitating one's ability to dance the varied dances and speak the shared languages, is the competency of empathy—*snukwnkhwtskhwts'mi'ls*. But it is something that may not come without great effort. To listen deeply is much more difficult than talking verbosely.

◆ ◆ ◆

Can we embrace the teachings of inclusion and interconnection, of equality and empathy, of intentional integrative engagement as easily as Tom and Susie and Allen and Cliff did? In our interactions with the many strangers amongst us, embroiled in the many seemingly entrenched schisms, can we not find compromise and consensus, as we respect the integrity of the many diverse, supple Spokes and speak the languages of the common, steadfast Hub? While we may never become competent in another's cultural and epistemological realities, we can strive to attain some level of relationship with one another and competency in each other's reality that can lead to mutual understanding, to mutual trust and respect, to empathy for the other, to integrative engagement. And that can result in effective communications and collaboration in pursuit of shared goals, and the possibility of grafting a branch from another tree onto the trunk of our own tree.

In today's society, stories that celebrate, bridge and reconcile differences, that speak to our shared spirit and common humanity, healing narratives of all kinds, seem to be in short supply. There are far too many strangers amongst us! But if there's truth to the old adage, doesn't it all start with each one of us, within us, with the stories you and I tell one another? One voice, then another, still another, and another yet can become an omnipotent choir. Let's re-affirm our highest and most noble aspirations, and each of us roll up our sleeves, and live our lives deliberately, intentionally, with *díakaashe*, re-telling stories akin to that of Tom and Susie Yellow-tail's Wheel, with its diverse Spokes and ubiquitous, transformative Hub, emanating throughout with an outflowing of empathy. Truly integrative stories, truly *basbaaaliíchiwé* stories. Stories, infused with empathy, that allow us to celebrate and respect our *differences*, while also facilitating a harmony of those differences, revealing our shared humanity, as there are *no differences,* stories that make *all the difference!*

◆ ◆ ◆

University of Idaho writer Brandon Schrand, a speaker at the "Turning of the Wheel" humanities series, introduced me to the literary genre known as the "personal essay." First articulated in 1580 when Michel de Montaigne coined the word, the "essay" can be a deeply personal and informal literary device that, through the revealing of one's own particular journey, seeks to evoke and engage the reader's own experiences, helping bring meaning to our shared humanity. While etched in the particulars of one's own story, as Montaigne wrote, "In every one of us is the entire human condition." A personal essay is therefore not so much a definitive statement, a formal treatise on the subject, confined within a standardized format, as a wondering exploration into one's inner territories, while asking universal questions.

In my own discipline of anthropology, Paul Stoller, along with other essayists such as Ruth Behar, have eloquently written and evocatively attested that, "As in ethnography, the memorable memoir is usually a text...in which the author constructs the personal as a bridge... that connects outer realities to inner impressions, others to selves, and readers to writers. In this way, these memoirs bring together disparate worlds and construct a deeper awareness of our common humanity" (Stoller 2009:164). They provide a strong argument for the role and importance of "memoir" and "story," of the "sensuous" and "emotive," and of the blurring of the observer-observed distinction in ethnography.

As re-told here, I see the text you now hold as having an affinity with the Western literary genres referred to as a personal essay and the memoir—an indigenous *basbaaaliíchiwé* genre. This is a re-telling of my journeys, of Cliff SiJohn and Allen Old Horn pointing the way into the Sweat Lodge and Tin Shed, of Tom and Susie Yellowtail pointing the way into the Big Lodge and a warmed wooden shed, and into the hallways of Hospitals, and of the wondrous story landscapes subsequently traveled—all pointing the way into the different, and through it, into the universal. Is it not the case that the deeper we travel within the distinctive Sweat Lodges and hallways of the many strangers amongst us, the deeper we can lay bare and acknowledge our inner stories, revealing that precious bundle of unconditional Love, discarding our distinguishing overt regalia? As we travel deeper into what is so different from our own upbringings, the farther out of the idiosyncratic we actually emerge, merged with what we share in common, with our adopted families? The farther up the Spokes of diversity we travel, the more we are fused with the Hub of our shared humanity.

◆ ◆ ◆

Would there be *something of value* in this essay, worthy of sharing? Only you can judge. I do hope that the stories I've shared with you throughout this *basbaaaliíchiwé* and *baaéechichiwaau*, this ethnography of my own landscape and of the landscapes of others—the Tin Shed and the Sweat Lodge, the halls of a Hospital and an Academy, the warmed wooden shed, *ashammalíaxxiia* and *baaxpée*, revealing the *miyp*, aligning the steadfast perennial bones and the resulting hierophany, *dasshússua* and orality, the

Tom at his cabin, tilling his garden and a story. Photo: with permission. *Frey 1993*

transitory intersection of those participating, have come alive, supple, and have swirled around you, a resuscitating of the bones. Story brought to life; life is story. And I hope those special words for me, *Awakkuléeshe* and *Bishée*, *Maakuuxshiichíilish* and *Kw'lk'ịl Sqqị*—have helped reveal some of the *Mystery* for you. *Mystery*—the inexplicable wonder and awe—yet another *miyp* huckleberry? It is my hope that these stories will now continue to be cherished and revered, something felt, experienced from the Heart. By adding such ideas as tribal sovereignty and cultural property rights, collaboration and giving back, as well as chaplaincy and General Education, and then adding the competency of the Spokes and the empathy of the Hub of the Medicine Wheel to the mixture, I hope you are brought a little closer to Tom and Susie's, and Cliff's experiences, and my own. With the coalescence of all these words, may they be resuscitated from the printed page, re-vitalized in their re-telling, words lifted off the page, coming alive, with you swirling among the many participants.

Let's all come together to re-tell some stories, *'me'y'mi'y'm*. With empathy, *snukwnkhwtskhwts'mi'ls*, let's swirl within the stories of Coyote, and talk with him and each other. Let's see what huckleberries, *st'shastq*, we can gather—huckleberries that might guide and nourish: for ourselves, for others, for those in need—huckleberries that might meet the challenges and chart the world—huckleberries that might even create the world. Let's carry forth the stories and do some re-telling, and see what awaits.

Rob Moran with grand-daughters, going out to do some huckleberrying. Photo, by permission, *Frey 2003*

As Cliff would always say at the completion of one of his wonderful public talks, "I now still my voice." I too now still my voice, bringing to a close this re-telling, having traveled the ethnographic landscapes of my story—*basbaaaliíchiwé*, and those of others—*baaéechichiwaau*, and close with the phrase, *tsi'łhnkhukhwatpalqs*, "the trail ends." But let's remember Tom Yellowtail's prophetic declaration, so elegantly and precisely spoken in 1993, just before his passing. We were at his cabin, far from the noise and bustle of the highway. Tom was re-telling his most cherished stories, culminating with that of Burnt Face. He wanted to leave these stories for his grandkids and for all of us. Late into the evening, after he completed his re-telling, Tom turned to me and affirmed, "If all these great stories were told, great stories will come!"

And I woke with *such…a…desire*!

Ahókaashiile, Qe'ciyéw'yew', Lim lemt.sh
"thank you"

Acknowledgments

This essay is as much a re-telling of my own story, a *basbaaa-liíchiwé*, as it is a re-telling of great stories shared with me by great storytellers, all gracious hosts, having invited me into their homes to then re-tell their stories, a *baaéechichiwaau*. Who I am is the culminating intersection of the lives of so many.

I am indebted to my family, to my parents Wallace and Jeanne Frey, to my wife Kristine Roby and son Matthew and his partner Kelly Graves. To my adopted "grandparents" Tom and Susie Yellowtail, of the Crow. To my many "brothers and sisters," from Coeur d'Alene country, Cliff and Lori SiJohn (Coeur d'Alene and Cayuse/Umatilla); from Crow country, Leonard and Regina Bends, Ada Bends, Alvin Howe, and Diane Medicine Crow-Reynolds (Crow); from Fort Washakie, Rayburn and Janet Beck, and her sisters, including Betty Glick, Theresa Plentyhoops and Zelma Robertson, and Janet's daughter Leonna Pretty Weasel-Armajo and her husband Martin Armajo, and their daughter, my "granddaughter," Jordan Armajo (Wind River Shoshone); from Warm Springs, Rob and Rose Moran (Little Shell Chippewa and Warm Springs); and always on the move, Heather Kae Binkley (Nakoda/Saami affiliation). And to *Bishée*, my "Medicine Father," and Burnt Face, my guide.

A very special thanks to the children and grandchildren of Tom and Susie Yellowtail for being "family" for me, including Bruce Yellowtail and his children, Jackie, Rudy, Dwayne, Merlin, Joey, and Thomas and his wife Amy; Virjama Wyles and her children, Kenny

Wyles and Linda Andrews; Connie Jackson and her children, David Small, Valerie, Tracy, Frank and Lesley Kabotie; and TR Glenn and his children.

Among the many others who have touched my life so deeply in some manner, teachers all, *family* all, a sincere *ahó*: to Johnny Arlee, Vic Charlo, Frank Finley, Agnes Vanderburg, and Clarence Woodcock (Bitterroot Salish and Pend d'Oreille); to Shaina Nomee (Cayuse/Umatilla); to John Abraham, Dianne Allen, Felix Aripa, Lawrence Aripa, Leanne Campbell, Michelle Clark, Lucy Finley, Jeanne Givens and her husband Ray, Roberta Juneau, Marceline Kevis, Chuck Matheson, Dave Matheson, Quanah Matheson, Caj and Kim Matheson, Chris Meyer, Richard Mullen, Lawrence Nicodemus, Alfred Nomee, Mariane Hurley Nomee, Norma Peone, Henry SiJohn, Frenchy SiJohn, CarylDene Swan, Dixie Saxon Stensgar, Ernie Stensgar, Audra Vincent, Jeannette Whitford, and Marjorie Zarate (Coeur d'Alene); to Tiffany Allgood (Cree/Cherokee affiliation); to Heywood Big Day, Rose Chesarech and her husband Steve, John Cummins and family, John Frost, Garland Howe, Bobby Howe, Louella Johnson, Marshal Left Hand, Joe Medicine Crow, Mary Helen Medicine Horse, John Old Coyote and his wife Sally and the Old Coyote family, Dan Old Elk and family, Allen Old Horn and family, Janine Pease, John Pretty On Top, Jonathan Pretty On Top, Lucy Real Bird and family, Jerome and Lois White Hip, and Bill Yellowtail and his wife Maggie (Crow); to Francis Cullooyah (Kalispel); to Basil White (Kootenai); to Horace Axtell, James Holt, Dan and Julie Kane, Mylie Lawyer, Ann McCormack, Aaron Miles, Sam Penney, Aaron Penney, Kevin Peters, Allen Pinkham, Josiah and D'Lisa Penney-Pinkham and their family, Diane Mallickan, Bob and Angel Sobotta, Leroy Seth, Vera Sonneck, Mari Watters, Silas Whitman, and Nakia Williamson (Nez Perce); to Dave Brown-Eagle, Pauline Flett, Buzz Gutierrez, Margo Hill, and Sam and Pat Peone (Spokane); to Thomas Morning Owl (Umatilla); to Evaline Patt, Elysia Moran, Roy Spino and his children "Mish," Bear, and Victoria, Lorraine Suppah, and Bridgett Whipple (Warm Springs and Wasco); to John Trehero (Wind River Shoshone); to Julian Pinkham

(Yakima); to Sue Ayer, Matt's mother; to Chris and Donna Bain; to Joseph and Elenita Brown, their daughter Marina Weatherly and their family; to Pierre and Connie Chesnel; to Brian Cleveley, Jeremy Kenyon, and Steven Daley-Laursen; to Michael and Judith Fitzgerald, and Joseph and Mariam Fitzgerald and their friends; to Raymond Brinkman, Phillip Cernera, Father Thomas Connelly, Ted Fortier, John Hartman, Gary Palmer, and Jill Wagner; to Davíd Carassco, Russell Coberly, Jack Schultz, Robert Theodoratus, and Deward Walker; to Father Randolph Graczyk, C. Adrian Heidenreich, G. Hubert Matthews, Tim McCleary, and Sister Karen Watembach; to Bob Chenoweth and Alan Marshall; to Lillian Ackerman, Suzanne Crawford O'Brien, Dell Hymes, Karl Kroeber, Robin Ridington, and Robert McCarl; and to so many others.

My deepest gratitude goes out to family, friends, and former students who so greatly assisted Rayburn and Janet, and Matt and Kelly, in helping support, and offer personal sacrifice and prayers in the 2009 Sundance: Chris Bain, Kathryn Barber, Monique Crumb, James Holt, Heather Kae Binkley, Jan Kirchhoff-Smith, and Mark Solomon and Jeanne Amie Clothiaux.

For assisting me with Indigenous terms, thank you to Tim McCleary (Apsáalooke), Cliff SiJohn and Audra Vincent (Schı̣t-su'umsh), and Angel Sobotta (Niimíipuu).

Thank you also to my colleagues and especially to my students over the past many years, who "underwent" earlier versions of this essay as a course packet, and whose reactions and suggestions helped reawaken and bring to print some of my life's stories now held in hand. In their honesty, students can be among our best teachers. Thanks to Ryan Richey for his edits on an earlier version of the course packet.

Special thanks also to Bob Clark, editor-in-chief, and Beth DeWeese, manuscript editor, with Washington State University Press, who from the start saw value in and were committed to this project, and for Beth's in-depth, insightful editing of this essay, helping bring it to life for you.

As a re-telling, inclusive of the many stories, terms, and concepts, gathered and re-arranged in this essay along a particular storyline, I give a special thanks to the Bitterroot Salish, Coeur d'Alene, Confederated Tribes of Warm Springs, Crow, Kootenai, Nez Perce, and Spokane elders, mentors, consultants, Cultural Committees, Circle of Elders, Tribal Councils, and/or Executive Committees, who had invited me to engage in collaborative, applied research, writing, and teaching, and who had previously reviewed and approved the stories, now re-told here, for public dissemination. Given the cultural sensitivity of the Jump Dance, Sundance, and Sweat House/Lodge, this includes previous approval by the associated tribal consulting elders, Cultural Committee, and Tribal Council to publically share the text descriptions and photographed images included in this essay. Thank you to the Confederated Tribes of the Colville Reservation for their permission to re-tell William Burks' Salmon story. Stories identified as "re-told" had originally appeared with permission in Frey 1979 and 1987; Frey, Aripa, and Yellowtail 1995; Frey and the Nez Perce 2001; Frey and the Schitsu'umsh 2001 and 2002; Frey and the Confederated Tribes of Warm Springs 2003; Frey and Pinkham 2005; Frey and Williamson 2005; Frey, Yellowtail, and SiJohn 2008; Frey and Campbell 2015.

This review process included permission to publically present my 1970s experiences with the *Awakkuléeshe* and *Bishée* (Frey 1979 and 1987). While my family and mentors knew of my "special visitors," I've since lamented the decision not to provide public attribution at the time. While receiving approval to publically identify individuals who participated in the 1970–80s research (which I did), I relied upon an ethnographic format within which there was generally no attribution assigned to any specific description, be it that chronicled in an interview with an elder or be it that derived from my participant observation at a giveaway or with the Little People. I suppose I could attribute the decision to a young person unsure of his footing along the then dichotomized professional and private paths. It followed "standard" ethnographic practice. And then an "awakening," and the acknowledging and telling of the evolution of the interweaving of my private personal with my public professional, of the blurring of the interwoven fibers of my familial and spiritual stories with my ethnographic stories. Held in hand are stories *basbaaa-liíchiwé* and *baaéechichi-waau*, all of whom make up the inseparable fibers of who I am. All of whose varied story sources and their attributions are thus acknowledged, I accepting responsibility for doing so, and are presented to you with humility and honest introspection as my personal essay, the blurred and interwoven rendered public, a "re-telling of my story." As with Tom's and Allen's, and Lawrence's and Cliff's, so with mine—a story told is only completed when attributing its teller, the one who sought to bring flesh to the bones.

"Coyote's Laugh," watercolor by Lawrence Aripa. A Christmas gift from Lawrence to the author, 1997.

While I'm the intellectual offspring of the Boasian family, and such exemplary teachers and mentors as Deward Walker and Davíd Carassco, to whom I am most grateful, I've been swaddled in the lessons of many great teachers and storyteller hosts, young and old, women and men, and acknowledge being awakened to the light and transformed as a Euro-American ethnographer and as a human being by the dark and heat of the Sweat House. It's been a truly humbling experience, one that I am forever indebted and most grateful to so many.

Ahókaashiile (Apsáalooke), *qeǎciyéw'yew'* (Niimíipuu), *lim lemt.sh* (Schitsu'umsh)—thank you with all my heart, for all the huckleberries.

Acknowledgements for the Expanded Edition

The *Ahkúxpatchiahche* chapter of this Expanded Edition could not have occurred without the Gritman Medical Center doctors, nurses and staff, including Kim Malm and Shelley McGregor, past and current Volunteer Directors, Danielle Breed, Administrative Chief of Staff, and all my fellow volunteer chaplains, especially Diane Lowe, Mary Beth Rivetti, and Elisabeth Berlinger, who first invited me to join the chaplain team. To them I owe a sincere thank you. Their companionship and support brought this writing to life. Also, a heart-felt gratitude to all the patients and their families I've served, who inturn shared their most vulnerable selves and offered invaluable lessons in the meaning of our Humanity. I also want to thank Father Randolph Graczyk, who has been with me since the beginning of my Sundance journey, for his review and editing of the *Ahkúxpatchiahche* chapter. To Rayburn and Janet Beck, Leonard and Regina Bends, the Yellowtail family, and the Frey family for their steadfast kindred love. And to Linda Bathgate, Editor-in-Chief, Washington State University Press, for her committed assistance throughout the Expanded Edition process.

While anchored and continuing to grow in Sundance spirituality and theology, I'm indebted to the threads of intellectual and theological traditions coalescing around Unitarian Universalism, World Religions, Perennial Philosophy as exemplified by Huston Smith and Seyyed Hossein Nasr, Process Theology as represented by Alfred North Whitehead and Charles Hartshorne, and Richard Rahr, reflective of both Perennial Philosophy and Process Theology. It is so gratifying to encounter so many asking similar questions about ultimate Reality. They encourage in me continual grow in the questions I ask.

Ahókaashiile, from all my Heart to their Heart.

Pronunciation Guide

The Apsáalooke language is part of the Siouan language family, with an alphabet composed of twenty-seven characters:

a aa b ch d e ee h i ii ia k l m n o oo p s sh t u uu ua w x ?

Almost all Apsáalooke words have a vowel that is stressed. The stressed vowel is identified by an accent mark. The accent is essential for meaning, pronunciation and spelling.

Vowels:

a	a**v**ailable
aa	**f**ather
e	b**e**t
ee	**a**ble
i	b**i**t
ii	b**ea**t
o	st**o**ry
oo	a**d**obe
u	p**u**t
uu	b**oo**ed
ia	**a**rea
ua	Nash**ua**

Consonants:

b	**b**ed
ch	**ch**urch (at beginning or ending of word)
ch	**j**ail (between vowels)
d	**d**og
h	**h**alf
k	**k**itchen (at beginning or end of word and when doubled within a word)
k	**g**uy (between vowels)
l	**l**eap (a sharper "l" than in English)
m	**m**an
n	**n**ot

p	**p**aper (at beginning or end of word and when doubled within a word)
p	**b**aby (between vowels)
s	**s**ize (at beginning or end of word and when doubled within a word)
s	**z**oo (between vowels)
sh	**sh**oe (at beginning or end of word and when doubled within a word)
sh	plea**s**ure (between vowels)
t	**t**ime (at beginning or end of word and when doubled within a word)
t	**d**ay (between vowels)
w	**w**ay
x	a**ch**t (German ch)
?	**uh-oh** (glottal stop)

From the Little Big Horn College Library "Apsáalooke Language Alphabet and Pronunciation Guide," lib.lbhc.edu/index.php?q=node/127.

Snchitsu'umshtsn is of the Salishan language family, spoken by the Schitsu'umsh or Coeur d'Alene. It has been spelled using at least three different systems—the "Reichard Orthography," the "Nicodemus Orthography," and the "Salishan Orthography." The Nicodemus Orthography was developed by Lawrence Nicodemus for use by the Coeur d'Alene community and is still in use today. Many of the sounds used in the Coeur d'Alene language are familiar to English speakers, but many others are not. Apostrophes following stop consonants or preceding sounded consonants signify glottalization.

a	**f**a**ther**
a̲	no example
b	**b**at
ch	**ch**urch
ch'	no example
d	**d**og
e	**egg**
e̲	no example
gw	lin**gu**ini
h	**h**ello
i	ma**ch**ine
j	**j**ar
kw	**qu**een
k'w	no example

kh   no example
khw   no example (like English wh, with hissing sound)
q   no example (like English ch in lock: lower than k; back)
q'   no example
qw   no example (like English qw)
q'w   no example
qh   no example (a guttural uvular sound, a bit like a snore)
qhw   no example (a guttural uvular sound, with a rounding)
l   like
'l   no example
ł   no example (like t and l pronounced together)
m   **m**om
'm   no example
n   **n**ow
'n   no example
o   la**w**
o̲   no example
p   **p**at
p'   no example
r   fa**r**
'r   no example
(no example (a growling sound, like r made in the throat)
'(no example
(w   no example
'(w   no example
s   **s**un
sh   **sh**ell
t   **t**ar
t'   no example
u   J**u**piter
ú   no example
w   **w**agon
'w   no example
y   **y**ard
'   uh–oh (a stop, like a constriction before a in "and")

From the Coeur d'Alene Online Language Resource Center, lasrv01.ipfw.
edu/COLRC/spelling.

Indigenous Term Glossary

Ahkúxpatchiahche: "attentive" (Apsáalooke)

Ahó: "thank you" (Apsáalooke)

Ahókaashiile: "thank you very much" (Apsáalooke)

Akbaalíak: "one who doctors" (Apsáalooke)

Akbaatatdía: "the one who made everything," the Creator (Apsáalooke)

Ammaakée: a giveaway ceremony; from *kée,* to give something away (Apsáalooke)

Amǫtqn: "the one who sits at the head mountain," the Creator (Schitsu'umsh)

Annashisée: "place of the big lodge," the Medicine Wheel (Apsáalooke)

'Apa'áal: "season of *'apá'* (loaf of ground cous cake), month of May (Niimíipuu)

Apsáalooke: "children of the large beaked bird," the Crow People (Apsáalooke)

Ashammalíaxxiia: "driftwood lodges," a kinship clan (Apsáalooke)

Ashé isée: "big lodge," Sundance Lodge, Medicine Wheel (Apsáalooke)

Ashkísshe: "representation lodge," or "lodge like" the Sundance Lodge (Apsáalooke)

Awakkuléeshe: the Little People; from *awakkulé* dwarf (Apsáalooke)

Baaéechichiwaau: "re-telling one's own," telling stories of the Animal First Peoples, though not frequently, but at a special time (Apsáalooke)

Baakáate: "my child" (Apsáalooke)

Baalaásdee, "compassion" (Apsáalooke)

Baaxpée: spiritual power; also, in good luck; Indian medicine (Apsáalooke)

Bacháxpak iilía "to share something with someone" (Apsáalooke)

Bakúpe: "my siblings" (Apsáalooke)

Basahké: "my mother," on the maternal side (Apsáalooke)

Basbaaliíchiwé: "telling my story" (Apsáalooke) *Basbía:* "my sisters" [male speaker] (Apsáalooke)

Biiké: "my elder brother" [male speaker] (Apsáalooke)

Biilápxe: "my father," clan uncle [male speaker] (Apsáalooke)

Bishée: "buffalo" (Apsáalooke)

Cemíitx: huckleberries (Niimíipuu)

Chatq'ele'; chatcolet: Lake Coeur d'Alene (Schitsu'umsh)

Chetche'in'nts: "to reveal" (Schitsu'umsh)

Cikáw'íiswit: "bravery" (Niimíipuu)

Chiwakíia: "beg for," to pray (Apsáalooke)

Chnis-teem-ilqwes: "I am your relative," a part of the human, plant, animal, fish peoples (Schitsu'umsh)

Dasshússua: "breaking with the mouth," the power of the spoken word (Apsáalooke)

Díakaashe: "doing it with determination" sincerity (Apsáalooke)

Diiawákaawik: "I'll see you later" (Apsáalooke)

Eeh: "yes" (Apsáalooke)

Hanyaw'áat: the Creator (Niimíipuu)

Hewléexhewlex: "spirit" (Niimíipuu)

Hischits: "it is my discovery" (Schitsu'umsh)

Hnkhwelkhwlnet: "our ways of life in the world" (Schitsu'umsh)

Hnleq'ntsutn: "sweat house" (Schitsu'umsh)

Ilúuppe "to be flexible" (Apsáalooke)

Isbaaaliíchiweé: "telling his story" (Apsáalooke)

Itchik: "good" (Apsáalooke)

'Itsk'u'lm: "doing" (Schitsu'umsh)

Qa'ánin': "respectful," "honor" (Niimíipuu)

Qe'ciyéw'yew': "thank you" (Niimíipuu)

Qém'es: camas (Niimíipuu)

Q'emiln: "throat," place name for Post Falls, Idaho (Schitsu'umsh)

Qawsqáaws: a medicine root (Niimíipuu)

K'u'lntsụtn: "he who creates himself," the Creator (Schitsu'umsh)

Léepwey: "butterfly creek," place name for Lapwai, Idaho (Niimíipuu)

Léewliks: salmon or any fish (Niimíipuu)

Lim lemt.sh: "thank you" (Schitsu'umsh)

'Me'y'mi'y'm: "telling stories" (Schitsu'umsh)

'Me'y'mi'y'm q'esp schint: "telling stories and learning about the time before human peoples" (Schitsu'umsh)

'Me'y'mi'y'm hu *schint*: "telling stories and learning about human peoples" (Schitsu'umsh)

Miyp: "teachings from all things" (Schitsu'umsh)

Niimíipuu: "the people" the Nez Perce People (Niimíipuu)

Niimíipuum 'inmíiwit: seasonal round of the Niimíipuu (Niimíipuu)

Pik'unmaayq'áal: "fish go downriver and salmon to ocean," September (Niimíipuu)

Pute-nts: "respect" (Schitsu'umsh)

Schitsu'umsh: "the ones found here" the Coeur d'Alene People (Schitsu'umsh)

Shéeluk: "it is said," "he/she said it" (Apsáalooke)

Smłich: "salmon" (Schitsu'umsh)

Snchitsu'umshtsn: the Coeur d'Alene language (Schitsu'umsh)

Snqhepiwes: "where the spirit lives, from horizon to horizon" (Schitsu'umsh)

Snukwnkhwtskhwts'mi7ls: "fellow sufferer," empathy (Schitsu'umsh)

Snukwnkhwtskhwts'mi7ls ł stsee'nidmsh: empathetic adaptability (Schitsu'umsh)

Shóotaachi, "greeting" (Apsáalooke)

Sp'ukhwenichelt: "son of light," Chief Child of the Yellowroot (Schitsu'umsh)

Sqha'wlutqhwe': camas (Schitsu'umsh)

Sqigwts: "water potato" (Schitsu'umsh)

Stmi'sm: "listening" (Schitsu'umsh)

Stsee'nidmsh: "adaptability" (Schitsu'umsh)

St'shastq: "huckleberries" (Schitsu'umsh)

Suumesh: spiritual power (Schitsu'umsh)

Talxtálx: "modest," "quiet," "responsible" (Niimíipuu)

Tamálwit: "the law" in a legal sense; also principles and teachings derived from the
    Creator and Animal First Peoples upon which the human people live (Niimíipuu)

Tatáche "to be solid" (Apsáalooke)

Téek'e: "to give and share [food with others]" (*píitek'e* is a giveaway) (Niimíipuu)

Tíwe: "tipi poles"; the central point at which the tipi poles come together, supporting
    each other (Niimíipuu)

Titwatityáaya: the Animal First Peoples (Niimíipuu)

Tsi'łhnkhukhwatpalqs: "the trail ends," the end of the story (Schitsu'umsh)

Tuk'ukín: "honesty," "honest," "impartial" (Niimíipuu)

Uchnek'we': "we are all relatives/we are all one" (Schitsu'umsh)

Unshat'qn: "we're all equal height at the head" "eye-to-eye" (Schitsu'umsh)

Wéeyekin: spiritual power (Niimíipuu)

Yei: "holy ones," the Animal First Peoples (Diné – Navajo)

Yéeye: suffix for descendants, family, and by extension kinship with all the "peoples"
    (Niimíipuu)

'ímes: deer (Niimíipuu)

Bibliography

Aoki, Haruo. 1979. *Nez Perce Texts*. Berkeley: University of California Publications in Linguistics 90.

Aoki, Haruo and Deward Walker. 1989. *Nez Perce Oral Narratives*. Berkeley: University of California Publications in Linguistics 104.

Barfield, Owen. 1965. *Saving the Appearances: A Study in Idolatry*. New York: Harcourt Brace Jovanovich.

Basso, Keith. 1996. *Wisdom Sits in Places: Landscape and Language among the Western Apache*. Albuquerque: University of New Mexico Press.

Behar, Ruth. 1996. *The Vulnerable Observer: Anthropology That Breaks Your Heart*. Boston: Beacon Press.

_____. 2007. "Ethnography in a Time of Blurred Genres." In *Anthropology and Humanism* 32 (2):145–55.

Berkes, Fikret. 2012. *Sacred Ecology,* 3rd ed. London: Routledge.

Boas, Franz and A. Chamberlain. 1918. *Kutenai Tales*. Washington, DC: Bureau of American Ethnology, Bulletin 49:1–387.

Boas, Franz and George Hunt. 1921. *Ethnology of the Kwakiutl*. Washington, DC: Smithsonian Bureau of American Ethnology.

Bronowski, Jacob. 1973. *The Ascent of Man*. New York: Little Brown and Company.

Brown, Joseph Epes. 1953. *The Sacred Pipe: Black Elk's Account of the Seven Rites of the Oglala Sioux*. Recorded and edited. Norman: University of Oklahoma Press.

Chief, Karletta, et al. 2014. "Guidelines for Considering Traditional Knowledge in Climate Change Initiatives." Department of Interior Climate Change Advisory Committee.

Coomaraswamy, Ananda. 1934. *The Transformation of Nature in Art*. Cambridge and London: Harvard University Press.

Dundes, Alan. 1966. "Texture, Text, and Context." In *Southern Folklore Quarterly* 28(4):251–65.

Eliade, Mircea. 1954. *The Myth of the Eternal Return or, Cosmos and History*. Princeton, NJ: Princeton University Press.

_____. 1958. *Rites and Symbols of Initiation: The Mysteries of Birth and Rebirth*. New York: Harper and Row.

_____. 1959. *The Sacred and the Profane: the Nature of Religion*. New York: Harcourt, Brace and World.

Evans-Pritchard, E. E. 1940. *The Nuer: A Description of the Modes of Livelihood and Political Institutions of a Nilotic People*. New York and Oxford: Oxford University Press.

_____. 1956. *Nuer Religion*. New York and Oxford: Oxford University Press.

Frankl, Viktor. 1959 [1946]. *Man's Search for Meaning*. Boston: Beacon Press.

Frey, Rodney. 1979. *To Dance Together: Ethnography in Apsáalooke (Crow) Culture.* PhD diss., Anthropology, University of Colorado, Boulder.

_____.1983 "Re-Telling One's Own: Storytelling among the Apsáalooke (Crow Indians)." In *Plains Anthropologist* 28(100):129–35.

_____.1987. *The World of the Crow Indians: As Driftwood Lodges.* Norman: University of Oklahoma Press.

_____. 1994. *Eye Juggling: Seeing the World through a Looking Glass and a Glass Pane.* Lanham, MD: University Press of America.

_____. 2004. "Oral Traditions." In *A Companion to the Anthropology of American Indians*, edited by Thomas Biolsi, 154–170. Malden, MA: Blackwell Publishing.

_____. 2014. "Southeast Salish, NR-19." In *Human Relations Area Files.* New Haven, CT: Yale University.

Frey, Rodney, with Lawrence Aripa, Tom Yellowtail and other Elders. 1995. *Stories That Make the World: Oral Literature of the Indian Peoples of the Inland Northwest.* Norman: University of Oklahoma Press.

Frey, Rodney, and Dell Hymes. 1998. "Mythology." In *Handbook of North American Indians, Plateau* 12, edited by Deward Walker, 584–99. Washington, DC: Smithsonian Institution Press.

Frey, Rodney, and the Nez Perce. 2001. Niimíipuu (Nez Perce) Lifelong Learning Online. Electronic document, www.lib.uidaho.edu/digital/L3/Sites/ShowOneSiteSiteID34.html.

Frey, Rodney, and the Schitsu'umsh. 2001. *Landscape Traveled by Coyote and Crane: The World of the Schitsu'umsh (Coeur d'Alene Indians).* Seattle: University of Washington Press.

_____. 2002. Schitsu'umsh (Coeur d'Alene) Lifelong Learning Online. Electronic document, www.lib.uidaho.edu/digital/L3/Sites/ShowOneSiteSiteID50.html.

Frey, Rodney, and the Confederated Tribes of Warm Springs. 2003. Warm Springs, Wasco, and Paiute Lifelong Learning Online. Electronic document, www.lib.uidaho.edu/digital/L3/Sites/ShowOneSiteSiteID81.html.

Frey, Rodney, and Josiah Pinkham. 2005. "Nez Perce Rituals and Ceremonies." In *Encyclopedia of American Indian Religious Traditions*, edited by Suzanne Crawford and Dennis Kelly, 147–51. Santa Barbara: ABC-CLIO.

Frey, Rodney, and Nakia Williamson. 2005. "Dances of the Plateau." In *Encyclopedia of American Indian Religious Traditions*, edited by Suzanne Crawford and Dennis Kelly, 213–220. Santa Barbara: ABC-CLIO.

Frey, Rodney, with Tom Yellowtail and Cliff SiJohn. 2008. "If All These Great Stories Were Told, Great Stories Will Come." In *Religion and Healing in Native America: Pathways for Renewal*, edited by Suzanne Crawford O'Brien, 185–205. Westport, CT: Praeger.

Frey, Rodney, ed. 2012. "'Turning of the Wheel': The Interplay between the Unique and Universal—a Humanities Exploration." Moscow: University of Idaho. Electronic document, www.lib.uidaho.edu/digital/turning.

Frey, Rodney and Robert McCarl. 2014. "The Confluence of Rivers: the Indigenous Tribes of Idaho." In *Idaho's Place: Rethinking the Gem State's Past*, edited by Adam Sowards, 13–41. Seattle: University of Washington Press.

Frey, Rodney, Leanne Campbell, et al. 2015. "Sqigwts.org." Coeur d'Alene Tribe and University of Idaho. Electronic document, www.sqigwts.org.

Gatzke, Jennifer. 2008. "'Voices that Soar with the Eagles' Women Drumming in the Coeur d'Alene (Schitsu'umsh) Indian Tribe of Idaho." Master's thesis, Anthropology, University of Idaho.

Geertz, Clifford. 1973. *The Interpretation of Cultures*. New York: Basic Books.

Hymes, Dell. 1981. *"In Vain I Tried to Tell You": Essays in Native American Ethnopoetics*. Philadelphia: University of Pennsylvania Press.

Kovach, Margaret. 2009. *Indigenous Methodologies: Characteristics, Conversations, and Contexts*. Toronto, Buffalo, and London: University of Toronto Press.

Kroeber, Alfred. 1944. *Configurations of Culture Growth*. Berkley: University of California Press.

_____.1963. *Anthropology: Culture Patterns and Processes*. New York: Harcourt, Brace and World.

Lewis, Oscar. 1951. *Life in a Mexican Village: Tepoztlan Restudied*. Urbana: University of Illinois Press.

Lowie, Robert. 1935. *Crow Indians*. New York: Holt, Rinehart and Winston.

_____. 1960. *Crow Texts*. Berkeley: University of California Press.

Medicine Horse, Mary Helen. 1987. *A Dictionary of Everyday Crow*. Crow Agency, MT: Bilingual Materials Development Center.

Momaday, N. Scott. 1969. *The Way to Rainy Mountain*. Albuquerque: University of New Mexico Press.

_____. 1970. "Man Made of Words." In *Indian Voices: The First Convocation of American Indian Scholars*, 49–62. San Francisco: The Indian Historian Press.

Mourning Dove. 1990 [1933]. *Coyote Stories*. Edited by Heister Dean Guie, with notes by L.V. McWhorter. Lincoln and London: University of Nebraska Press.

Narayan, Kirin. 2007. "Tools to Shape Texts: What Creative Nonfiction Can Offer Ethnography." In *Anthropology and Humanism* 32(2):130–144.

Needham, Rodney. 1972. *Belief, Language and Experience*. Chicago and Oxford: University of Chicago Press.

Parsons, Elsie Clews, ed. 1967 [1922]. *American Indian Life*. Lincoln and London: University of Nebraska Press.

Phinney, Archie. 1934. *Nez Perce Texts*. New York: Columbia University Contributions to Anthropology 23.

Pinkham, D'Lisa. 2012. "Indigenous Woman's Perspective." Colloquium talk presented at "Turning of the Wheel: a Humanities Exploration." University of Idaho, Moscow, April 10.

Ray, Verne. 1933. "Sanpoil Folk Tales." *Journal of American Folk-Lore* 46 (180):129–187.

Redfield, Robert. 1930. *Tepoztlan, A Mexican Village: A Study of Folk Life*. Chicago and London: University of Chicago Press.

Reichard, Gladys. 1946. "Coeur d'Alene Texts," Part II, xvii–xxiv. Bloomington: University of Indiana, Archives of Languages of the World.

_____. 1947. *An Analysis of Coeur d'Alene Indian Myths*. Philadelphia: Memoirs of the American Folklore Society 41.

Schrand, Brandon. 2011. "Removing the Mask: The Personal Essay as an Epistemological Instrument in the Unique and the Universal." Colloquium talk presented at "Turning of the Wheel: a Humanities Exploration," University of Idaho, Moscow, November 2.

Smith, Linda Tuhiwai. 2012. *Decolonizing Methodologies: Research and Indigenous Peoples*. 2nd. edition. London and New York: Zed Books.

Stoller, Paul. 2007. "Ethnography/Memoir/Imagination/Story." In *Anthropology and Humanism* 32(2):178–91.

———. 2009. *The Power of the Between: An Anthropological Odyssey*. Chicago: University of Chicago Press.

Taylor, Barbara Brown. 2019. *Holy Envy: Finding God in Faiths of Others*. New York: HarperCollins.

Tedlock, Dennis. 1972. *Finding the Center: Narrative Poetry of the Zuni Indians*. New York: Dial.

Turner, Victor. 1967. *The Forest of Symbols: Aspects of Ndembu Ritual*. Ithaca, NY: Cornell University Press.

———. 1969. *The Ritual Process: Structure and Anti-Structure*. Hawthorne, NY: Aldine de Gruyter.

Van Gennep, Arnold. 1960 [1909]. *Rites of Passage*. Chicago: University of Chicago Press.

Wilson, Shawn. 2008. *Research Is Ceremony: Indigenous Research Methods*. Halifax and Winnipeg: Fernwood Publishing.

Yellowtail, Thomas, and Michael Fitzgerald (recorded and edited). 1994. *Yellowtail, Crow Medicine Man and Sun Dance Chief: An Autobiography*. Norman: University of Oklahoma Press.

Indigenous Interviews/Story Sources

Lawrence Aripa, Schitsu'umsh (Coeur d'Alene)
Janet and Rayburn Beck, Shoshone
Vic Charlo, Bitterroot Salish
Frank Finley, Bitterroot Salish
Lucy Finley, Schitsu'umsh (Coeur d'Alene)
Rob and Rose Moran, Little Shell Chippewa and Warm Springs of Oregon
Allen Old Horn, Apsáalooke (Crow)
D'Lisa Penny Pinkham, Niimíipuu (Nez Perce)
Josiah Pinkham, Niimíipuu (Nez Perce)
Leroy Seth, Niimíipuu (Nez Perce)
Cliff SiJohn, Schitsu'umsh (Coeur d'Alene)
John Trehero, Shoshone
Agnes Vanderburg, Bitterroot Salish
Mari Watters, Niimíipuu (Nez Perce)
Basil White, Kootenai
Tom and Susie Yellowtail, Apsáalooke (Crow)

Thanks also to the many consultants and hosts who wish to remain anonymous.

Index

About the Author

Rodney Frey is emeritus professor of ethnography and Distinguished Humanities Professor at the University of Idaho. He is a lay chaplin at the Gritman Medical Center in Moscow, Idaho. He holds a doctorate in anthropology from the University of Colorado, and since the mid-1970s has partnered with tribal communities including the Crow, Coeur d'Alene, Nez Perce, and Warm Springs. His books include *Landscape Traveled by Coyote and Crane: The World of the Schitsu'umsh (Coeur d'Alene Indians)*; *The World of the Crow Indians: As Driftwood Lodges*; and *Stories That Make the World: Oral Literature of the Indian Peoples of the Inland Northwest as told by Lawrence Aripa, Tom Yellowtail and other Elders*. He is the recipient of the Idaho Humanities Council's 2024 award for Outstanding Achievement in the Humanities, the council's highest award.

Printed in the USA
CPSIA information can be obtained
at www.ICGtesting.com
LVHW010353260524
780890LV00002B/2